# Comparative Perspectives
# on the Academic Profession

edited by
**Philip G. Altbach**

Praeger Special Studies Series in Comparative Education
Series editor: Philip G. Altbach
Published in cooperation with the
Center for Comparative Education,
State University of New York at Buffalo

The Praeger Special Studies program, through
a selective distribution network, makes
available to the academic, government, and
business communities significant and timely
research in U.S. and international economic,
social, and political issues.

# Comparative Perspectives on the Academic Profession

PRAEGER SPECIAL STUDIES IN INTERNATIONAL ECONOMICS AND DEVELOPMENT

Praeger Publishers   New York   London

95074

Library of Congress Cataloging in Publication Data

Main entry under title:

Comparative perspectives on the academic profession.

    (Praeger special studies in international economics and development)
    Includes bibliographies.
    1. College teachers.  2. Comparative education.
I. Altbach, Philip G.
LB2331.7.C65         378.1'2         77-83481
ISBN 0-03-040781-8

Much of the material in this book appeared
as a special issue of *Higher Education*

PRAEGER SPECIAL STUDIES
200 Park Avenue, New York, N.Y., 10017, U.S.A.

Published in the United States of America in 1977
by Praeger Publishers,
A Division of Holt, Rinehart and Winston, CBS, Inc.

789 038 987654321

Printed in the United States of America

# Acknowledgments

Most of the essays in this volume are reprinted from *Higher Education,* 6 (May 1977), a special issue on the academic profession, and from *Higher Education,* 6 (August 1977). I am indebted to the publisher, Elsevier Publishing Company, Amsterdam, for their kind permission to reprint these essays.

# Contents

# LIST OF TABLES AND FIGURE

# Comparative Perspectives on the Academic Profession

# Introduction
## Philip G. Altbach

## THE ACADEMIC PROFESSION: AN UNCERTAIN FUTURE

This volume consists of studies about the academic profession. Its chapters deal with countries as diverse as India, Argentina, and the United States. Challenges such as student enrollment growth, unionization, the problems of professionalism in a bureaucratic environment, and others are considered. The authors of the studies in this volume differ in their methodological orientations and perspectives. They are united, however, by their concern for a professoriate everywhere facing problems. It is our conviction that the kind of analytical attention offered by these essays can at least provide the basis for constructive thought. The purpose of this short introduction is to delineate some of the themes discussed in this volume and to discuss some of the general currents facing the academic profession.

Research on the academic profession is at present a small subspecialty of a growing field of studies on postsecondary education. There is no doubt some resistance within the academic world itself to research on the professoriate. Social scientists have long conducted research on juvenile delinquents, tribal aborigines, and religious sects: They have seldom turned their analytical tools on themselves and their colleagues. It is widely assumed that academics know about their own institutions by virtue of working in them. There is no doubt some fear about exposing academic mores to public scrutiny and a feeling that academic work is somehow above critical analysis.

The scope of existing research on the academic profession remains limited in most countries. A bibliography containing about 1,700 listings of materials published in 1974 concerning higher education outside of the United States contains only 54 listings on the professoriate (Altbach 1976). There is generally more research available for the industrialized nations of North America and Western Europe than for the rest of the world, and it is probable that half of the world's published research concerns the United States.

Another characteristic of research on the academic profession is that much of it has been conducted by social scientists who analyze the professoriate narrowly according to, for example, socialization or social interaction theory. These social scientists are interested in the academic profession as an available population for research and not necessarily to shed light on the nature of academe. Some of the best of this work, such as Ladd and Lipset's (1975) research on the politics of the professoriate in the United States or Williams, Blackstone, and Metcalf's (1974) study of the academic labor market in Britain, deal with only limited aspects of the subject. Specialists on higher education, on the other hand, often see the professoriate as just one element in studies of governance, curriculum, or collective bargaining. They seldom attempt to analyze the academic profession as a whole.

There is no question that research on the academic profession is crucial for an understanding of higher education, and recently there has been a flurry of interest in the topic. This volume is an indication of that concern. The time for reticence about engaging in research on the professoriate is past; the challenges to the academic profession require both self-study and self-understanding, and without careful research and analysis, such understanding is impossible. In addition, those outside of the profession who have increasing power over the future of the university must have a realistic appraisal of the role of academics in the universities and in society.

The academic profession, let it be stated, remains crucial to the university. Even with the current difficulties, the professoriate, and particularly the senior teaching and research staff, remain at the heart of the academic enterprise. They have control over the curriculum, and in most universities a key role in governance. They generally dominate the department or faculty structures that constitute the basic building blocks of the academic structure. Because they control the curriculum and the departments, the professoriate in some respects control the processes of knowledge production and dissemination. If the academic staff is unqualified, standards of education and research will necessarily suffer. If academics are demoralized, the atmosphere of the university is affected. If the professoriate is engaged in political disputation the university will be politicized. If the professoriate has lost its commitment to academic goals and its sense of cohesion, the university will suffer from drift.

The historical role of the academic profession has traditionally been paramount. The dominant academic model, that of the medieval University of Paris, was founded and controlled by professors. The other historical model, the student-dominated Bologna University, remains an exception in history, with little influence in the modern world (Haskins 1965). More than any other group, the professoriate, and especially the senior faculty, has been responsible for maintaining historical continuity in the idea of the university. When changes have occurred, the professoriate has had influence in shaping them even when they were initiated by forces external to the university. Such innovations as the German research-oriented university (Ringer 1969), the American land-grant model (Veysey 1965), and the Latin American reformed university of 1918 (Walter 1968) were the result of a combination of external pressures and academic responses to them. In these and other instances, the professoriate has been able to shape changes so that they reflected, at least in part, their image of the university. In many cases, academics have been able to circum-vent or weaken changes that they did not favor.

The traditional structure of the academic system and the models of academic governance have reinforced the power of the professoriate. The growth of such structures as faculties, departments, colleges, and other mechanisms for academic decision making has been the result of a long historical process. In almost all of these structures throughout the world the professoriate has a major, if not a dominant, voice. These structures have tended to control such key functions as appointments of academic staff, decisions about curriculum, and policies concerning academic programs.

Why, one might ask, have the 1960s and 1970s proved to be so difficult for the academic profession in many countries? As the university has evolved from a bastion of training for a small elite to a key credentialing and training institution, it has come under increasing scrutiny. In the post-World War II period, societies have relied increasingly on higher education for technological training and research, and this has meant that universities have grown both in numbers and in their functions. Along with increased funds there has also come government interest in the affairs of academe and demands that the universities account for their activities. The university curriculum has expanded to include many applied subjects previously thought inappropriate for higher education, thereby diminishing the intellectual unity of the faculty. The university has become a means of providing access to remunerative and prestigious occupations and to upward social mobility. This has increased pressure for admission from social groups previously excluded from higher education and has contributed to expansion.

Growth has meant many things, and has affected the academic profession very directly. As the number of teachers in postsecondary education increased in many countries, the sense of community has been weakened. The socioeconomic background of the professoriate has changed, as individuals who are not from the educated upper middle class have obtained academic jobs. Women, minority groups, and the working class, previously virtually barred from academic work, have obtained an increasing number of positions. A kind of generational conflict has developed as large numbers of young teachers entered the system during the great expansion of the 1960s. Many of these individuals were at odds with the values, orientations, and experiences of their senior compeers (Ladd and Lipset 1975). The academic staff at a single university in the United States, and increasingly in other countries as well, may include more than 1,000 individuals. Such large numbers make traditional forms of faculty governance difficult and virtually preclude a sense of community. Although rapid expansion has ended in many countries, the impact of the cohort of young faculty who entered academe in the 1960s and of the general problems of large numbers will continue to affect the universities.

The crisis of the university is, in a sense, a penalty of success. Universities in the post-World War II period were called on to contribute to rapid technological development, and to produce highly skilled graduates and research to fuel this development. Governments provided funds for expansion, research facilities, and enhanced salaries for professors. Research grants became commonplace. Professors were called on for advice and consultation by government and industry, and occasionally participated in important political and social events. The professoriate felt a new sense of power and prestige. As Robert Nisbet (1971) has argued, the traditionally accepted academic dogma concerning such issues as curriculum, norms of behavior, and the role of the university in society became threatened by the very success of the university in attracting resources, and the unwillingness or inability of the professoriate to control and limit expansion. The traditional undergraduate liberal arts curriculum in the United States, for example, was attacked by students seeking "relevance" and by business interests and others seeking technologically trained personnel. The faculty, concerned more with graduate education and research, neither defended the traditional curriculum nor suggested alternatives.

The traditional notion of the professor as an individual teaching in a university has changed dramatically. The "ivory tower," if it ever existed, is a relic of the past. It is difficult to define the professoriate in a cross-national context, because academics have taken on many new roles and have different tasks in various countries. Most of the chapters in this volume deal primarily with academic staff in universities. However, as the chapters on India and Australia make clear, in many countries university teachers constitute only a small part of the academic community. Teachers in colleges, technological institutions, teacher training institutions, and other postsecondary establishments are part of the academic community. As David Riesman (1958) pointed out, the academic profession is somewhat like a snake, with the head giving direction and leadership to the rest. Thus, the norms and values of the university-based academic staff in many countries influence the larger teaching profession despite the fact that university professors are now a minority. The top of the profession generally sets standards and provides role models.

In the United States, teachers in community colleges and other nonuniversity postsecondary institutions constitute the majority of the academic profession. The Indian college instructors, working in undergraduate institutions, constitute 90 percent of the academic community. In Australia, Canada, and Britain teachers in teacher training colleges, technological institutions, and others are an increasingly large part of the total teaching staff.

During the 1960s efforts in Britain, West Germany, Australia, and other nations were made both to democratize the academic system by upgrading many postsecondary institutions to university status and to improve the condition of teachers in these institutions. These efforts added to the size of the profession and in some cases contributed to confusion about academic standards and norms.

The inclusion of such groups as research workers, teaching assistants, and librarians in the academic profession has been the subject of controversy. In the Soviet Union, there is a clear differentiation between teachers and researchers, but this is uncommon in other countries. The addition of groups not traditionally part of the academic hierarchy has caused some confusion concerning such issues as remuneration and job responsibilities. These groups have further swelled the profession.

The authors in this volume use terms such as "professor," "teacher," "lecturer," "academic staff," and "faculty" rather interchangeably. Actually, the connotations of some of these terms may differ according to national setting. The American practice of appointing a number of "full professors" in a single academic department differs substantially from the British and German tradition of a single "professor" for a given discipline or department in a university. The American practice of granting tenure (limited job security) after a maximum of six years is by no means the international norm. In most other countries the equivalent of tenure is granted earlier, and it often is a stronger guarantee of continuing employment. Academic salaries differ considerably from country to country. It has been said that the Dutch professoriate is now the most highly paid in the world. Academics in Europe and North America can generally afford to live in a middle-class style on their academic salaries alone. This is not the case in much of Latin America, Japan, and India, where even senior professors often work at several jobs in order to maintain a middle-class standard of living.

As Lewis and Ryan (1977) point out in this volume, academics are among the few professionals who function in a large bureaucratic organization. This helps to define the nature of academic work and the ethos of the university. Universities have always had some bureaucratic structure, but in many countries the density and pervasiveness of the academic bureaucracy has expanded dramatically. Large numbers of administrators, many of whom no longer come from academic backgrounds, have responsibility for financial affairs, student services, and other functions. While academics maintain major control over the curriculum, there is often conflict between the professoriate and the newly enlarged and powerful administrative staff of the university.

Comparative analysis of higher education in general and of the academic profession in particular is rare, and difficult to undertake because of the many national differences involved and the expense of such research (see Altbach 1977). The chapters in this volume are case studies of specific countries, and it is left to the reader to discern relevant comparisons. Nevertheless, a few general themes are evident in these chapters.

"Academic drift", as Grant Harman (1977) defines it, is a theme of many of the chapters. Academics seem to accept the various, and often conflicting, demands placed on their institutions without much debate or objection. As long as the new demands resulted in added resources, they were accepted without a clear understanding of the long-term consequences.

Numerical growth in the academic profession has resulted in a loss of community, broadening of the social class base of the profession, increased differentiation by discipline or speciality, and in general a weakening of common interests.

The professoriate has tended to oppose reforms which change the traditional patterns of university governance, curriculum, or other elements that affect working conditions and privileges. The profession has tried to deal with increased numbers of students and new academic functions without changing organizational patterns.

The professoriate has had mixed success in protecting academic autonomy from governmental and other demands for accountability, and from the growing power of administrators.

There has been a trend toward democratization of the professoriate by extending participation in governance to junior ranks and upgrading some academic staff (such as librarians and research personnel) to professorial ranks. This democratization has often been opposed by senior professors, but in general this opposition has not prevented change.

Because of expansion during the 1960s, the average age of the professoriate has temporarily declined. This had led to some generational conflict and tension between established academics and their younger colleagues.

There is an international trend towards emphasis on research and publication as a criteria for academic advancement, at least at the university level. This is changing academic systems, especially in the Third World, that had not traditionally stressed the research function.

There are significant national differences in the traditions, roles, remuneration, working conditions, and other variables concerning the academic profession. Attitudes, values, socialization patterns, and responsibilities vary. Even within national academic systems the profession may be segmented by institution, discipline, or function. These variations make generalization difficult and have mitigated against the emergence of an international academic consciousness.

Higher education reached a peak of public attention and support in the 1960s. That decade was marked in many countries by dramatic increases in expenditures for postsecondary education, by enrollment increases, and by an emphasis on higher education as a means of solving national problems. This period was also marked by student unrest and a growing dissatisfaction with the internal operation of universities.

At present, there is much criticism of higher education. General economic problems have caused governments to cut back on funding for universities. Demographic and economic factors have caused a downturn in enrollments in the industrialized nations. Economists and others have questioned the contribution of higher education either to the growth of individual income (Bird 1975) or to national development. Ideas of "deschooling" have led to questions about the role of formal education. Accusations of elitism have been leveled against universities.

These criticisms have affected the universities. Not only have they led in many cases to curtailment of resources, but they have led to increased government intervention in internal affairs, often with the aim of controlling the expenditure of funds. The academic community has been demoralized, and has not come persuasively to the defense of the universities. A decade or more of growth, increased prestige, and seemingly unlimited funds for research resulted in complacency.

The research reported in this volume indicates that the crisis is not limited to a single nation and that the academic profession is undergoing change in many countries. Latin American nations are trying to establish a professional academic staff on a full-time basis and to encourage research as part of the academic role. The Japanese have been concerned about the results of low professorial salaries and resulting moonlighting by academics. West Germany, the Netherlands, France, and other Western European nations have to deal with expansion and democratization in academic governance. The United States, Britain, and Canada face a steady state of enrollments and declining resources for higher education.

The academic profession is directly affected by all of these changes. As Edward Shils (1975) has pointed out, the academic ethos is under considerable strain. It is hoped that this volume, by focusing attention on the professoriate, can help to stimulate the careful analysis that is needed to face the problems confronting postsecondary education.

## REFERENCES

Altbach, Philip G., ed. 1976. *Comparative Higher Education Abroad: Bibliography and Analysis.* New York: Praeger.

―――. 1977. "Studying the Academic Profession: Comparative Perspectives." Paper presented to the annual meeting of the American Educational Research Association, New York, April 8, 1977.

Bird, Caroline. 1975. *The Case Against College.* New York: McKay.

Harman, Grant. 1977. "Academic Staff and Academic Drift in Australian Colleges of Advanced Education." This volume, pp.76–98.

Haskins, Charles. 1965. *The Rise of Universities.* Ithaca, N.Y.: Cornell University Press.

Ladd, Everett and Lipset, Seymour Martin. 1975. *The Divided Academy: Professors and Politics.* New York: McGraw-Hill.

Lewis, Lionel and Ryan, Michael. 1977. "The American Professoriate and the Movement Toward Unionization." This volume, pp. 208–33.

Nisbet, Robert. 1971. *The Degradation of the Academic Dogma.* New York: Basic Books.

Riesman, David. 1958. "The Academic Procession." In *Constraint and Variety in American Education,* ed. David Riesman, pp. 25–64. Garden City, N.Y.: Doubleday.

Ringer, Fritz.1969. *The Decline of the German Mandarins: The German Academic Community, 1890–1933.* Cambridge, Mass.: Harvard University Press.

Shils, Edward. 1975. "The Academic Ethos Under Strain," *Minerva* (Spring), pp. 1–37.

Veysey, Laurence. 1965. *The Emergence of the American University.* Chicago: University of Chicago Press.

Walter, Richard J. 1968. *Student Politics in Argentina: The University Reform and Its Effects, 1918–1964.* New York: Basic Books.

Williams, Gareth; Blackstone, Tessa; and Metcalf, David. 1974. *The Academic Labor Market: Economic and Social Aspects of a Profession.* Amsterdam: Elsevier.

# 1

# Gentlemen and Players:
# The Changing British Professoriate
Gareth Williams

In many ways the development of the academic profession in Britain has followed a pattern similar to that in the United States since the establishment of the Association of University Teachers (AUT) in 1919 (compare American Association of University Professors in 1915). The central dilemma of the AUT, as with its U.S. counterpart, has been deciding whether its main function is to represent the intellectual, professional, or narrowly economic interests of its members.

The view of the official historian of the AUT (Perkin 1969) is that in its first 50 years the AUT saw the gradual professionalization of university teaching, or, as he later claimed, its re-professionalization (Perkin 1973). By the beginning of the 1970s, according to Perkin,

> there can be no doubt that university teaching is nothing like the tiny, isolated and dispersed, and almost irrelevant occupation it was at the beginning of this century. It has become not merely *a* profession but *the* profession towards which all the rest must look for the supply of new recruits and of new ideas on which the future of our society depends (1973).

Undoubtedly the AUT played a major part in this development, but an equally important part was played by the massive expansion of universities

---

*Non-English readers may not know that it was long the practice in English cricket for amateur players to be designated as gentlemen while their professional colleagues on the same team were called players. The latter were segregated into separate changing rooms and subjected to other minor indignities, such as being referred to by their surnames only in newspaper reports. This practice, like much else in the traditional British way of life, fell into disuse during the 1960s.

during the 25 years after World War II, and particularly during the 1960s. The effect of this expansion on the sociology of the British university profession has been documented in Halsey and Trow (1971) and the effect on its economic situation has been analyzed in Williams, Blackstone, and Metcalfe (1974). Halsey and Trow's "thesis about the evolution of British university teaching is that it is a traditional, gentlemanly profession informed by the norms of a democratically self-governing guild which is in the process of adapting itself to internal and external pressures towards bureaucracy and specialization." The democratically self-governing guild to which they refer is the collegiate system of Oxford and Cambridge that dominated thinking about universities in Britain until the mid-1960s.

Williams, Blackstone, and Metcalfe believe that the effect of expansion was more direct.

In the last analysis academics benefitted from the operation of the ubiquitous economic laws of supply and demand. During the 1960s academic jobs were plentiful and well qualified recruits were scarce. There are always economic benefits in belonging to an expanding industry. University teachers have a special advantage from expansion in that increased demand for dons caused by more students precedes an increase in supply of potential recruits when these students graduate. The increased number of students itself normally results at least in part from a high labour market demand for graduates, which means that universities have to compete with other employers for this category of manpower by bidding up salaries and otherwise offering attractive conditions of employment (1974, p. 79).

We have, therefore, in the three major books on the British academic profession published in the past decade, three rather different views of the changes that were taking place. Perkin sees the growth of what is essentially industry-based trade unionism bringing together individuals with diverse intellectual interests into a single profession applying professional standards of competence. Halsey and Trow see expansion and increased specialization bringing about formalized bureaucratic career structures, while Williams, Blackstone, and Metcalfe consider that many of the assumptions made about the economic and intellectual independence of the academic profession result from the boom conditions of the 1960s.

Clearly these three analyses of the profession are not mutually exclusive, as institutional, sociological, and economic developments were taking place simultaneously and interacting with each other.

What is undeniable is that by 1971 a massive expansion in the number of university teachers had been proceeding for ten years. Williams, Blackstone, and Metcalfe state, "allowing for wastage and recruitment over 20,000 new academics must have been recruited between 1962 and 1968. In each of the years 1962–1965 more than 10 percent of the academic staff of universities . . .

had less than a year at the job" (1974, p. 80). This expansion was accompanied by almost equally great changes in the composition of the academic profession by subject of specialization. In 1961 14 percent of British academics were in social studies faculties. By 1969 the figure was 21 percent. In 1961 25 percent of staff were in humanities and 17 percent in medical faculties. By 1969 the figure was 12 percent in both cases.

Yet these substantial changes had not been accompanied by equivalent changes in the way that British university teachers perceived themselves. The dominant view remained that of the independent scholar, cushioned from economic necessity, pursuing and teaching truth wherever he thought it lay. Perkin, for example, concludes his history of the AUT thus:

> To most university teachers the highest academic responsibility is neither to the students nor to society, important as they are, but to the subject itself, and in the final analysis to truth, or, if that is too absolute and abstract a concept in a relativistic age, to mankind's total stock of objective knowledge. We have seen that the academic stands above all for the professionalization of independent thought and discovery, and has inherited the independence and some of the time free from the slavery to income-earning of the now defunct gentleman-amateur. But that independence and free time for study are now under great pressure from politicians, civil servants, industrialists and others who want higher education, preferably of an immediately vocational kind, and research, preferably of an immediately "useful" application, on the cheap. This is the academic profession and the AUT must resist with all their might. Society has a right to ask university teachers to do its thinking and discovering for it, but it has not the right to fore-ordain what shall be thought or discovered. The academic has had thrust upon him the mantle of the Old Testament prophet: he has a higher duty than blind obedience to secular authority, and must speak the truth as he sees it, whether or not it is comfortable or acceptable to the powers that pay. At bottom, society has no choice: it must either pay for truly independent thought and discovery, and adequate time and resources for academics of integrity to do it, or it must do without, or make do with second-rate hacks and yes-men who will ensure the rapid decline of science, culture and higher education, and so the deterioration of society itself. An uncivilized society is a contradiction in terms, a body without a soul, a rotting corpse. It is not merely dying, it is dead already, killed by its own hand.
>
> The academic profession's final responsibility, to society, therefore, is to stand no nonsense from it, but to tell it, firmly and fearlessly, what it costs to do those things which alone justify its existence, the endless improvement of our knowledge of ourselves and our world and the enrichment of the quality of life in it (Perkin, p. 246).

Halsey and Trow also take the view that no fundamental changes had occurred.

Staff/student ratios in British universities are high and formal obligations light. There is freedom in the sense of personal autonomy of an order to be found rarely, if at all, in other occupational groups. These conditions permit the essential elements of what is considered a "gentlemanly" way of life. They also make professionalism possible in that, with assured income, both the self-respect of the university teacher and the pressure on him to work beyond the unexacting minimum of his formal duties derive in large measure from his reputation among his colleagues (1971, p. 169).

Perhaps the most conclusive evidence of the dominant attitude in the British university profession at the beginning of the 1970s is provided by the results of a referendum in 1971 on whether the AUT should affiliate with the Trades Union Congress (TUC) of labor unions. This was decisively defeated by a 2–1 majority and the public pronouncements of many academics at the time demonstrated that Perkin and Halsey and Trow accurately interpreted the prevailing ethos.

In 1976, however, proponents of affiliation with the TUC managed to obtain a new referendum and on this occasion the vote went in favor of affiliation by a 5–3 majority. This represented a remarkable change of opinion and, even allowing for new members of the association, suggests that over a quarter of the members changed their minds between 1971 and 1976. The purpose of the present paper is to explore this move away from "professionalism" towards trade unionism.

## THE INSTITUTIONAL HOMEWORK OF THE BRITISH ACADEMIC PROFESSION

In Britain as elsewhere there is always some difficulty in deciding exactly what is meant by the academic profession. Since the time of the Robbins Report (HMSO 1963) higher education in Britain has explicitly been considered as consisting of three sectors, the universities, the colleges of education (for teacher training), and the heterogeneous collection of institutions called advanced further education. Since 1967 government policy has focused on creating a sharp division between the so-called public sector of higher education and the universities. In terms of educational philosophy the so-called binary line that separates the autonomous universities from the public sector is very blurred. Much of the work of universities and polytechnics (the leading institutions in the public sector) overlap in content, level, and methods of teaching. Similarly, there is no sharp distinction in their financing. Although the universities receive their money via the University Grants Committee and the polytechnics via the local education authorities, both ultimately receive at least 90 percent of their financial resources from the central government.

## Professional Affiliations: Unions

There is, however, a clear distinction between the two categories of institutions in their professional affiliations. About three-quarters of university teachers belong to AUT.* The union to which most teachers in the public sector belong is the National Association of Teachers in Further and Higher Education (NATFHE), which has for many years adopted a fairly militant trade union stance. The weight of NATFHE membership is amongst the teachers in what is technically called non-advanced further education (that is, technical and vocational education at secondary level). Their wages and conditions of work have for many years been determined by national collective bargaining and are related to those of school teachers. NATFHE has therefore had to campaign on two somewhat contradictory fronts. On the one hand, along with other teacher unions, it has pressed for increases in teachers' salaries generally. On the other, it has had to advance the special claims of teachers in further education as opposed to those of teachers in ordinary primary and secondary schools.

One result of this orientation of NATFHE is that some teachers in polytechnics (institutions that the government explicitly intended to have parity of esteem with universities) have formed the separate Association of Polytechnic Teachers. The aim of this association is partly to promote the special economic claims of the advanced education part of further education, and partly to further professional, as opposed to narrowly economic, interests. Information about the strength of this association is scarce, but it is widely believed that compared with NATFHE it has made relatively little headway amongst polytechnic staff.

A more important thorn in the flesh of the two major academic unions is the Association of Scientific, Technical, and Managerial Staff, one of the most vocal general white-collar unions. In higher education it has acquired a dual role. It is widely recognized as the main union representing the interests of technicians and para-academic staff. In addition, although in general it represents the interests of a privileged class of workers and its national stance is a defence of the status quo against the narrowing of earnings differentials, it has in recent years attracted a small membership amongst academic staff of universities and polytechnics who consider themselves politically to the left of most of their academic colleagues.

------

*There is some dispute about the figure. Williams, Blackstone, and Metcalfe found a membership of about 60 percent in 1970, while the AUT was claiming nearly 80 percent. Much of the difference is illusory. Much depends on whether medical staff and part-time and temporary staff are included. The former normally belong to specialist unions (or professional associations) and the latter often do not belong to any union.

In this paper, as with most previous work on the British academic profession, attention is concentrated on university teachers. An important exception is Whitburn, Mealing, and Cox (1976), which provides a statistical description of staff in polytechnics, but unfortunately does not include their trade union affiliation or attitudes towards union membership. However, the changing attitudes of university teachers with respect to trade union activities can be fully understood only in the context of developments in higher education more generally.

## Employers and Employees

There is an ambiguity in the legal and institutional position of British university teachers. Unlike their colleagues in many European countries, they are not government employees. However, neither do universities have substantial autonomy in establishing the salaries and work conditions of academic staff. University teachers are employed by individual universities and are paid by them, but the salary scales are determined nationally and the grant which universities receive from the central government takes into account any nationally agreed changes in academic salaries.

Nearly all the general income of British universities comes from the central government and is paid through the University Grants Committee, whose traditional role is to act as a buffer between the universities and the government, enabling them to accept a massive public subsidy while guaranteeing their institutional autonomy.

The net result of this situation is that it is very difficult to identify who are, in practice, the employers of university teachers. Individual universities are able to appoint their own academic staff and they have some degree of freedom in determining conditions of employment. The life tenure that well over three-quarters of British university teachers enjoy (Williams, Blackstone, and Metcalfe 1974) is tenure with the individual university and not with the University Grants Committee or central government. If a university were unable to honor its financial commitments, its tenured staff would be vulnerable just as they would in any commercial enterprise. In this the university teachers are in a somewhat worse situation than their colleagues in the public sector who are local government employees.

However, individual universities have little freedom in determining the pay or career structure of their academic employees. All lecturers, who comprise about two-thirds of the profession, are paid according to a nationally negotiated salary scale. While individual universities are free to appoint lecturers at various points on the scale they are thereafter to all intents and purposes committed to pay a substantial annual increment until the lecturer reaches the top of the scale where he remains unless he is promoted to one of the senior grades of lecturer, reader, or professor. The proportion of staff that a university may have in one of these senior grades is fixed nationally at 40 percent. The salaries of professors are determined as individual bargains but they are subject to a nationally imposed constraint on the minimum and average salaries that a university may pay its professional staff as a whole. Thus if a university wishes to attract a particular scholar by paying him a salary much above the average it can do so only by paying at least some of his colleagues less than the average.

There is thus little scope for collective bargaining at the level of the individual institution. The national machinery for salary negotiations attempts to reconcile the confusion between legal responsibilities for contractual arrangements with staff and the sources of finance for their salaries. The actual machinery is a two tier system of negotiation in which representatives of the AUT and the Committee of Vice-Chancellors and Principals meet under the chairmanship of the University Grants Committee to hammer out an agreed salary claim. Subsequently the claim is presented jointly to the Department of Education and Science, which represents the government. When a higher level of academic salaries is agreed the government grant to the universities is supplemented by an amount enabling the increased salaries to be paid.

Much of the history of the academic profession during the present century has been the growth of this nationally standardized career structure and the gradual development of nation-wide collective bargaining in which the university teachers are represented by their professional association, the AUT.

## ALTERNATIVE VIEWS OF THE ETHOS OF THE PROFESSION

### Political Stance

In Britain as in the United States the academic profession has long been situated somewhere to the left of the political spectrum. Ladd and Lipset (1975) have shown that from 1944 to 1972 well over half, and occasionally as much as three-quarters, of the professors in U.S. universities voted for the Democratic Party. In Britain such enduring consistency does not exist. However, Halsey and Trow (1971) show that in 1965 53 percent of university teachers in Britain considered themselves left of center, compared with 19 percent who considered themselves right of center. In 1970, Williams, Blackstone, and Metcalfe (1974) found that 60 percent of university teachers consider themselves to be in the labor or liberal camps, compared with 23 percent whose allegiance was to the Conservative Party. On the eve of the October 1974 general election that showed some movement towards the left nationally, 75 percent of university teachers claimed that they intended to vote labor or liberal, while the proportion of conservatives remained at 23 percent (*Time Higher Education Supplement,* 1974).

Thus in both Britain and the United States the proportion of university teachers who claim to be left of center is higher than that for the population as a whole, but more interestingly is much higher than that of corresponding income groups. In 1970, for example, the proportion of all social classes in Britain claiming to support the Labour and Liberal Parties was 52 percent and the proportion of professional and managerial supporting these parties was only 20 percent (Butler and Pinto-Duschinsky 1970). Although the three surveys cited above are not strictly comparable they do appear to suggest some movement leftwards in the political orientation of university teachers. In the light of this increasing leaning to the left it ought perhaps to cause little surprise that in March 1976 the members of the AUT voted by a substantial majority to affiliate with the TUC and thus narrow the gap between their theoretical political orientation and their practical political stance. In fact the change in the voting figures between 1971 and 1976, as noted, was much greater than can be explained by a gradual leftward drift.

## "Locals" and "Cosmopolitans"

The conventional view of the British academic profession is that it is rooted in two, to some extent contradictory, ideals.

> On the one side there was the creation of . . . the professional principle of a powerful lecturing and researching professoriate. On the other, there was the . . . principle of the working college tutor, which goes back beyond the college system to the regent masters of the earliest days, whose "catechetical lectures" were really tutorials and who were solely responsible for the pastoral care of the undergraduates. Both forms appealed to the professionalism of university teaching, the professorial to the principle of expertise and, ultimately, of a hierarchy of experts, which characterises all modern professions; the tutorial to the principle of fiduciary service to the client . . . (Perkin 1969, p. 14).

The notion of the contrast between the gentlemen scholar and the specialist researcher is a common feature of the literature of the academic profession in Britain and many other countries. One version is the distinction between "locals" and "cosmopolitans." The prime loyalty of a local is to his own university and the students in it, whereas as that of the cosmopolitan is towards his particular specialty and other specialists wherever in the world they are located (compare Halsey and Trow 1971, p. 390).

In Britain the difference between the two ideals shows itself in differences in attitudes towards teaching undergraduates. The much-lauded Oxford and Cambridge tutorial system depends essentially on university teachers who are willing to discuss intelligently a wide range of issues with their undergraduate students one or two at a time. By contrast the civic university archetype is a lecturer or professor whose academic integrity makes him unwilling to presume to teach outside the area in which he has a specialist's first-hand knowledge gleaned from his own research. It has been shown that promotion to professorial rank is associated with success as a cosmopolitan (see Williams, Blackstone, and Metcalfe 1971, pp. 120, 520).

We may therefore take as representative of the two ideals the university teacher at Oxford and Cambridge on the one hand and the professor on the other. Neither of these two groups was particularly enamoured of the idea of trade union membership in 1976. An opinion poll taken at the same time as the 1976 AUT referendum found that only about a third of Oxford and Cambridge teachers intended to vote in favor of TUC membership and only just over a third of the professors in all universities intended to do so. It is, of course, possible that Oxford and Cambridge dons and professors in other universities are not necessarily the only representatives of the two academic traditions.

## Economic Considerations

However, it is also possible that there is currently an alternative ethos that is even more widespread in the profession. What has often been ignored, or at best insufficiently taken into account in the literature, both fictional and nonfictional, is that in many respects and for many people it is simply the job at which they have the greatest comparative advantage in earning their salary. The passage already quoted from Perkin about the academic profession's responsibility to society, contains the phrase that the rest of society wants its higher education "on the cheap." It is not excessively cynical to claim that what Perkin is concerned about and what many academics have been really worried about in recent years is exactly the same thing that has been worrying the coalminers and other skilled workers of all kinds in Britain—that society, which in the academic profession is usually personified as the civil servants in the Department of Education and Science, has been underestimating the economic value of their services.

Williams, Blackstone, and Metcalfe go much further in emphasizing the importance of economic considerations. Their position is that university teaching is not a single profession but a loose federation of individuals with different craft skills who are in fact competing in a variety of outside labor markets. Their book shows that during the 1960s university teachers with specialist skills in areas that were in high demand outside the universities (for example economics and applied science) were, even within the constraint of fixed national salary scales, likely to be economically better off than their colleagues in other disciplines. The mechanisms by which these adjustments can come about are: first, more rapid promotion—second, initial appointment on a higher point on the salary scales—third, through greater opportunities for earnings outside the university. Finally, those areas in which there were considerable employment opportunities outside the university experienced considerably greater wastage of staff (1974, chaps. 12, 13).

The picture painted here is not of a profession whose primary loyalty is to an academic way of life, nor particularly to scholarship within a particular specialization. Rather, the majority of university teachers see themselves as performing one of a range of possible jobs for which their educational background qualifies them.

Halsey and Trow show that during the period from the 1920s to the early 1960s the relative financial position of British academics deteriorated considerably. In 1928 the average university salary was 3.7 times that of the average worker in manufacturing, whereas by 1956 it was 2.0 times as much. However, one effect of the great expansion of demand for higher education in the late 1950s and early 1960s was that the relative position of academics improved somewhat and by 1966 their earnings were 2.1 times those of the average worker in industry. The relevant information is shown in Table 1.1.

Academics, however, do not usually compare their earnings with those of average manual workers. Even an income difference of only 100 percent is sufficient to open up differences in style of life sufficiently great for there to be no serious threat to the self-esteem of the more favored group.

Halsey and Trow go on to claim that the university teacher usually compares himself with either the administrative civil servant, industrial manager, or scientist. These are the groups with which the AUT most commonly makes comparisons when submitting pay claims. This is, however, only part

## TABLE 1.1

### Average Salaries of Academic Staff, 1928–77

| Year | Average Earnings | | |
|------|------------------|---|---|
| | University Teachers (A) | Manufacturing Industry (B) | A/B |
| 1928–29 | 584 | 156 | 3.7 |
| 1938–39 | 612 | 184 | 3.3 |
| 1951–52 | 1,091 | 455 | 2.4 |
| 1956–57 | 1,323 | 648 | 2.0 |
| 1966–77 | 2,368 | 1,102 | 2.1 |

*Source:* Halsey and Trow 1971, p.173.

of the truth. Table 1.2 shows for the main subject groups the areas in which British university teachers thought they would be employed if they were not working in universities. Overall the civil service has a fairly low position and so does industry. Other education on the other hand, which in effect means teaching in schools or further education colleges, is a very important alternative occupation, particularly for those in the humanities and social sciences.

University teachers' salaries have declined relative to those of manual workers during much of the present century, as part of a general narrowing of differential between white-collar and manual occupations until the late 1960s. The position of university teachers compared with other while-collar workers remained relatively stable and in some cases even improved somewhat (see Halsey and Trow, p. 174).

Since the boom years of the mid–1960s, the relative economic position of university teachers has declined sharply. This is what the economic hypothesis would predict: "Contraction or deceleration in the growth rate will hit this occupation particularly severely" (Williams, Blackstone, and Metcalfe, 1974, p. 79).

Table 1.3 shows that between 1965 and 1975 the average posttax income of university professors declined by 19 percent, while that of manual workers rose by 13 percent. If we assume that professors' earnings moved roughly in line with those of other university teachers (which is broadly true during the period in question) we can very crudely link these figures to those of Table 1.1. This suggests that the potential living standards of academics relative to those of manual workers deteriorated over this ten-year period, from 2.1 times to 1.4 times. Furthermore, they also declined relative to those of many of the more directly competitive workers in other occupations. Clearly, with such a major change over such a short period the material life-style of university teachers

TABLE 1.2

Alternative Occupations by Faculty, 1969 (percent)

| Alternative Occupations | Humanities | Social Studies | Pure Science | Applied Science | Medicine | All Faculties |
|---|---|---|---|---|---|---|
| Sample number | 556 | 624 | 1015 | 481 | 361 | 3037 |
| Other education | 35 | 21 | 10 | 4 | 3 | 15 |
| Civil service | 14 | 19 | 11 | 6 | 1 | 11 |
| Industry | 7 | 14 | 16 | 31 | 5 | 15 |
| Professions | 30 | 26 | 10 | 20 | 72 | 26 |
| Research | 3 | 10 | 48 | 31 | 16 | 26 |
| Other | 11 | 10 | 5 | 8 | 3 | 7 |

## TABLE 1.3

Changes in Real Net-of-Tax Pay, 1965–75

| Profession | Percent Change |
|---|---|
| University professor | −19 |
| Hospital consultant | −14 |
| Senior managers in | |
| Chemicals | −14 |
| Oil | −12 |
| Nationalized industry | −12 |
| Food | −11 |
| Senior civil servant | −8 |
| Senior hospital administrator | +1 |
| Senior bank manager | +2 |
| Senior accountant in practice | +2 |
| Average manual worker | +13 |
| Real gross domestic product | +26 |

*Source:* Comparisons of British medical and industrial salaries in 1965–76 are from Gerald D. Newbould, *British Medical Journal* (February 19, 1977).

was no longer safely above the strains and stresses of everyday life. Although no relevant information is yet publicly available it is virtually certain that the severe incomes policy of 1976 and 1977 will have worsened still further the relative economic position of British academics. Clearly Perkin's ideals are being subjected to a severe test.

## Polytechnics and Parity of Esteem

It is not, however, only in relation to incomes that the economic position of university teachers has seriously deteriorated since the late 1960s. The key to changing attitudes about trade union membership is partly in the creation and rising fortunes of the directly competitive occupational group of teachers in polytechnics.

The polytechnic policy of building up public sector institutions to rival the university and have parity of esteem with them, while at the same time devoting themselves to more directly vocational studies, has been written from several different angles—see, for example, Robinson (1968), Pratt and Burgess (1974), and Whitburn, Mealing, and Cox (1976). With the exception of the last, little has been written about the staff of polytechnics and virtually nothing has appeared in the academic literature so far about the comparative career opportunities, conditions of service, and salaries of what have become the two main branches of the British academic profession.

One of the accidents of history is that the polytechnics are considered to be public sector colleges and therefore the salaries of their teachers are linked to those of the numerically much greater school teaching profession. When the polytechnics were first established in the late 1960s, this link was seen as a factor inhibiting a career in polytechnics from being as attractive as that in universities. In general, while starting salaries were relatively good the prospects of people in mid-career and above were much worse than those in universities. This created an inherent contradiction in the polytechnic policy. Parity of esteem with universities was being sought with a pay scale similar to that of school teachers, though at a somewhat higher level. This is no doubt one of the reasons why they were far less attractive than universities to well-qualified staff. In 1970, 73 percent of university teachers possessed a "good honours degree." The corresponding figure for teachers in polytechnics was 46 percent. Whitburn, Mealing, and Cox (1976).

In 1974, as part of a general restructuring of teachers' pay recommended by the official Houghton Committee, polytechnic teachers received very substantial increases amounting to as much as 50 percent within a 12 month period. This brought many of them to a level of earnings that, with similar qualifications and experience, they would have been unable to obtain in universities. It certainly brought parity of esteem as far as salaries were concerned.

In normal circumstances this award might have been welcomed by those conducting salary negotiations on behalf of the universtiy teachers. After all, what better basis for a national pay claim in an occupation where productivity is notoriously difficult to measure, than that a directly competitive public sector occupation is earning more? Unfortunately, before university teachers were able to take advantage of this newly acquired weapon government incomes policy froze the wages and earnings structure broadly into its 1974 pattern, allowing relative increases only for those at the very bottom.

## CONCLUSIONS

Since the late 1960s, therefore, university teachers have labored under a general feeling of rapidly declining relative economic position and, since 1974, a specific salary grievance. It is not at all clear that this deterioration in their economic position has anything to do with collective bargaining power. After all, as we have seen, their position improved somewhat during the boom of the

1960s. However, it does appear that in recent years those workers who have been organized in the largest collective bargaining organization have fared best. There can be little doubt that this sense of economic grievance was the major factor behind the 1976 decision to ally themselves with organized labor.

The first year of these new arrangements saw no dramatic changes. There was no improvement in the relative earnings of university teachers. In fact, they have almost certainly declined still further. On the other hand, academics have not yet been called upon to join a general strike, while the trade union movement shows little sign of being influenced by the persuasive powers of the professors, which was one of the reasons put forward to support the case for joining the TUC. This episode is a demonstration that claims about the special nature of university teaching as an occupation should be viewed with suspicion. Most British academics are concerned with the pursuit of truth and its dissemination to their students. They also see many advantages in the great flexibility which their profession allows them. In this respect it remains a job for gentlemen; however, when their economic self-interest is threatened they behave like any other group of employees and seek economic betterment through collective action.

## REFERENCES

Butler, D. and Pinto-Duschinsky, M. (1970). *The British General Election of 1970.* London: Macmillan.

Halsey, A. H. and Trow, M. A. (1971) *The British Academics.* London: Faber and Faber.

HMSO. (1963). Report of the Committee on Higher Education (Robbins Report), Cmnd. 2154. London: Her Majesty's Stationery Office.

Ladd, E. C. and Lipset, S. M. (1975) *The Divided Academy.* New York: Norton.

Perkin, H. J. (1969). *Key Profession.* London: Routledge and Kegan Paul.

————. (1973). "The Professionalization of University Teaching." In *Education and the Professions,* ed. T. G. Cook. London: Methuen.

Pratt, John and Burgess, Tyrrell. (1974). *Polytechnics: A Report.* London: Pitman.

Robinson, E. (1968). *New New Polytechnics.* London: Penguin.

*Times Higher Education Supplement.* (1974). "Teachers in the British General Election of October, 1974." London: Times Newspapers.

Whitburn, J.; Mealing, M.; and Cox, C. (1976). *People in Polytechnics.* London: Society for Research into Higher Education.

Williams, G. L.; Blackstone, T. A. V.; and Metcalfe, D. (1974). *The Academic Labour Market.* Amsterdam: Elsevier.

# 2

# The Robed Baron: The Academic Profession in the Italian University
## Guido Martinotti & Alberto Giasanti

The relationship of the highly formal and centralized structure of the Italian academic system and the informal practices which in fact govern this system is the focus of this article. The key role of the academic profession in the system is our primary concern. We shall not concentrate on the political attitudes of Italian academics, or on the decision-making processes in the universities. We shall, rather, focus mainly on the nature of the academic system and the role of the academics in its informal operation.

## BACKGROUND OF THE CURRENT SITUATION

It is necessary to provide some background concerning the Italian academic system prior to analyzing the role of the professoriate. Italian universities are in a long period of considerable strain. We hesitate to use the word crisis, since this connotes some inevitable solution. It is, rather, our view that the period of strain can go on for a long time. Italian higher education is moving from an elite to a mass system (Trow 1973; Burn 1973), but it is our impression that although the Italian system remains essentially elite in nature, it serves a population larger than its organizational resources allow.

This situation may be best understood through a short historical analysis of the stages of development of the Italian university (Martinotti 1972, pp. 172–75). In the twentieth century we can identify four periods in the development of the Italian university. The first covers the years until just before World War II, and could be defined as a period of balanced growth. The system grew

Data for this paper have been collected as part of a research grant, no. 73.00982.09 from the Consiglio Nazionale delle Ricerche.

23

steadily and slowly, the student body increasing by about 5 percent a year. During this period the Italian university system was in fact an elite one, embedded in a largely hierarchical and elitist society, the social development of which was kept in check by the fascist regime. But, as one always tends to forget, it was precisely in this period that the institutional characteristics of the Italian university system were fixed. The present organizational structure can actually be traced back almost entirely either to the Law Casati (1859) or, to a much larger extent, to the 1923 reform of the Italian school system by the philosopher Giovanni Gentile.

The second period, from the years immediately preceding the war to 1954, is characterized by growth and recession, both caused by the war; first a marked increase of the student body in the years up to 1947 and then a slump due to a serious crisis of intellectual unemployment in the reconstruction years. After 1954 there is a third period of sustained expansion of the student body and of the university system in general. These are the years of the "Italian economic miracle," and the prevailing social philosophy was an expansionist one; the unchallenged view on education was the theory of "human capital," and the expectations were that there would be a shortage of this capital in the 1970s (Barbagli 1970; 1974). This period, which came abruptly to an end around 1967, was also marked by the major, and totally unsuccessful, effort by the Italian ruling class to reform the university—the famous (or infamous) Project 2314 that had been planned for several years, which aborted in 1967 due to student opposition.

The great 1967 student struggles against 2314 contributed to the much larger explosion of 1968 that marks the start of the last and current period. This is characterized by the failure of the system to find an institutional reorganization based on a general reform law. Instead piecemeal adjustments were made and this led to the lack of any coherent overall plan. First came the law passed in 1968 to open up entry (which was already quite large), which thus accelerated—but by no means initiated—the explosive growth of the student body. Next, the so-called urgent provisions (*provvedimenti urgenti*) hurried through in 1973 tried to ease the situation by raising the salaries of teachers, giving tenure to the senior groups of the nontenured teachers, providing (in fact promising) more teaching jobs, and establishing very moderate rules for expanding participation in the decision-making process.

Table 2.1 provides an indication of the main trends in the Italian universities in the two last periods mentioned above. We have selected three rows of indicators: input, structure, and output. During the period up to 1967 all these indicators increased, but at different speeds. The percentage of students from the secondary school who decided to go on to the university grew from just above one out of two at the beginning of the period to almost four out of five at the end; the number of first-year students increased more than threefold, and that of the entire student body two and one-half times, but the full professors

## TABLE 2.1

### Some Parameters of the Italian University System

| Year | Percent Graduates from Lower-level School Enrolling in University | Input Number of First-Year Students | Input Total Number Regular Students | Structure Full Professors | Structure Total Teaching Personnel | Output Graduates |
|---|---|---|---|---|---|---|
| Base Value 100 = | -- | 35.893 | 136.458 | 1.852 | 16.682 | 20.203 |
| 1954-55 | 56.9 | 100.00 | 100.00 | 100.00 | 100.00 | 100.00 |
| 1955-56 | 59.3 | 112.93 | 101.88 | 105.13 | 105.13 | 109.31 |
| 1956-57 | 59.2 | 123.01 | 106.53 | 107.18 | 112.53 | 100.86 |
| 1957-58 | 58.9 | 135.10 | 113.32 | 108.96 | 114.04 | 96.45 |
| 1958-59 | 57.3 | 139.95 | 120.14 | 112.04 | 125.58 | 103.15 |
| 1959-60 | 59.2 | 157.61 | 129.12 | 104.10 | 136.96 | 104.63 |
| 1960-61 | 59.6 | 166.35 | 140.44 | 107.61 | 144.95 | 108.31 |
| 1961-62 | 63.5 | 181.69 | 150.94 | 112.90 | 156.17 | 113.92 |
| 1962-63 | 71.6 | 209.11 | 165.47 | 118.84 | 153.78 | 118.66 |
| 1963-64 | 74.6 | 215.15 | 175.05 | 125.97 | 161.74 | 129.24 |
| 1964-65 | 76.2 | 240.70 | 190.05 | 133.26 | 167.32 | 138.21 |
| 1965-66 | 79.6 | 293.87 | 218.22 | 140.82 | 187.39 | 143.81 |
| 1966-67 | 78.4 | 333.87 | 248.07 | 147.24 | 218.91 | 154.64 |
| 1967-68 | 73.4 | 354.56 | 271.20 | 157.79 | 219.34 | 198.95 |
| 1968-69 | 74.6 | 397.43 | 304.60 | 167.65 | 217.63[b] | 236.82 |
| 1969-70[c] | 84.5 | 488.24 | 357.87 | 170.68 | -- | 235.21 |
| 1970-71 | 86.2 | 541.26 | 410.82 | 180.77 | -- | 279.23 |
| 1971-72 | 92.2 | 596.81 | 462.52 | 190.98 | -- | 300.21 |
| 1972-73 | 87.8 | 594.05 | 481.91 | 201.24 | -- | 319.60 |
| 1973-74 | 82.2 | 595.24 | 494.78 | 235.85 | -- | 311.56 |
| 1974-75 | 82.8 | 632.22 | 519.39 | 232.07[b] | (253.99) | 327.67 |
| 1975-76 | -- | 662.50[a] | 545.91[a] | -- | -- | -- |

Note: the left "Percent Graduates..." column base value row shows 56.9; the Number of First-Year Students column base value is 35.893 with 1954-55 = 100.00, 1955-56 = 104.22, 1956-57 = 104.04, 1957-58 = 103.51, 1958-59 = 100.70, 1959-60 = 104.04, 1960-61 = 104.74, 1961-62 = 111.60, 1962-63 = 125.83, 1963-64 = 131.11, 1964-65 = 133.92, 1965-66 = 139.89, 1966-67 = 137.78, 1967-68 = 129.00, 1968-69 = 131.11, 1969-70 = 148.50, 1970-71 = 151.49, 1971-72 = 162.04, 1972-73 = 154.30, 1973-74 = 144.46, 1974-75 = 145.52.

[a] Provisional data. [b] Due to changes in the breakdowns it is not possible to construct the time series. [c] From this year on data are for the solar year. *Source:* ISTAT vols. 9–29.

increased only 50 percent and the total teaching body barely doubled. The output increased by 50 percent.

This pattern indicates strain on the system: pressure from outside, a huge increase in the services requested (quantity and quality) and, on the other hand, a very slow growth of the resources put into the university system.

The 1970–74 period generally followed the pattern set in the previous period. Despite the so-called mini-reform of 1973 that promised the creation of new teaching posts, the number of professors did not increase considerably, thus indicating that the structural response of the university to the new demands had been insufficient. Growth in the Italian system of higher education does not differ greatly from growth in other national systems in the Western countries. An international comparison would show that apart from one indicator (De Francesco 1976), the rate of growth in the Italian university has not been one of the largest in Europe. Also, the popular image of the Italian university as a "hyper-democratized" mass university system is not supported by the data, which show, among other things, that the widening of access has resulted in a steady increase in the drop-out rate (De Francesco and Trivellato 1976) and that the system has reacted with a high degree of internal differentiation in terms of social selection (Martinotti 1969; De Francesco and Trivellato 1976).

What is peculiar to the Italian situation is the fact that these substantial developments took place in a highly centralized and rigid system that has remained practically unchanged, from the legal and institutional point of view, throughout this period. In other words, with the exception of a few innovations, mainly legal, the Italian university is still organized as it was conceived by Giovanni Gentile in 1923. The corollary of this is that after 1967 university professors had to manage the strains between the students' demands and the almost absolute rigidity of a centralized system where even the slightest change in the curriculum of one *facoltà* has to be approved by a national law signed by the president of the republic. This role of working out the compromises demanded by the situation has become an important trait of the Italian academic profession.

## THE CHAIR SYSTEM AND THE FORMAL CAREER STRUCTURE

Although the chair system in use in Italy and in several other countries is fairly well known (Giasanti 1974; Martinotti 1972), it is necessary to get into some of its intricacies to understand the workings of the academic profession in Italy. One difficulty in this description lies in the fact that the basic linear system has been rendered somewhat more complicated through successive small and often relatively short-lived adaptations to pressures to expand the teaching body. This is due to one of its basic traits, the fact that virtually all universities in Italy are integrated into the national system of state education. Therefore all professors are civil servants and, in addition to depending on the national Ministry of Education for their salaries, civil service rules govern important aspects of academic careers. The evaluation of scientific merit has to be made within this rigid and cumbersome formal structure. Academic recruitment is determined by national examinations (*concorsi*). These are the same for all Italian universities, and no local initiative (such as the creation of new professorships) is possible.

One consequence of this system is that each teaching job is made available only at the end of a long chain of multi-level bargaining on the sharing of resources: first between the university system as such and the rest of the public administration, then among universities, then among faculties and disciplinary areas, and finally among disciplines within each faculty. Each teaching post corresponds to one specific course (*corso* or *insegnamento*) with a precise label that cannot be changed except by a procedure that takes years, again involving a long decision-making process. The teaching jobs can be held by a full professor or chair-holder (*cattedratico* or *professore di ruolo*) or by temporary appointment that is by an *incaricato*. Thus we can say that the career consists of three echelons: the *professori ordinari,* the incaricati (both of these being teaching roles), and the third, which is a much larger and rather undefinable mass of nonteaching roles—assistants, tutors, fellowship-holders—called "subordinates" (*docenti subalterni*).

At the pinnacle of the profession we find the professore ordinario. This is a full-fledged civil servant and thus he has tenure; that is, he cannot be removed from office until retirement age (70 for professors). In addition, professors cannot be removed from office except for serious criminal offenses. The ordinario is recruited through a national concorso that is the crucial point of his career. In 1974–75 there were 4,298 full professors, almost all males— 2.2 women for 100 males in 1968 (Marbach 1973, p. 51) and 1.9 in 1968–69 (ISTAT 1975). The basic gross salary ranges from 6.5 m. to 9.5 m. lira a year.

The second layer consists of professori incaricati; that is, teachers who have not got a permanent post but teach a university course, in that role having exactly the same functions as a chair-holder. This is a body more difficult to describe because the incaricato can be a person with different qualifications: he can be a professore ordinario appointed to teach a second course; an assistant also appointed as a teacher (in both cases these would be called *incaricati interni*); and incaricato quite simply (these are called *esterni,* with differences of salary and attributions); or even a person belonging to a private or public administration who teaches part-time. Due to the fact that the number of teaching jobs given out as *incarichi* is larger than the aggregate number of persons having these jobs, accurate statistics on the number of incaricati do not exist. A recent estimate shows 11,544 posts for 1970–71, and 8,933 persons. The percentage of women is a little higher among the incaricati group, 13.7 percent in 1971 (Marbach 1973, p. 51). The incaricati are also recruited through a public *concorso,* but instead of a special committee appointed or elected at the national level they are appointed yearly by the local faculty. In 1973, by the so-called urgent provisions, incaricati who at that time had held a teaching post for at least three years were given automatic tenure, and became *incaricati stabilizzati.* The salary of a professore incaricato is 4.5 m. lira a year.

The third echelon consists of a rather large and differentiated body of nonteaching jobs. These are difficult to define because the logic of the system has been one of coping with new demands for an enlarged teaching body, yet not creating new tenured posts (*posti de ruolo*)—which were difficult to create due to the national bargaining system from which they had to be extracted. The original role in this echelon was that of *assistente.* This was a tenured job and could be a career in itself, not leading to a teaching post. The assistente was attached to a chair and was dependent on the professor. This post was also obtained through a national public concorso, but the judging committee consisted of the professor holding the chair, another full professor of the faculty, and another assitente of the same faculty. Despite this procedure, appointments were essentially in the hands of the professor. In recent times these posts, being tenured, became very coveted and, being relatively scarce, were no longer the entry point in the career, but a good intermediate job to be reached even as much as ten years after graduation. In 1964–65 only 25 percent of the assistenti were less than 30 years old (Marbach 1969, p. 42), and the average age was 36 years (39 in medicine).

The creation of the category of assistant was a response to the need for more university staff in the postwar years. An assistant was appointed directly by the professor, without the usual committee system. Assistants were unpaid, and therefore called voluntary. Their number expanded rapidly. In 1964–65, there were 13,099 voluntary assistants out of a total of 22,610 assistants (5,337 of whom were tenured). By 1973–74, the number of voluntary assistants was 10,406 out of a total of 26,151 (Marbach 1969, p. 29; ISTAT 1975, p. 123).

The 1973 mini-reform tried to put some order into this area by abolishing assistants and similar posts and by creating 8,000 posts with four-year contracts and 4,000 two-year fellowships to be given to young graduates, who had been working in precarious positions up to that moment. In 1974–75 there were still 24,057 assistants of all sorts—not to be replaced—and 11,831 in other precarious roles.


## THE DYNAMICS OF THE ACADEMIC CAREER

The essence of the Italian academic profession is a bureaucratic structure in which is embedded a system of plutocratic prerequisites, like those that characterized the German professoriate at the time of Max Weber. We must go beyond the structural elements of the academic profession and carefully examine the realities of the informal system. The hierarchical pyramid of the profession consists, as we have seen, of a body of about 4,000 full professors, 8,000 incaricati, and 36,000 others in precarious roles. From the organizational point of view it is, however, a pyramid without a base because, in organizational terms, the entry is not clearly defined.

## Entering the System

The ideal career pattern is to graduate, become an assistant to some chair-holder, and then to obtain more permanent academic appointments culminating in a professorship. The usual pattern, however, is more complicated. The entry point is usually in an institute. The institute is the fundamental building block of the Italian university, handling basic teaching and research. Institutes are often under the control of a single chair-holder, and they receive a regular budget from the university. Administrative arrangements regarding students, syllabi, and other matters are generally handled through institutes. Like the university at large, the institutes are hierarchically organized, with a director at the head. Because secretarial and other support personnel are very limited, the institute is burdened with a considerable amount of work which must be handled by teaching staff, and as a result there is usually room for young scholars to take on some of these responsibilities. Thus, many young scholars gravitate to an institute and "hang around," hoping to attract favorable attention and thereby be promoted in their academic careers.

The young scholar's best strategy is to be spotted by one of the older teachers, which is not difficult because they are always on the look-out for new helpers, and become "attached" to him. The first stage of the recruiting process is usually very informal, with no precise engagements being made on either side. After a while, however, the professor will have to arrange things with the young follower, and there will be a fatherly talk about the hardships of the profession. This attitude of discouraging young scholars from going on has the ritual meaning of limiting the moral responsibility of the professor in case of an immediate or later failure by the assistant.

Even at this slightly more formalized stage there will rarely be any stable stipend available. This obviously will depend on the power of the single institute and professor: rich and powerful institutes usually are the product of enterprising professors who can augment the basically poor endowment of the institute with research grants, consulting, editorial activities, and so on. Thus, in exchange for services within the institute the professor will help the young assistant find some source of revenue outside the institute, and the assistant himself will have to get busy in looking for external sources of income.

Stable jobs within the institute are only infrequently available at this stage, and any external full-time job would damage the recipient's chances to work in close contact with the professor (*maestro*) within the institute (or solve the delicate internal problems of competition). Thus a subtle and peculiar kind of highly personal tie is formed and this is so because of the lack of institutional resources. The consequence of this situation is, of course, a highly personalized and fragmentary cultural experience. It is not rational for the actors involved in this structure to find horizontal connections with other scholars in the same or other faculties. All efforts in this sense are to a certain degree wasted, because they subtract energy from the major task of establishing oneself within the institute. This occurs usually when some kind of institutional job is made available in the institute, in the form of an assistantship, fellowship, or, in more recent years, as one of the four-year contracts established in 1973. This second step occurs fairly late in the career for the assistenti, and a bit earlier for the contracts or the fellowships. None of these jobs, however, provides a stipend sufficient for a living, the more so the later the stipend is obtained. The only really good job in this echelon, that of assistente ordinario, is obtained, as we have seen, at the average age of 36. The salary, which would be reasonable for a very young graduate, is totally insufficient for a person in his mid-thirties. Thus the need for external support is not diminished if and when the young scholar has finally entered into the bureaucratic system. Survey data show that in 1964–65, 65 percent of the whole body of assistants had incomes from outside the university (Marbach 1969, p. 68).

The need for noninstitutional forms of support also means continued dependency on the professor to whom the assistant is attached, in order to allow the taping of the resources controlled by the latter. This personal tie between the professor and his assistants (instead of an organizational tie between the young professional and the institution) is one of the trademarks of the Italian academic system. It is referred to in the current language in Italy as a "feudal" relationship: powerful chair-holders are called *baroni.* Although in a sense this term could also be accepted technically, in the precise meaning of exchange of protection for services and loyalty, it is obvious that the more general concept of Weber's patrimonialism is the most suitable interpretative model, with the proviso that in the Italian academic profession there is a marked mixture of the patrimonial and legal-rational models. Patrimonial practices and relations are embedded in a rigid central bureaucratic example of the legal-rational model.

## Becoming an Incarico

The next important phase of the development of the career comes when the now not-so-young scholar achieves a teaching position by becoming incaricato. This step usually requires leaving the internal structure of the single institute and the faculty for the larger arena of the national academic community. Traditionally the appointment to an incarico was preceded by the achievement of the *libera docenza,* a title which embodied the old *venia legendi,* and was given by a national committee of four full professors and one libero docente appointed by the Ministry of Education. The libera docenza was not a formal position, but an honorary title that was then taken into consideration by the formal structure as a priority prerequisite for the assignment of an incarico.

The incarico is obtained through a yearly public contest that each faculty sets up, usually in late spring, to fill its academic teaching requirements. Anybody can run for this post, including persons who have no formal education (in this case they must be more than 35 years of age), professors, previous incaricati, assistants, or foreign lecturers. The faculty examines the publications and curricula of the candidate, decides upon strict relevance to the subject matter that is to be taught, and then establishes priority levels rigidly indicated by the law. Within these levels it gives a ranked judgment, and finally votes to choose the candidate. The incarico is a yearly appointment, except that since 1973 professors who at that date had held the incarico for three years were granted a special tenure, called *stabilizzazione,* with the rationale that in view of the fact that the same law promised the creation of a considerable number of chairs, there should be a period of security for the large body of incaricati who were the likely candidates for these chairs.

The incarico, because it is the first step into the national academic community, is highly significant for the young applicant. It is important not only that he is relatively well known, but also that his patron or the professor to whom he is attached should have a national reputation sufficient to obtain support for his candidate in another university. A professor asking or obtaining support for his candidate in one university must be ready to give support for a candidate moving from that university to his own or to a third university. In other words he must control a certain number of jobs in his own faculty or other faculties. Thus the yearly assignment of *incarichi* takes place in a complex national network, which should be conceived not as a market, but as a complicated chess game in which the actors control a certain number of cells and combine this power in an exchange that involves the internal power structure of the faculty, as well as its external power in the community.

Although this is not a written rule, the best strategy of a young scholar from one of the major universities has traditionally been to seek a job in a minor university where he stands more chance for promotion to professor later. Actually this pattern has undergone substantial modifications in recent years, due to the creation of new universities, the expansion in jobs in the existing ones, and several other factors. In 1971–72 the percentage of incaricati who graduated from the same university was 74.4, and the pattern described persisted only in the more traditional faculties such as law, with 66.7 percent teaching in the alma mater (but 33.3 percent in a region different from the one where graduation was obtained), and humanities with 63.8 percent and 33.4 percent, respectively.

The salary of an incaricato varies, as we have seen, depending on the type of position. The basic gross salary range (before a recent increase) was from 1.8 m. to 3.3 m. lira. It is not surprising, therefore, that only 45.6 percent of the incaricati survive on their academic salaries alone.

It is only at the level of appointment as professore incaricato that there is some degree of autonomy from the patron. But even at this level, the patron is still needed in order to enter the last phase of the academic career, that of the concorso. At this level the academic will often direct an institute, hold research grants, and employ lower-level academic staff. In order to keep open options for possible appointments to a chair, the pinnacle of the profession, the professor will often commute between institutions. The goal is to transfer from a provincial university to a metropolitan city like Rome, Naples, or Milan.

## Becoming a Full Professor

The final step is the acquisition of a chair, which in the current revealing language is referred to as the "winning" of a chair. The formal procedure involves a three-step procedure. First, a faculty declares one chair vacant for concorso; second, a national committee is set up to decide which of the various candidates are eligible; third, the faculty appoints or calls the winner of the contest, and at that point the professor becomes a cattedratico. All the three steps require many complex strategies. The important fact to underline here is the interplay between the local level (designation and appointment by a faculty) and the national level (concorso and final inclusion in the tenured role of ordinari).

The typical strategy of a prospective candidate would be first to have one faculty declare the vacancy of the chair. This can more easily be achieved in a small university. Chairs can become vacant as a result of the death or transferral of a previous chair-holder, in which case the faculty can decide to fill the vacant job with some professor who already has a chair in another university, or with a newly-to-be-created cattedratico. The minister of education may also create some new chairs—again, the faculty then decides whether to assign these to professors in other faculties or to create new professors.

Once the chair has been declared vacant the prospective candidate still has to see that the committee decides favorably: if he is not included in the list of eligible candidates, he not only loses the chair, but he loses it to someone else who will block his way in the faculty in the future. Patient years of work have sometimes been wasted by a premature vacancy. The best way, and practically the only safe one, to avoid this situation is to have the patron included in the committee. This is considered an almost necessary prerequisite, because the competition is so strong that any full professor being elected or appointed to the committee will very likely have his own candidate to support and will not have much freedom to help even worthy and friendly outsiders.

Until 1973 this committee was elected by all full professors in Italy of that specific discipline or related disciplines (which included all disciplines taught at the same faculty). This election—which would appear a very universalistic procedure—had in fact created a huge electoral machine in Italian universities, one that negated the possibility for marginal persons in the profession to be elected to the committee. Since 1973 the committees have been chosen at random among the professors of that or related disciplines. Quite predictably, however, this development has not produced more universalism but has simply randomized the clientele, and thus weakened some of the great electoral empires. Once the list of eligible candidates is agreed in the committee, the faculty that has the vacant post calls the person it prefers, who can be the candidate of the faculty or another person.

This complex mechanism has many disadvantages, although the general feeling is that by some miracle the net product is not worse than that of other systems of selection. One of the drawbacks is the enormous amount of energy expended in the process. Another is the fact that the committee itself is not liable for the consequences of the promotion; the members of the committee are not going to work with the candidate elected. On the contrary, to hand out a chair is often the only way for a patron to get rid of a dull assistant. All this makes for a rather late entry into the chair position: in 1969 only nine out of a thousand got to the chair under 30 years of age, while 2.1 percent only reached it after they were 61 years old or more. Only one-third of the full professors in 1969 had become cattedratici at 40 or younger, and almost two in five got their chair after 46 years of age.

## THE SOCIOLOGY OF THE FULL PROFESSOR

The age distribution of chair-holders varies greatly, according to the different faculties. As can be seen from Table 2.2, there is a marked difference between law and medicine in terms of the seniority of full professors. In law one out of five cattedratici is 40 or less, while in medicine only slightly more than one out of twenty-five has a chair at that age. Thus, with exactly the same rules governing the careers of professors in all the disciplines, it is clear that selection within the academy varies greatly from one discipline to the other. As a matter of fact, age distribution is only a rather rough indicator of these differences, and can probably be accounted for by the intellectual structure of the discipline. In those disciplines where achievement is dependent on a high

TABLE 2.2

Full Professors by Age and Faculty

| Faculty | Less than 40 | 41-50 | 51-60 | 61-70 | Over 70 |
|---|---|---|---|---|---|
| Law | 20.1 | 26.4 | 27.9 | 23.3 | 2.3 |
| Humanities | 8.4 | 34.0 | 30.0 | 21.4 | 6.2 |
| Magistero | 10.1 | 40.5 | 28.5 | 17.7 | 3.2 |
| Sciences | 15.3 | 41.3 | 25.7 | 15.0 | 2.6 |
| Medicine | 4.3 | 30.1 | 32.5 | 26.2 | 7.0 |
| Engineering | 11.5 | 35.3 | 25.7 | 22.4 | 5.1 |
| Economics | 17.9 | 24.0 | 32.3 | 23.1 | 2.6 |

*Source:* Giasanti 1974.

degree of cumulative experience, as in medicine, the humanities (especially the historical disciplines), or the applied scientific disciplines (engineering and architecture), the pinnacle of the career is achieved rather late. In disciplines where the cumulative experience is less important than the grasping of the logic and handling of a theoretical system, as in pure sciences or in legal science as it is conceived in Italy, advancement can be faster.

Despite the numerical development that has taken place in recent years the academic profession, if compared with other elite groups, is quite old. Only 11.3 percent of the full professors in 1969 were under 40, compared with 40.2 percent of lawyers, 36.1 percent of judges, and even 18.0 percent of such stately professions as notaries. It is true that the full professors represent the top layer of the profession and in this sense they are not totally comparable with these other groups, but it is interesting to note that from 1960 to 1970, in the case of business executives, the percentage of the younger group (under 40) increased from 4.4 percent to 33.6 percent, and the relative strength of the older group (61 and over) was cut in half, from 22.4 percent to 11.3 percent (see Table 2.3). The body of full professors, in a comparable span of time, remained more or less the same, and the strength of the older group even increased slightly, from 25.0 to 26.7 percent.

If we compare the regional origin of the same professional groups (see Table 2.4), we can see that full professors tend to come from the more industrialized regions of the north (see Table 2.5). In this sense they are much more similar to the industrial executive than to other members of the bureaucracy, like judges and executives of the central administration, who come predomi-

## TABLE 2.3

### Full Professors and Industrial Managers by Age, in Two Different Periods of Time

| | Industrial Managers | | Full Professors | |
|---|---|---|---|---|
| | 1960 | 1970 | 1963 | 1970 |
| Less than 40 | 4.4 | 33.6 | 11.7 | 11.3 |
| 41-50 | 22.5 | 28.5 | 24.5 | 33.6 |
| 51-60 | 50.7 | 26.6 | 38.8 | 28.4 |
| 61 and over | 22.4 | 11.3 | 25.0 | 26.7 |
| | (Sample) | (Sample) | (N=2,373) | (N=3,328) |

*Sources:* Data on managers, Invernizzi 1971. Data on professors, Giasanti 1974.

nantly from the southern regions. The regional mobility of professors is quite strong; less than one in five actually teaches in the same town where he was born (see Table 2.6).

The greater attraction of the place of origin is exerted by the northern universities, where 57.3 percent of those teaching in 1969 were also born there, while in the central region— dominated by the city of Rome, with its mammoth university—55 percent of the professors came from other regions (see

## TABLE 2.4

### Regional Origins of Full Professors and Other Selected Elite Groups (percent)

| Area of Birth | Industrial Executives | Full Professors | Members of Parliament | Lawyers | Judges | Central Administration Executive |
|---|---|---|---|---|---|---|
| North | 78.4 | 64.4 | 42.2 | 33.0 | 14.3 | 9.0 |
| Center | 14.4 | 23.3 | 18.6 | 19.0 | 12.8 | 13.7 |
| South | 8.2 | 29.3 | 37.5 | 46.1 | 70.5 | 76.5 |
| Foreign | -- | 2.9 | 1.5 | 1.2 | 2.4 | -- |
| | (Sample) | (N = 3328) | (N = 1358) | (Sample) | (N = 6039) | (N = 256) |

*Sources:* Data for: industrial executives, Invernizzi 1971; professors, Giasanti 1974; MPs, Somogi 1963; lawyers, Prandstraller 1967; judges, Martinotti 1968; and central administration executives, Ammassari 1959.

## TABLE 2.5

Comparison Between Social Origins of
Full Professors and Business Executives

|  | University Professors | | Executives | | Total Italian Population | |
|---|---|---|---|---|---|---|
|  | 1958 | 1972 | 1961 | 1970 | 1961 | 1968 |
| Middle and upper class | 92.0 | 76.0 | 94.0 | 78.0 | 33.8 | 35.7 |
| Lower class | 5.5 | 21.0 | 5.4 | 22.0 | 66.2 | 64.3 |

*Source:* Giasanti 1974.

Table 2.7). One of the consequences of the national system is that the allocation of incarichi and chairs and the distribution of personnel in the 50-odd Italian universities is the result of a complex interplay of factors, including the relative strength of each patron's group, or "school." Thus the product of a national system for the profession is the creation of dependent universities; that is, smaller universities that serve mainly as stepping stones to larger, more central

## TABLE 2.6

Regional Mobility of Full Professors:
Birthplace and Teaching Place, 1969

| Birthplace | Percent |
|---|---|
| Foreign countries | 3.1 |
| In a geographical area different from that of the teaching place | 46.5 |
| In region different from that of the teaching place | 12.6 |
| In province different from that of the teaching place | 13.5 |
| In town different from that of the teaching place | 4.5 |
| In the same town where the chair is located | 19.8 |

N=3328

*Note:* N = 3328          *Source:* Giasanti 1974.

## TABLE 2.7

Regional Mobility of Full Professors: Region of
Birth and Teaching Region, 1969 (percent)

| Teaching Region | Foreign Countries | North-west | North-east | Center | South | Islands |
|---|---|---|---|---|---|---|
| Northwest | 3.0 | 57.3 | 14.8 | 14.6 | 5.6 | 4.6 |
| Northeast | 4.1 | 19.1 | 47.0 | 15.0 | 9.4 | 5.3 |
| Center | 2.7 | 16.1 | 14.0 | 44.5 | 15.4 | 7.4 |
| South | 1.6 | 6.8 | 10.1 | 19.1 | 56.9 | 5.4 |
| Islands | 3.5 | 10.2 | 6.3 | 12.6 | 16.1 | 51.3 |

*Source:* Giasanti 1974.

universities, and which in turn have personnel coming from the larger universities. This accounts for the regional mobility.

## THE POLITICAL ECONOMY OF THE PROFESSION

The formal structure is highly centralized and answers the strict prerequisites of a bureaucracy. Italian university professors are in fact civil servants dependent on the state. They perform functions delegated to them by the state. Their entire career is patterned on criteria for recruitment and advancement similar to that of judges or top officials of the central administration. On the other hand, however, careers, especially at the beginning stage, are strongly conditioned by the fragmentation and basic material poverty of the organizational structures of higher education. This produces a very high degree of organizational insecurity. The young scholar at the start of his career has to find external sources of revenue in order to survive. The difference is that now these sources will rarely be plutocratic, in terms of family riches, and more often will come from the professional-intellectual market. When the first secure institutional jobs are obtained external sources are still needed to complement the insufficient university salary, and when finally the chair is obtained it is necessary for the cattedratico to control a wide range of resources, in order to be able to feed the reproduction cycle in his own institute. Thus the university as an organization is weak and vulnerable vis-a-vis the external world, and this accounts, in our opinion, for the unusually high degree of involvement in politics and in other nonuniversity activities that characterizes the Italian academic. This particular variable, then, appears to be one of the major explanatory dimensions for the analysis of the Italian academic system and of the academic profession in particular. The behavior and attitudes of professionals who are so obviously in the position of gatekeepers to a complex network of relations cannot but be deeply influenced by the conflicting requirements of such a position.

One should not, however, automatically extend this particular model to all professors in the Italian university. In a highly centralized institutional system like the Italian one, differences in behavior and attitudes tend to be underestimated. It is generally assumed that since all professors have the same career structure and depend economically on the Ministry of Education, they should form an homogeneous interest group. Important differences are to be found if one examines the various aspects of the profession. Giglioli, in his survey of Italian academics, found that the political orientation of the respondents in his sample was predicted by the degree of professionalization of that particular discipline.* We tend to agree with Giglioli. It seems to us that when we are talking of the academic profession we are in fact talking about different professions, each with its own institutional setting, norms, career patterns, specific income, and values. We think that it is possible to identify three major settings, each with its own type of academic man: the professional, the scientist, and the intellectual.

The first type, the professional, is identified by the fact that it has two separate offices or bureaus. These can, and usually do, mutually support themselves, but are at the same time different organizational entities—one inside the academic institution and the other outside. The typical Italian embodiment of this pattern is the lawyer-professor, who has a chair and an institute within the university, and a professional office elsewhere. Correlates of this double life, so to say, are the following: very little time is spent in the academic establishment and therefore there is resistance to more teaching intensive innovation in the university; publication and research are rather limited, and concentrated at the beginning of the career; there is a tendency to limit scientific production to esoteric kinds of articles or books directed to a restricted public; publication is of individual as opposed to team, works; the professional has specific clients in professional life; and there is a high ratio of external to internal income. In the Italian situation one necessary correlate is that contacts with the international scientific community are limited (academic parochialism).

At the opposite pole we would put the scientist type of academic. Here there is practically no separation between the academic and not-strictly-academic offices. The teaching and research establishments are separated by a very thin line; usually there is an effort to integrate both aspects in the

---

*Personal communication to the author.

university institution, consequently the time spent within the academic institution is very large. Publication lists are very long: research continues throughout the academic career but it is still directed to a specialized public, although
for different reasons. Collaborative research is often stressed. There is no
specific client and a low ratio between external and internal income. As the
life of this kind of academic man is spent almost entirely within the university,
there is usually no resistance to changes that would render the university
establishment more efficient. Finally, one should find in this type a strong
allegiance to the international scientific community (academic cosmopolita-
nism).

The third type is that of the academic intellectual. Again in this case there
are no separate offices. Actually, there is no second office at all, in the sense
that this academic's nonteaching activities do not require an office in the
organizational sense, but simply an individual workshop (usually at home)
plus a good library service (usually in the university establishment). A lot of
time is spent in the university, although not necessarily in teaching or collective research activitity. The scientific modus operandi is individual and there
is no specific client. However, contrary to both of the preceding types, the
public is diffuse and nonspecific. Publication lists tend to be very long and
directed to a diffuse and general public. A low ratio of external to internal
income and fairly wide contacts with the international scientific community
are typical. The main aspects of these three types are summarized as in Figure
2.1.

Although we have framed these three types in terms of faculties they in
fact do not fully overlap—there are faculties in which the professional type
prevails but in which the other two types are also present, depending on the
disciplinary field of specialization of each individual professor. Another re-
mark that should be added is that this basic ambiguity of the academic career
begins at the beginning: the scheme has nothing to do with the career patterns.

## FIGURE 2.1

### Engagements in University Institutions

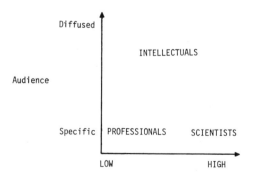

Despite the unique feature of the Italian system that does not require formal educational qualifications to become a university professor, nonprescriptive career types are very rare, as can be seen from the previous posts held by university professors (see Table 2.8).

A very small minority comes from outside the university, but, being in the university does not mean that the personnel is not involved in other kinds of activities. There is no doubt that such an arrangement is very costly in terms of returns for the basic aims of the academic institution and is also rather a heavy strain on the individuals involved.

This is not to say that there are no positive aspects, both from the organizational, and from the individual points of view. From the organizational point of view this weakness of the boundary between the academic

TABLE 2.8

Full Professors in 1969: the Two Jobs Previously Held

|  | Last Job Held | Second to Last Job Held |
|---|---|---|
| Assistant | 54.8 | 27.0 |
| Incaricato | 26.0 | 54.0 |
| Professor in foreign universities | 1.0 | 3.6 |
| High-school teacher | 10.3 | 7.6 |
| Executives in the administration of the Education Ministry | 0.9 | 2.6 |
| Executives of other public administrations | 4.2 | 0.0 |
| Professor in "free universities" | 0.4 | 1.3 |
| Other | 2.4 | 3.9 |
| N= | 3328 | 3328 |

*Source:* Giasanti 1974.

profession and the external world, means a deeper involvement of the Italian university in society. The fact that this has been due mainly to the privilege of those in a position to exploit the professional advantages of this ambiguous situation does not necessarily mean that under changing conditions this could not be an asset for the academic system. From the personal point of view it is also obvious that, despite the strains of the situation, all levels of the pyramid have vested interests in the maintenance of this situation.

Thus one of the reasons behind the repeated failures of reform laws seems to lie precisely in the fact that the Italian academy is in a state that is not very satisfactory to anybody. But any real change would start by rendering, in the short run, almost everybody a little less satisfied. Whether under the pressures of an increasingly demanding body of students the strains of this internal-external overlapping of demands will become unbearable, to the point at which a radical change towards a more clear-cut differentiation between the university and nonuniversity roles of the professors is brought about, remains to be seen. So far the enforcement of a full-time commitment for the teaching body has proven to be the weak spot of all reform projects.

## REFERENCES

Amato, Vittorio. 1952. *Sulla distribuzione dei professori universitari in Italia nel 1951.* Pubblicazioni della Facoltà de Economia e Commercio dell'Università di Catania, Catania.

Ammassari, Paolo. 1959. *L'estrazione sociale dei funzionari delle stato degli enti locali.* AAVV, Milan, ISAP.

Barbagli, Marzio. 1970. "Scuola e occupazione intellettuale." *Il Manifesto* (December), pp. 51–58.

———. 1974. *Disoccupazione intellettuale e sistema scolastico in Italia.* Bologna: Il Mulino.

Bonaguidi, Alberto. 1972. "La struttura dei professori universitari in Italia." *Studi di Statistica,* no. 8 (Pisa), pp. 181–209.

Burn, Barbara B., ed. 1973. *The Emerging System of Higher Education in Italy: Report of a Seminar.* New York: International Council for Educational Development.

Comitato di studio dei problemi della università italiana. 1960. *La popolazione universitaria.* Bologna: Il Mulino.

De Francesco, Corrado. 1976. "1960–1970: Lo sviluppo dell'istruzione superiore in alcuni paesi capitalistici." *Quaderni di Sociologia* 25, no. 1: pp. 41–55.

——— and Trivellato, Paolo. 1976. "L'università di massa degli anni '70 in Italia." *Inchiesta* (January-March), pp. 74–83.

Del Conte, Roberto. 1972. "La transformazione dell'attività del notaio." Ph.D. dissertation, University of Milan.

De Pasquale, Antonio. 1948. *La distribuzione dei professori universitari secondo l'età il luogo d'origine.* Annali della Facoltà di Economia e Commercio di Palermo, Vol. 2, no. 2.

Giasanti, Alberto. 1974. "Social Characteristics of Italian University Professors." Paper presented at the Eighth World Congress of Sociology, Toronto.

Invernizzi, Emanuele. 1971. "Le ricerche empiriche sui dirigenti italiani." *Studi organizzativi* 3, no. 4: pp. 75–94.

ISTAT. 1955–75. *Annuario statistico dell'istruzione italiana 20–21. Roma.*

Marbach, Giorgio. 1969. "Gli assistenti universitari in Italia—indagine campionaria." *Biblioteca del Metron* 4. Roma: Università degli Studi, pp. 17–186.

———. 1973. "I professori incaricati nell'università italiana." *Biblioteca del Metron* 5. Roma: Università degli Studi.

Martinotti, Guido. 1968. *Caratteristiche sociali dei magistrati italiani.* Varese: CNPDS.

———. 1969. *Gli studenti universitari: profilo sociologico.* Padua: Marsilio.

———. 1972. "Italy." In Margaret Scotford Archer, ed., *Students, University and Society.* London: Heinemann.

Prandstraller, Giampaolo. 1967. *Gli avvocati italiani.* Milan: Angeli.

Somogyi, Stefano. 1963. "Costituenti e deputati 1946–1958: analisi statistica." In *Il Parlamento italiano,* Sartoni, G. et al. Naples: Esi.

Trow, Martin. 1973. "Problems in the Transition from Elite to Mass Higher Education." *Conference on Future Structures of Post-Secondary Education.* Paris: Organization for Economic Cooperation and Development.

# 3

# The Changing Role of
# the Japanese Professor
## William K. Cummings & Ikuo Amano

The Japanese university tradition is scarcely 100 years old. The first modern institutions of higher education were established soon after the Meiji Restoration (1868), largely for the purpose of studying Western learning, especially science and technology. Throughout the Tokugawa period (1600–1868) Japan had intentionally isolated herself from these bodies of knowledge. In 1877 several of the government-established institutions were combined to establish Tokyo University, and this institution was reorganized as the Imperial University in 1886. By 1891, the Imperial University had acquired the structural characteristics that were to serve as the ideal model for all subsequent Japanese universities.

The basic educational, research, administrative, and political unit of the Imperial University was the academic chair headed by a full professor (*kyōjyu*), who might have his efforts supplemented by an assistant professor (*jokyōjyo*), a lecturer (*kōshi*), and one or two assistants.* In the 1891 regulations, 123 academic chairs were recognized as responsible for teaching and

The authors wish to thank Kazuyuki Kitamura and the other members of the Research Institute for Higher Education of Hiroshima University for so generously supplying unpublished data on university governance for their inspection. Also they acknowledge the stimulation they have experienced in reading Shigeru Nakayama's (1974) important comparative analysis of university traditions.

*While we identify the chair as the basic unit, we wish to emphasize that we disagree with those who in recent years have leveled extreme charges against the chair as the root of the stagnation and inflexibility of higher education in Japan. Especially in recent years the chair is often little more than a bureaucratic unit. In many faculties chairs tend to be joined into departments and these become the principal units for teaching, research, and personnel selection. Of course, in some faculties of some universities, the chair holders still wield considerable power—especially in well-known medical faculties—but the cases should not be overgeneralized.

research in different fields. The chairs of related fields were combined to create the faculties of law (22 chairs), letters (20), science (17), engineering (21), medicine (23), and agriculture (20). The full professors of each faculty constituted the membership of the faculty meeting and the dean was appointed by the minister of education. At a third level the deans, other administrative officers, and several faculty representatives made up a faculty council. The president of the university, who also acted as chairman of this council, was appointed by the minister of education (acting for the emperor).

By and large, the chair holders of this institution commanded a respectable level of expertise in their specialities, but few were at the frontiers conducting original research. Nevertheless, within Japan they were usually the leaders in their fields—in some cases, the only practitioners.

## A COMPARISON OF THE JAPANESE AND WESTERN UNIVERSITY TRADITIONS

During this foundation era, there emerged three major contrasts with the Western university tradition that have special relevance in an analysis of the role of academics in Japan. First, in the West most of the early universities tended to be established by private bodies such as the church, private individuals, or associations, whereas in Japan the most prominent modern universities were established by the state. In Japan the state explicitly declared that its universities were "to seek knowledge widely for the sake of the state," thereby indicating that there were limits to the scope of intellectual inquiry. Moreover, the state, through its system of educational inspectors and its authority over charters, exercised pressure towards intellectual orthodoxy in all higher educational institutions. Over time, university professors challenged the state's limitations on academic freedom, and this led the state to make some concessions —for example, state-supported universities were allowed greater autonomy in the selection of their officers and personnel—but it never conceded with respect to this basic principle. From the early 1920s, the state obtained the resignations of many academics who, in its judgment, published materials or made statements that violated the state's interests. In contrast, in the West the principle of academic freedom was relatively firmly established by this time. Though governments gradually became supporters and even establishers of universities, they found it necessary to respect this principle.

As a late starter, the Japanese government adopted the strategy of developing a single high-quality state university to play the key role in introducing Western learning (Amano 1975). This institution became the feeder institution for lesser institutions established by the state, as well as for most private institutions, as they lacked sufficient resources to achieve self-sufficiency in faculty development. The state's prime institution was lavishly funded, whereas the lesser government institutions received much smaller budgets. The state refused to offer direct aid to private institutions. Similarly the state, which was a major employer of university graduates, discriminated in favor of its own institutions. Imperial University graduates were given important posts as a matter of course, whereas the graduates of private institutions were virtually ignored (Spaulding 1967). To some degree, employers in the private sector followed the state's biases.

In most Western systems, as we have noted, the early universities tended to be developed by nongovernmental bodies, and while in England and to a lesser degree in France a small number of universities towered over all others no single institution was able to achieve the dominance of Japan's Imperial University. Except for Napoleon's abortive effort, no Western government attempted so clearly to bring the nation's institutions of higher education under the domination of the state as did Japan. Partly this was because Western governments began to develop higher educational institutions only after many institutions had become established and had developed independent bases of popular support. Western governments, in the laissez-faire tradition, also tended to take the view that they should promote institutional competition through rewarding excellence wherever it appeared, instead of favoring a single institution in the hope that this would lead to excellence.

The Japanese state modified the hierarchy by establishing a second imperial university at Kyoto in 1897 that ultimately achieved a status close to that of the original Imperial University at Tokyo. Prior to the end of World War II, five other imperial universities with more specialized focuses were established within Japan. Also, beginning in 1918 the state extended official recognition to several of the more successful private institutions. However, these modifications did not alter the fundamental hierarchical structure of the system: institutional budgets and privileges continued to be graded. Explicit in the concept of the Japanese hierarchy was a differential specification of duties for professors. Those at the elite imperial universities were expected to conduct research, keep abreast of international developments in their fields, and educate the nation's future leaders. For this purpose, the imperial universities had graduate schools, research institutes, and special research budgets. In contrast, lesser institutions were merely expected to train people for medium-ranking occupations, and their faculty were expected to concentrate on teaching. Private universities outside the state umbrella had a hierarchy all their own, but the peak of this hierarchy was much lower than that of the government universities.

A final contrast between the two traditions—and in many respects the most important in terms of our subsequent discussion—involves the respective emphasis on university activity as against activity in one's profession or relative to professional or disciplinary activity, and the extent to which faculty perceived themselves as locals, as contrasted to cosmopolitans. In the West, organizations to promote the professions preceded the establishment of universities, and in many ways the universities had to accommodate to this situation (Nakayama 1974). Thus Western universities became organized in chairs or departments which conformed to the prevailing trends in professional organization, and as new specialties emerged the universities altered their structures. Western professors, at least at the leading universities, often felt a stronger identification with their professional work than with their university activities, and thus would abandon their university when it served their professional interests. In the postwar U.S., this tendency has become so evident that several observers feel America's universities have lost their distinctive identities and merely serve as holding companies for professors to hang their shingles on. Of course, the Western situation is more complicated than these brief comments imply, but for the purpose of contrast these generalizations will suffice.

In Japan at the beginning of the modern period there were no professionals. Indeed the universities were established to train people to become professionals, or at least to develop a command of specialized knowledge. In the very early days of the modern Japanese university, professors engaged in a great diversity of activities, writing popular articles and translating Western materials for popular audiences, giving public lectures, consulting with the government, conducting their basic research, and of course teaching. While many of these activities were externally oriented, they were not guided by professional standards as professional societies were in their infancy. Gradually, the professors' involvement in these external activities declined. In part this decline was due to the increasing self-sufficiency of external institutions—the government bureaus achieved greater intellectual depth, free lances emerged to serve the popular media, newspapers expanded their staffs. Thus the external institutions placed fewer demands on the professors. At the same time, it is important to note the various steps universities took to capture the energies of their faculty.

The founders of these new universities assumed that their institutions had unique missions—to develop leaders, critics, or citizens of exceptional character—and for this reason they strove to build up their institution's integrity. This concern was reflected in the development of special entrance examinations to select students. These exams emphasized academic ability but, especially in the private sector, they also took into account the character and social commitments of students. In order to foster distinctiveness, the new universities favored former students when recruiting faculty. Some, such as the imperial universities of Tokyo and Kyoto and the private universities of Waseda and Keio, became almost fully inbred. The universities also offered various rewards to their faculty. The distinctive Japanese chair system that resulted in a one-to-one ratio between junior and senior positions virtually guaranteed promotions to all faculty. Moreover, as deans and other academic officers were chosen from within, many could look forward to an ultimate ascent to one of these honorary positions.

In the formative stages these institutions also offered various opportunities to ambitious faculty. For those professors interested in research, clever grantsmanship might lead to the construction of a custom-made research facility such as Waseda's Shakespeare Theatre, Keio's hospital, or the various research institutes attached to the national universities. For those interested in promoting specific academic fields, the chances of witnessing substantial growth in the number of colleagues in the same discipline employed at their institution were reasonably good so long as they played smart university politics.

Another reward, essentially a carry-over from the feudal days, was the respect that students paid to their professors. While in the classroom the professors taught specialized subjects, outside the classroom their relations with students often became quite diffuse. Students looked upon their professors as men of great wisdom (calling them *sensei*), and sought their advice in matters ranging from career planning to the selection of an appropriate marriage partner. Even long after the students graduated from school, they might come back to visit and seek the advice of their professors. Needless to say, the devotion of the students gave professors a sense that their university-centered educational activities were important.

In the formative period, individual professors could look forward to rewards of this kind as a matter of course. As the universities matured, they developed other institution-specific rewards. For example, each university in the private sector developed a distinctive salary scale and separation pay program; common to these was the principle of increasing annual increments according to length of service. These provisions clearly encouraged professors to stay for a long period giving loyal service to a single workplace, for if they moved they would forfeit their seniority at their original place and have to start from zero years of service in the new place. In the national sector, all institutions shared a common scheme, and thus movement was eased between national schools. But moving outside the national sector resulted in loss of tenure just as in the private sector.

Another important institution was the *daigaku kiyoo,* or university journal. These journals, either managed by individual universities or the faculties within them, enabled professors to publish whatever they wrote without an external review. Moreover, universities often paid modest fees to the authors. The early establishment of these university-specific journals actually tended to inhibit the growth of academic societies and journals. An excellent example is the field of law, where successful society journals were not launched until after the war; even today the most prestigious academic journals in this field are the *Tokyo University Law Faculty Journal* and the *Chuo University Law Faculty Journal.*

In combination with the increasing institutional differentiation of intellectual activity, these various mechanisms tended to channel the energies of professors towards their university. Professors looked upon themselves primarily as members of their universities and only secondarily as experts in a speciality. Of course, the numbers of specialists in the various fields gradually multiplied. Professional societies were established, with their journals, annual meetings, and the other trappings. However, through much of the prewar period these societies tended to be mere extensions of the particular universities where the specialists had been trained. Many of these societies located their central headquarters in the office of an imperial university chair. The head of the chair would be the permanent society president and the members of the executive board would be his former students. The professional societies had little existence independent of the social networks radiating from the chairs of these leading universities.

The university-centered pattern allowed Japan to develop several universities of respectable quality in a surprisingly short period. However, the professional components of the professorial role were neglected during this period. While professors spoke of values such as academic freedom, value-free analysis, and civility, these were at best weakly institutionalized. And as Japan approached World War II, the university world offered remarkably little resistance as the state systematically violated these academic values. Indeed, Ienaga (1967) argues that the faculty of individual universities where professors were persecuted willingly sacrificed the academic freedom of the accused in order to protect their university's autonomy.

## THE DECLINE OF UNIVERSITY CENTEREDNESS

Many of the practices that sustain university centeredness—special entrance exams, particularistic criteria for recruiting faculty and placing students, diffuse student-professor relations, salary and retirement schedules based on seniority, exclusive journals—continue to affect the orientations of professors to the present day. The careers of Japanese professors tend to revolve around a single institution, as do most of their personal contacts. Michiya Shinbori's comparative study of the career patterns of elite professors in five advanced countries found that the Japanese sample had the most restricted careers of all, being most likely to study at only one university, most likely to spend their entire academic career at one university (and more often than in the other countries this was their alma mater), and second least likely to have ever taken up employment outside of higher education (Shinbori 1964). While a subsequent study suggests that elite scholars in Japan may have more restricted mobility than the average professor, whereas the reverse tends to be true in the West, it nevertheless concludes that the Japanese scholar's career and social contacts are geographically restricted (Cummings 1975).

Nevertheless, many contemporary professors do not feel an especially strong attraction to their workplaces. Partly this is because the expansion of higher education has led to a decline in the attractiveness of many of these workplaces. Moreover, various outward-oriented opportunities have emerged to direct their energies away from their universities. We will now examine these changes and their consequences for the integrity of the academic role.

## THE POSTWAR EXPANSION OF HIGHER EDUCATION

At the end of World War II, there were but 49 universities employing 6,000 faculty. While these institutions varied considerably in size, the largest (in 1947) employed only 798 faculty and enrolled no more than 13,500 students (General Headquarters 1948, pp. 316 ff). The universities also varied in quality and level of financial support, but all manifested a quiet pride in their accomplishments.

Most of these old-system universities suffered plant damage or endowment deflation during the late years of the war and the early occupation. Partly to cope with this situation, but also to facilitate an expansion of higher educational opportunities, the Occupation's postwar reforms lowered the minimum standard for university education and eased the conditions for establishment. At the same time, the Occupation's new educational regulations eliminated all types of higher educational institutions other than the university. Given this situation, virtually all the old-system higher educational institutions sought to obtain university status, and nearly all were finally granted this status (though some were placed on probation or given a temporary status as junior universities). Almost overnight the number of universities quadrupled and by 1952, when the Occupation left, Japan had 220 universities and 205 junior colleges employing 26,733 full-time faculty and enrolling 446,281 students. By 1974, there were 413 universities, 506 junior colleges, and 65 technical colleges enrolling nearly 2 million students, or approximately 30 percent of the 18-22-year-old cohort. These institutions employed a full-time staff of 105,397.

### From Elite to Mass Higher Education

This vast postwar expansion of Japanese higher education has embodied many of the changes outlined in Trow's (1973) analysis of the transformation from elite to mass higher education. Overall statistics suggest a declining average condition in research facilities and funds, and even some decline in educational conditions. But, as in other systems, the fate of individual institutions had varied. In some respects the situation of a small cluster of elite national institutions has improved remarkably, while many new institutions constantly struggle for funds.

The Japanese shift towards mass higher education has its special characteristics. Whereas in the West governments took the lead in expanding opportunities, Japan's central and local governments have acted with restraint
(Cummings 1973). After the initial upgrading of several government institutions to university status during the Occupation, these governments have
established no more than a handful of new institutions. Over the past 20 years
they have allowed enrollments in government institutions to increase by only
104 percent, and most of these new places have been in the applied sciences.

Also, apart from grants to build facilities for science education and a
modest loan program, the government refused to provide financial assistance
to private institutions until 1970. In 1970 the government began a program of
substantial aid to private institutions that will presumably narrow the public-
private differences in educational facilities and costs to students. On the other
hand, the government has been very tolerant in approving private sector
applications for expansion or new establishments. As a result, much of Japan's
shift from the elite to the mass system has been accomplished by the private
sector, and thus generally under inferior conditions. For example, compared
with national universities where the average student to full-time-teacher ratio
was 8.0 in 1974, the ratio averaged 31.3 in the private sector. National universities had 22.2 square meters of floor space and 84.3 square meters of campus
per student, compared respectively with 7.3 square meters and 29.9 square
meters in the private sector (RIHE of Hiroshima University 1976).

Within the private sector, there is considerable variation. Several of the
old established private institutions have taken extreme steps towards becoming
mass institutions, while maintaining that these expansionist measures were
essential in order to upgrade faculty salary levels and research conditions.
Seven private institutions have enrollments exceeding 20,000 and Nihon University is reported to have over 80,000 students. Student-teacher ratios have
risen sharply—for example, at Waseda between 1935 and 1967 from 14.7 to
47.5, at Keio from 15.9 to 39.2, at Nihon from 10.9 to 56.9 (Jiyu Minshutō
1969, p. A11)—and teaching loads have increased, often to twelve in-class
hours a week. These mammoth private institutions suffer from many of the
familiar problems of large-scale organizations—bureaucratization, imperson-
ality, and poor communication and integration of programs. They have sadly
departed from their proud heritage as idealistic institutions concerned with
character education, and their faculty recognize this.

## The Changing Workplace

Some professors, despite the decline of their universities, remain deeply
committed to attributing problems to sources beyond their control. The committed serve willingly on the various administrative and planning committees

—and from among them a new class of faculty managers who actually derive some pleasure from administrative work has emerged (Amano 1976). On the other hand, others tend to believe their institution's decline is attributable to the greed and incompetence of the managers, for whom they have little sympathy. These professors tend to be disappointed and critical of their universities, and are unmoved by appeals for greater loyalty or service. Members of this latter group play a leading role in the faculty-staff unions that have continued during the whole postwar period to fight for better working conditions.

In addition to the established private universities there are a large number of other private institutions. Some, while lacking tradition, have managed to grow into strong and attractive institutions with a reasonable balance between facilities and responsibilities. Especially notable are Sophia University and the International Christian University, which have respectable student-teacher ratios and employ many well-known faculty members. Among the newer private universities, however, many are quite marginal both as educational and research enterprises. A small inner core of managers is likely to be firmly committed to the fate of these institutions, but most professors merely view them as places to expend routine effort and receive a pay check.

Relative to the private sector, public sector institutions have enjoyed superior funding, but this does not mean that they are more attractive institutions. In fact, government agencies have not given higher education a high priority and thus the total amount of funds has been modest—as a percentage of the national income, public expenditures on higher education actually declined through 1972. Many of the local government institutions have experienced stringent times, and several have had to abandon their independence to become incorporated as components of national universities. The universities supported by the national government are divided into two groups—an elite sector composed of former imperial universities, other full universities, and famous specialty schools such as Hitotsubashi and Tokyo Kogyo University (Japan's equivalent of MIT), and an ordinary sector of partial universities located in rural areas. Many of the institutions of the latter group have difficulty in recruiting staff. As national universities they offer the same basic salaries as the first group, yet in many respects they are unattractive: they tend to be located in peripheral areas far from the metropolitan centers of intellectual life, usually they consist of but two or three faculties with applied orientations, their staffs tend to be provincial, and their research facilities and budgets are modest. Above all, they suffer from the split institutional personality of being locally oriented yet supported by the national government (Shimizu 1975).

Among the public sector institutions, only the elite sector provides generally attractive working conditions: tradition, qualified colleagues, relatively generous research funds, bright undergraduate students, and graduate schools. These institutions are undoubtedly the most attractive workplaces in Japan, but even here there are problems. For example, many now find that their campuses are no longer adequate; while centrally located, the campuses often are small and plagued by noise and urban pollution. To escape these problems, several institutions, including the University of Tokyo and Hiroshima University, have developed plans to relocate all or part of their facilities on new campuses located outside the central cities. Others, such as Tokyo Education University and Tohoku University, have actually moved to new locations. For one account, see Cummings (1974).

These institutions have increased in complexity during the postwar period, but there have been few improvements in their governing procedures; thus, the professors complain that an excessive amount of their time is being absorbed by faculty and committee meetings (Tomoda 1976). The faculty of these institutions are at the center of national academic and intellectual life, and this subjects them to many pressures. Yet they receive no more in terms of basic salary than others who work in more peaceful settings. A small but growing number of the faculty at the elite institutions openly wonder whether their position is worth the personal strains they experience, and a few have moved down to lesser institutions or out of higher education altogether.

## RESEARCH FEVER AND THE ACADEMIC SOCIETY BOOM

Growing interest in research is another postwar trend that has played an important role in eroding university-centeredness. In the prewar system a formal division was established between elite research-oriented imperial universities and ordinary teaching-oriented institutions. However, it was not until the 1920s that the research-oriented universities began to acquire substantial research equipment of international caliber, and only in the mid-1930s did the government and certain private foundations begin to grant special funds for research projects beyond those automatically channeled to the universities for their routine work. As these funds became available, many scholars—especially the younger ones in the natural and applied sciences who had received special training in European laboratories—began to devote increasing portions of their energy to research. At the Imperial University at Tokyo several new research institutes and centers were founded and across the nation many new academic societies were created. As Japan became involved in the war, however, research conditions deteriorated and opportunities for publishing and keeping in contact with the international scientific community were virtually eliminated. One source of postwar research fever has been the explosion of activity by the professors at elite universities who had experienced those wartime deprivations.

Another reason is to be found in the postwar structural reform of the higher educational system. As we have noted, the Occupation attempted to level the traditional hierarchy by relabeling all old-system higher educational institutions as universities. While very little was done to actually bring the facilities of the various institutions to the same level—Table 3.1 shows that Tokyo University has continued to enjoy a substantial edge in terms of operating expenses—or to achieve greater balance in the distribution of talented scholars, the staff at many of the newly elevated universities came to perceive themselves in a much more exalted light. No longer were they mere teachers, but now researchers as well, and hence these professors also began to reach outwards for ways to improve their research situation. The new system for training professors contributed to this attitude. In the old system, many of those who taught at higher educational institutions assumed their posts immediately upon graduation from a university, and without extensive formal training in research. The reforms of the new system established a formal graduate school system with course work and research papers leading to master's and doctoral degrees. The new and more systematic program of academic training has naturally tended to cultivate a deeper interest in research. Surveys by the Ministry of Education indicate that the proportion of academics in four-year universities with advanced degrees increased from 16.3 percent in 1953 to 46.0 percent in 1965.

## The Academic Societies

As can be seen in Table 3.2 more academic societies were established in the brief period between 1946 to 1950 than at any other time in the short history of modern Japanese higher learning. The Occupation was impressed by this research fever, and by and large did what it could to facilitate it. Special rations of paper were issued to the academic societies to allow them to begin a program of publications. By 1949, according to a Ministry of Education survey, some 1,158 journals were being published by learned societies and individual universities (General Headquarters 1952, p. 367). Special programs were also established to send Japanese students and scholars overseas.

The trend in the establishment of new academic societies has continued down to the present. In many instances, these new academic societies have been formed as expressions of protest against the old university-centered system of academic cliques and school journals. Often their constitutions include provisions limiting the number of professors from any single university that can sit on the board of councilors or the executive committees in charge of programs, publications, and so on. Moreover, the chief officer is usually not allowed to succeed himself. These provisions have been designed to maximize academic society participation. A similar spirit goes into the preparation of annual meetings and society publications. In many societies the organizers of annual meetings try to solicit papers from all the members, rarely imposing any quality restrictions. Similarly, the society journal committees tend to adopt very egalitarian criteria when accepting manuscripts—rather than seek

## TABLE 3.1

### Total Operating Expenses of the Largest Japanese Universities Relative to the University of Tokyo's Operating Expenses in 1928, 1948, and 1965

| | 1928 | | 1948 | | 1965 | |
|---|---|---|---|---|---|---|
| Rank | University Name | Expenses Relative to Tokyo | University Name | Expenses Relative to Tokyo | University Name | Expenses Relative to Tokyo |
| **National Sector** | | | | | | |
| 1 | Tokyo | 1.000 | Tokyo | 1.000 | Tokyo | 1.000 |
| 2 | Kyoto | 0.565 | Kyoto | 0.603 | Kyoto | 0.496 |
| 3 | Kyushu | 0.477 | Kyushu | 0.381 | Osaka | 0.301 |
| 4 | Hokkaido | 0.434 | Nagoya | 0.343 | Nagoya | 0.294 |
| 5 | Tohoku | 0.394 | Osaka | 0.337 | Hokkaido | 0.287 |
| 10 | Nagasaki Ika | 0.131 | Tokyo Kogyo | 0.143 | Shinshu | 0.145 |
| **Public Sector** | | | | | | |
| 1 | -- | | Kyoto Fu Ika | 0.170 | Osaka Shi | 0.220 |
| 2 | -- | | Hyogo Ken Ika | 0.103 | Osaka Fu | 0.105 |
| 5 | -- | | -- | | Kobe Ika | 0.090 |
| **Private Sector** | | | | | | |
| 1 | Keio | 0.357 | Nihon | 0.261 | Nihon | 1.280 |
| 2 | Waseda | 0.146 | Waseda | 0.216 | Chuo | 0.393 |
| 3 | Meiji | 0.077 | Nihon Ika | 0.135 | Keio | 0.291 |
| 4 | Tokyo Jikei Ika | 0.067 | Keio | 0.118 | Waseda | 0.283 |
| 5 | Nihon | 0.059 | Chuo | 0.117 | Tokai | 0.216 |
| 10 | Doshisha | 0.024 | Tokyo Jikei Ika | 0.061 | Tokyo Ika | 0.140 |

*Sources:* 1928—Mombusho, *Teikoku Kyoiku Nempo, Showa 3-Nen;* 1948—Abraham Flexner, ed., *Universities of the World;* 1965—Daigaku Kijun Kyokai, *Daigaku Soran,* 1968.

## TABLE 3.2

### Founding Dates of Japanese Academic Societies

| Period of Establishment | Humanities and Education | Law and Political Science | Economics and Commerce | Pure Science | Engineering | Agriculture | Medical Science | Total Number | Total Percent |
|---|---|---|---|---|---|---|---|---|---|
| Through 1900 | 3 | 2 | -- | 8 | 5 | 1 | 7 | 26 | 8 |
| 1901-10 | 1 | -- | -- | 1 | -- | -- | 4 | 6 | 2 |
| 1911-20 | 1 | -- | -- | 3 | 7 | 2 | 3 | 16 | 5 |
| 1921-30 | 6 | -- | 2 | 7 | 7 | 11 | 13 | 46 | 15 |
| 1931-40 | 5 | -- | 7 | 6 | 9 | 2 | 6 | 35 | 11 |
| 1941-45 | -- | -- | 2 | -- | 4 | -- | 2 | 8 | 3 |
| 1946-50 | 25 | 12 | 6 | 11 | 15 | 3 | 12 | 84 | 27 |
| 1951-60 | 20 | 5 | 5 | 10 | 19 | 7 | 16 | 82 | 27 |
| 1961-64 | 3 | -- | -- | -- | 3 | 1 | 1 | 8 | 3 |
| Total | 64 | 19 | 22 | 46 | 69 | 27 | 64 | 311 | 100 |

*Note:* Societies of national stature existing in 1964 were included; those restricted to individual universities or local areas were not included. Societies of "other fields" are not included.

*Source:* Nihon Gakujutsu Kaigi, 1966, *Zenkoku Gakukyokai Sōran* (Directory of learned societies), Tokyo.

referee judgments and make selections based on quality, the journal editors accept all the manuscripts they can afford to publish. When the editors reject manuscripts, it is likely to be because the author has already been published in the past or because the manuscript's focus is outside the journal's scope.

## Research Funds

Soon after the academic societies began to organize, some of their leading figures went to the Occupation to suggest the establishment of the Japan Science Council, to represent the basic research community to the government and to society at large (Kelley 1949). In the spirit of the times, a democratic\ council was developed composed of all the academic disciplines, not just certain segments as in the case of America's National Academy of Sciences. Moreover, the 210 members of the council were to be chosen through triennial elections by all the active researchers in the nation.

The first session of the council was held in 1949, and from the beginning it took bold and often provocative stands on scientific and social issues, to the considerable displeasure of the central government. Partly for this reason, the council's influence has slowly declined. But in the early years its recommendations attracted considerable attention, and among these was its request for the government to exert a bolder effort to promote scientific research.

The Occupation echoed this view, thus placing considerable pressure on the government to provide funds for basic research. Needless to say, in the immediate postwar period this proved extremely difficult. The government's first concern was to provide sufficient funds for salaries and other basic operating expenses. Beyond that, the government placed a high priority on nurturing the handful of elite national universities that had a long tradition of excellence. Thus more than 60 percent of the small amounts the government could spare for research went to these universities as normal research expenses for chairs and research institutes. Since then the government has continued to favor these sites, thus limiting the environment within the academic system in which researchers can enjoy relatively generous funding.

Yet at the same time the government did create a small budget for special research projects, to be awarded on a competitive basis to all researchers regardless of their workplace. The government turned the responsibility for making preliminary recommendations on these funds over to the Science Council. Reflecting its grass-roots democratic character, this organization decided to forego any serious effort at identifying priorities or establishing guidelines, and instead delegated the allocative responsibility to key academic societies. While the formal records of the deliberations of these societies are not available for public review, it is generally understood that they adopted an egalitarian *junban* allocative principle. The applications of scholars were filed according to date of receipt and small fixed amounts were awarded until the funds were exhausted. Those who failed in a given year could expect to be higher on the list the succeeding year. This system aimed to spread the funds as widely as possible, with little regard for the actual amounts requested or the quality of the proposed projects. As in the case of academic society meetings and journals, these procedures emphasized the equality of researchers rather than the differential quality of their work.

Several of the postwar reforms operated to foster interest in research as well as to democratize its conduct. A number of the structural conditions that we have mentioned continue to promote research fever. Academic societies continue to be established at an impressive pace. Research funds allocated on a competitive basis by the Ministry of Education have continued to grow even faster than the regular research funds. In addition to the ministry's funds others are provided by other government organs (especially the Ministry of International Industry and Trade, the Science and Technology Agency, and the newly established NIRA) and several newly established private foundations (such as Nihon Keizai Shimbun Foundation and the Toyota Foundation). Two recent surveys (1967 and 1973) of Japanese professors indicate that nearly half of them view research as the most important component of their role, and the component to which they devote the greatest amount of their time.* In the 1967 survey, professors listed their actual weekly time budget. When asked to indicate their ideal schedule, nearly all shifted some of their time towards research; 49 percent shifted over 13 hours a week towards research. The interest in research is especially strong among the young faculty and those with the position of assistant, at the bottom of their institution's hierarchy.

## Pure Research and Popular Research

The 1967 survey (which excluded assistants) provided evidence on the outcome of this research fever. Of the respondents in this survey, 95 percent said they had published at least one article and nearly three-fifths said they had published a book. Nearly half said they had published 19 or more academic papers. Differences by field are indicated in Table 3.3. This sample was reliable in most other respects, and hence there is no special reason to doubt these figures. They suggest, at least in terms of sheer number of pages, that the Japanese professoriate is one of the most prolific in the world.

---

*The 1973 survey conducted by the Research Institute for Higher Education of Hiroshima University has not been fully published yet; however, one brief summary in English can be found in the Research Institute for Higher Education *Research Bulletin* (1976). The 1967 survey is reported in Cummings (1972). Also see Nakano (1974).

## TABLE 3.3

### Several Indicators of Research Orientation, by Field (percent)

| Report of the Scholars | Humanities | Social Science | Engineering | Agriculture | Medicine | Science | Other Fields | Total |
|---|---|---|---|---|---|---|---|---|
| Have published 19 or more papers | 35.7 | 44.1 | 47.4 | 68.0 | 69.8 | 55.3 | 31.3 | 48.8 |
| Have published at least one book | 66.9 | 76.4 | 52.5 | 84.0 | 58.7 | 44.8 | 56.9 | 60.9 |
| Have published five or more books | 22.2 | 32.3 | 6.8 | 20.0 | 20.2 | 11.2 | 20.3 | 18.4 |
| Over 29 percent of publications for general audience | 62.7 | 71.4 | 11.7 | 10.3 | 10.5 | 20.3 | 30.3 | 32.2 |
| Most typical publication is original research | 33.3 | 29.0 | 57.3 | 53.2 | 62.0 | 71.3 | 39.1 | 48.4 |
| Most typical publication is theory | 21.5 | 33.1 | 11.2 | 2.1 | 3.0 | 4.9 | 14.5 | 14.6 |
| Most typical publication is an academic report | 25.7 | 21.8 | 12.6 | 14.9 | 27.0 | 12.3 | 10.1 | 18.7 |

*Source:* 1967 Representative Study.

Of course, not all of these are pure research publications. Among advanced industrial societies the Japanese people are possibly the last nation of readers. Not only do they consume newspapers (519 per 1,000 people in 1972 compared to 319 in the United States), but they also are avid readers of journals, books, and translations. Throughout the postwar period, approximately 20,000 new book titles have been published annually in Japan (24,593 new titles in 1971, including 2,228 translations—compared to 31,619 new titles, including 2,285 translations, in the United States, with twice Japan's population) and a half-dozen quasi-intellectual monthly journals have continued to prosper with circulations ranging (unofficially) from 50,000 to 300,000. Japanese professors are a major source of the copy for these commercial media, and as far as many professors are concerned the commercial media are at least as satisfying a place to publish as the academic journals—their expressive abilities are put to a greater challenge, they reach a wider audience, and, not so incidentally, they get paid (often on a page-count basis). The 1967 RIHE survey suggested that one-third of Japan's professors are frequent writers for the commercial presses, and among these nearly one-third write exclusively for these media.

## PROFESSIONALISM AND SHOWMANSHIP

Research, regardless of its content, tends to draw the professor into contact with colleagues at other universities and in the broader society. In the case of basic research, this can be seen at every stage of the process, from obtaining funds to publishing results. In deference to postwar equality, granting agencies restrict the maximum amount they will award to a single scholar, so those intending major research find it necessary to write group grant applications listing the names of several active researchers in the area of the grant's objectives. To strengthen the application's credibility, group members are selected from several different workplaces. In the actual conduct of the research, some of the members will be more active than others, but usually a respectable effort is exerted to maintain the group's integrity. Thus a foreign observer cannot help being impressed with the numerous *kenkyukai* (research groups that meet periodically) which Japanese professors belong to; as often as not, these groups are underwritten by a grant and are composed of members from several universities.

Increasingly scholars consider academic societies to be the appropriate places for publishing the fruits of their research, or at least announcing them. Annual society meetings are well attended, and while the formal debates and criticisms are often restrained, the more informal discussions are spirited and often serve to foster relations between men of different backgrounds. While there are no studies of the interpersonal networks of Japanese professors, it is of some interest that in recent years many academics say that both their performance and their acquaintances through academic societies were critical factors in landing their present job (Cummings 1975).

Publishing in the commercial media also broadens the professor's circle. Moreover, those who are skillful in these presentations can look forward to becoming "talents," with frequent invitations to give lectures to nonuniversity groups, to participate in seminars and working groups sponsored by business firms and government bureaus, and to appear on television and radio talk shows. Opportunities of this kind are extraordinarily plentiful in Japan and often quite lucrative (Passin 1975). Every year a handful of professors find these popular activities so attractive that they abandon their university posts to become full-time free lances (the reverse is also true).

## POLITICS AND THE JAPANESE ACADEMIC

### Academic Freedom

Many Japanese intellectuals were deeply disturbed by the military regime's success in reversing the late Taisho democratic trend and leading Japan into war. The more outspoken tended to argue that the military could have been halted if the intellectuals had demonstrated greater courage. Others observed that the institutional framework for guaranteeing freedom of speech was insufficient.

These points of view were appreciated by the Allied Occupation, and it took bold steps to respond to them. In the new constitution, the Occupation promoted articles which guaranteed both freedom of speech and academic freedom. In the new laws and regulations on university governance, the Occupation attempted to limit the role of the central Ministry of Education to that of financial supporter and adviser, while turning basic policy decisions over to the National Diet and every-day decision making to the universities. Steps were taken to increase the autonomy of individual universities. For example, the ministry was relieved of its former role as inspector of higher educational institutions and its chartering authority was weakened. Universities of the national sector were guaranteed the privilege of selecting their own officers and staff, subject only to pro forma government approval, whereas private institutions were allowed complete freedom in these matters.

### Political Activities of Professors

In the first years of the Occupation, most academics were pleased with the Occupation's basic reforms and also with the signs of a progressive trend in the electorate. Within the universities they formed various associations to discuss how they should promote their interests. On the practical side, they formed labor unions to fight for improved salaries and working conditions and a democratization of the hierarchical relations between senior and junior faculty and between faculty and students. These unions had an immediate impact on procedures for governance at many universities—junior faculty were allowed to participate in university elections and in certain cases even in faculty meetings. It might be noted that the trend towards democratization has continued during the whole postwar period so that by 1975 it was the exception for a faculty meeting to exclude junior staff (except in the medical sciences). Another steady trend has been towards reduced salary differentials by academic rank (Kokuritsu Daigaku Kyokai 1966).

Apart from the unions, many left-oriented university intellectuals established more ideological research groups to discuss ways to promote further social reform. The best known among these was the Democratic Scientists' Society or Minka (Hiroshige 1960, pp. 134ff.; Onuma, Fujii, and Katō 1975). At its peak Minka had over 10,000 members. This group was especially sensitive to the problem of promoting world peace. Astounded by the awesome destructive power of the atomic bomb, a weapon that had been developed by American university scientists, Minka vowed that the Japanese university would never cooperate with militarists in arms research. Minka also showed much interest in the Marxist picture of class relations, and its leaders defined university professors as "intellectual workers" distinct from the ruling class of managers and professionals. As workers, Minka maintained, the professors would have to engage in militant struggles to improve their working conditions and ultimately to transform the social order.

In contrast with Minka, some 5,000 liberal academics established the Association of University Professors (General Headquarters 1952, pp. 331 ff.). This organization shared many of the progressive ideals of Minka, but rather than a militant approach it stressed the need to settle disputes through rational means (that is, no strikes or violence), as such conduct was more appropriate to those people entrusted with the "noble duties of research and education of students."

Through 1947 the Occupation seemed to encourage these faculty and student associations, but thereafter its attitude changed. For example, in 1948 it forbade a general strike in which many academic unions intended to participate and began to take a more forward role in the plans for university reorganization by proposing the establishment of boards of trustees to govern each university and the abolition of the academic chairs. The most shocking step was the Occupation's request in 1949 that the Japanese government carry out a purge of all communists in educational positions. With tortured logic, the Occupation argued that committed communists were not capable of a value-free approach to intellectual work. Whatever the merit of these arguments, the plan for a purge clearly violated the spirit of the constitutional guarantees on academic freedom. This contradiction was appreciated by most Japanese academics, and thus they became quite cool to the Occupation as well as to those liberal bodies that had in the past cooperated with the Occupation. The immediate outcome was the effective dissolution of the liberal Japanese Association of University Professors, and a sharp elevation of Minka's status. One indication of this shift was that in the elections for the Japan Science Council a sizable minority of candidates approved by Minka obtained seats (Kobayashi 1956). The council's previously mentioned tendency to issue provocative declarations on social issues is in part explained by Minka's success.

These developments during the late years of the Occupation created a heightened sensitivity to broad social issues among Japanese professors and motivated many to take a more active role in politics, especially of the Left. Most felt it sufficient to participate in politics with their pens, but a small minority became more actively involved as consultants to progressive associations such as the Japan Teachers' Union and other labor unions.

Following the Occupation's departure, there was a decline in the Left's dominance as growing numbers of liberal and "realistic" professors gained the courage to poke their heads out from underneath the rocks of political controversy. Nevertheless, the 1967 RIHE survey indicates that the professoriate was still far to the left of the general public. Of the 95 percent in the sample who said they voted in the 1967 elections for the Lower House, 5 percent supported Communist Party candidates, 40 percent supported Socialist Party candidates, 22 percent supported Democratic Socialist Party candidates, and only 33 percent supported the ruling Conservative Party (which gained a majority of the popular vote). Another indication of the leftward inclination of professors —more accurately, of the polarization of the academic community between radicals and liberals—comes from a question on the social service component of their role. Given the alternatives: one should serve society (a) by working with the government to develop better social policies, (b) by criticizing official social policies, or (c) by some combination of the two, only 8 percent chose the neutral orientation, while 47 percent chose the critical orientation and 46 percent the cooperative position.

The 1967 survey was conducted just as student unrest began to be felt on Japan's campuses. Partly due to student pressure, in the 1968--71 period professors once again became openly involved in politics; for the first time since the Occupation several stood as candidates in important local elections. It was in this period that Ryokichi Minobe, a former professor of economics at Tokyo Education University, became mayor of Tokyo; Masao Motoyama, a former professor of education at Nagoya University, became mayor of that city; and Ichiji Nagasu became governor of Kanagawa Prefecture. Since then several professors have been elected to important public offices. Thus one might say that another postwar trend has been the forging of alliances between sectors of the professoriate and external political groups.

## Politicization of University Decision Making

Before the purge of communists, differences between liberal and progressive intellectuals had largely been aired at an abstract level and over broad social issues. After the purge, however, these differences came to be reflected in internal university politics as well. Debates over candidates to be selected for new positions or academic offices began to acquire strong political overtones as each side tried to extend its revolution into the university. The best known example is economics, where faculties split into Marxist and Keynesian factions. Similar distinctions appeared throughout the social sciences and the humanities, and to some degree even in the basic sciences.

Following the Occupation's departure, the intensity of ideologically-oriented university politics seemed to wane, but at various points since then it has resurfaced. Two subsequent peaks were in 1959–60 and 1967–70, the two periods of energetic student activity. Internal political activities were especially intense during the latter peak, leading to the selection of leftist presidents for many of Japan's well-known universities, especially in the private sector. On the other hand, differences in the national sector led to a situation where at one point nearly a score of universities were without elected presidents.

In contrast to the harmony of the essentially apolitical old-system university, the intrusion of politics has created a special dimension of strain for the contemporary academic, especially at the well-known universities. There is always the fear that someone will take one's lecture, one's personal opinions, or one's writings and warp them through the lenses of some ideological prism to the point where they are no longer recognizable—and then hold the author responsible. In a sense, the guarantees of academic freedom have created a latent fear that one will be misunderstood and maligned, not so much by society as by one's colleagues. For many academics, this politicized situation has robbed them of much of the satisfaction they hoped to derive from the university-centered aspects of their work.

## CONCLUSION

In Japan the role of university professor was initiated by the state and a small number of educational pioneers after 1868. Gradually these founders developed a system of regulations and rewards that channeled the energies of individual professors inwards towards their universities, rather than outwards towards academic disciplines and society. Over the last two to three decades the centripetal pull of the universities has weakened. Nevertheless, most professors continue to believe that their basic commitment should be to their university, and thus they particularly rally behind their university in times of crisis. The campus turmoil of the late 1960s was a revealing example: many professors abandoned their research altogether to participate in daily skull sessions with angry students. During this period, attendance at faculty meetings was close to perfect even though the meetings often lasted a full day and sometimes extended much longer.

In normal times, a minority of professors exhibit exceptional devotion to their universities. Indeed, it seems clear, especially in the private sector, that a new class of faculty managers who actually enjoy university administration has emerged. Most universities also have their great teachers who year after year continue to deliver polished lectures and spend endless hours chatting with their students.

In today's normal situations, however, many professors have an ambivalent attitude towards their university-centered activities. While they recognize the importance of these activities, they find them neither especially interesting nor sufficiently remunerative to justify special effort. Most indicate a desire to decrease the amount of time they spend in teaching and, especially, in university-related administrative work. Some, like the so-called academic *salariman,* appear content to put in a 9–5 day at their university and avoid all other challenges.

Yet a large number seek to engage in the growing volume of externally oriented opportunities—to conduct research, consult, write for popular audiences, to speak to the public through lectures and on television, and even to engage in politics. The diversity of these opportunities and the energy with which some academics, called "talents," participate in them staggers the imagination. A successful talent's diary is likely to be filled from morning till evening with a minimum of three external events for several weeks in advance. At least two-thirds of his annual income will come from these engagements. Other professors tend to specialize in one or the other of these areas, at least for some period in their careers. They may devote themselves exclusively to basic scientific research or to politically oriented activity. The successful academic is even likely to go through stages, from being a serious and committed researcher in his early years to becoming a quasi-popular writer by his late thirties and a public speaker and consultant in his fifties.

Significantly, it is difficult to predict how a Japanese professor will play his professorial role by merely knowing his institutional affiliation and his specialty. In Japan's great national universities, one finds many popularists who do little serious research. On the other hand, in some of the smaller colleges one can find avid researchers.

In other mass systems, such as in the United States, one finds a similarly increasing diversification of the activities taken up by academics. In these systems, however, this diversification has tended to take place along with a complementary process of differentiation in the purposes of individual institutions. Thus the purposes of individual institutions tend to shape the way professors play their roles. In research-oriented universities, professors devote much of their time to research, and relatively less to teaching, popular writing, and showmanship. In central city universities, professors are closer to the media and the mass market. Small liberal arts colleges stress excellent teaching, and the professors who seek employment in these institutions attempt to live up to the institutional expectations. Thus there appears to be a more ordered differentiation of roles within the American higher educational system.

The growing diversity of opportunities and of personal styles in Japan defies systematic analysis or neat generalization. In many respects, this diversity is attractive, yet it also raises basic questions and generates obvious strains. What are the responsibilities of a university professor? Which aspects of his work are worthy and which less so? Is it permissible for a professor to skip his classes in order to appear on a television program for which he will receive a fee? In order to engage in political activity?

Beyond these questions of role confusion generated by practical opportunities, there are fundamental ambiguities generated by an academic system under political stress. Both the internal and external activities of professors tend to be evaluated in political terms by their colleagues and their students, even when the individuals concerned think their actions are politically neutral. Particularly in times of radical student protest, those who manage universities suffer through arduous ordeals in trying to navigate through the political interpretations attached to their actions. This politicization extends even to the realm of basic scientific research, causing some areas of inquiry in, for example, physics and biology to be considered reactionary because new discoveries might contribute to the plans of the nation's militarists.

The university-centered principle has proved too weak to regulate these strains and ambiguities. Whereas in the old system universities were managed by wise and authoritative founding figures, today they tend to be faculty-controlled democracies. At individual institutions, issues such as those we mention tend to manifest themselves on a case-by-case basis. In the old system, the authoritative figure might have delivered some judgment, but in the new democratic system, faculty courtesy defers to the conscience of the individual professor. He can consider many standards—those of his university, his discipline, his political ideology, and the interests of his family—but he will find there is no universal standard for the academic profession. Possibly this is because, as Nakayama suggests (1974), the foundation of universities and the university-centered principle preceded the formation of professions and the articulation of their standards. Possibly it is because political ideologies and academic activities have become so tightly intertwined. Regardless of the cause, we conclude that Japan still lacks widespread agreement on the ideals and standards to guide professorial activities.

## REFERENCES

Amano, Ikuo. 1975. "The Structure of Japanese Higher Education: Its Formation, Continuity, and Changeability." Paper presented at the International Conference on the Changing Japanese University, Tokyo, 1976.

————. 1976. "Daigaku Kyōin no Yakuwari Kozo" (The Structure of the university professor's role). Report prepared as part of "Daigaku no Soshiki Unei ni Kansurn Sogoteki Kenkyu (University organization and management), issued by Hiroshima University's Research Institute for Higher Education, as Research Note no. 26.

Cummings, William K. 1972. "The Changing Academic Marketplace and University Reform in Japan." Ph.D. dissertation, Harvard University.

————. 1973. "The Japanese Private University." *Minerva* 11:348–71.

————. 1974. "The Conservatives Reform Higher Education." *Japan Interpreter* 8:421–31.

————. 1975. "Understanding Behavior in Japan's Academic Marketplace." *Journal of Asian Studies* 34:313–40.

General Headquarters, Supreme Commander Allied Powers, 1948. *Education in the New Japan.* Vol. 2.

————. 1952. *Postwar Developments in Japanese Education.* Vol. 2.

Gouldner, Alvin W. 1957. "Cosmopolitans and Locals: Toward an Analysis of Latent Social Roles." *Administrative Science Quarterly* 2:281–306, 444–80.

Hearn, Lafcadio. 1973. *Japan—An Attempt at an Interpretation.* Boston: Houghton Mifflin.

Hiroshige, Tetsu. 1960. *Sengo Nihon no Kagaku Undō* (Japan postwar science movement). Tokyo: Chuōkoronsha.

Ienaga, Saburo. 1967. *Daigaku no Jiyu no Rekishi* (The History of academic freedom). Tokyo: Koshobo.

Jiyū Minshutō Bunkyō Seido Chōsakai. 1969. *Kokumin no Tame no Daigaku* (Universities for the Japanese nation). Tokyo: Jiyū Minshutō Jōhō Iinkai Shuppankyoku.

Kelley, Harry C. 1949. "A Survey of Japanese Science." *Scientific Monthly* 6.

Kobayashi, Tetsuya. 1956. *General Education for Scientists and Engineers in Japan.* Ann Arbor: University of Michigan Comparative Education Dissertation Series.

Kokuritsu Daigaku Kyokai. 1966. "Kokuritsu Daigaku Kyokan no Kyuryo Kaizen Ni Kansuru Ikensho" (Memorandum on the improvement of salaries of national university faculty members). *Jurisito* 356:96–99.

Mombusho. Annual. *Nempo* (Ministry of Education statistical yearbook).

Mombusho Gakujutsu Kokusaikyoku. 1975. *Wagakuni no Gakujutsu* (White paper on the learned activities of our nation). Tokyo: Nihon Gakujutsu Shinkokai.

Nagai, Michio. 1969. "Chishikijin no Seisan Rūtō" (The Production of Japanese intellectuals). In Michio Nagai, ed., *Kindaika to Kyoiku* (Modernization and education). Tokyo: Tōkyō Daigaku Shuppankai.

———. 1971. *Higher Education in Japan: Its Take-off and Crash.* Trans. Jerry Dusenbury. Tokyo: University of Tokyo Press.

Nakano, Hideichiro. 1974. "Japanese University Professors Today." *Kwansei Gakuin University Annual Studies* 23:1–10.

Nakayama, Shigeru. 1974. *Rekishi to shite no Gakumon* (University traditions). Tokyo: Chūō Koronsha.

Ogata, Ken. 1976. "Shigakū Zaisei to Kenkyuhi" (Private university budgets and research money). *IDE* 165:23–28.

Onuma, Masanori; Yōichiro Fujii; and Kunioki Katō. 1975. *Sengo Nihon no Kagakushi Undoshi* (The Postwar movement of Japanese scientists). 2 vols. Tokyo: Aoki Shoten.

Passin, Herbert. 1975. "Intellectuals in the Decision-Making Process." In Vogel, Ezra F., ed., *Modern Japanese Organization and Decision-Making,* pp. 251–83. Berkeley: University of California Press.

RIHE of Hiroshima University (1976). Summary of 1973 survey data, full publication forthcoming. *Research Institute for Higher Education Research Bulletin.*

Shimizu, Yoshihiro, ed. 1975. *Chiiki Shakai to Kokuritsu Daigaku* (National universities and their local communities). Tokyo: Tōkyō Daigaku Shuppankai.

Shinbori, Michiya. 1964. "Comparative Study of Career Patterns of College Professors." *International Review of Education* 10:284–96.

Spaulding, Robert M. 1967. *Imperial Japan's Higher Civil Service Examinations.* Princeton: Princeton University Press.

Terasaki, Masao and Tokiomi Kaigo. 1969. *Daigaku Kyōiku—Sengo Nihon no Kyōiku Kaikaku* (University education: Change in postwar education). Vol. 9. Tokyo: Tōkyō Daigaku Shuppankai.

Tomoda, Yasumasa. 1976. "Democratization and Efficient Organization of the Governance in Individual Institutions." Paper presented at the International Conference on the Changing Japanese University, Tokyo, 1976.

Trow, Martin. 1973. "Problems in the Transition from Elite to Mass Higher Education." Carnegie Commission on Higher Education Reprint.

U.N. Secretariat. 1974. *Statistical Yearbook of 1973.* 25th issue. New York: U.N. Secretariat.

# 4

# Academic Staff and Academic Drift in Australian Colleges of Advanced Education
## Grant Harman

There are now over 20,000 university and college of advanced education teachers and researchers in Australia, apart from some 4,000 to 6,000 part-timers. These 20,000 people, usually referred to in Australia as academic staff or academics rather than as professors (the title professor is reserved for the top rank of university teachers and researchers), constitute a relatively high-income and high-status elite in Australian society. Within their institutions, most of them enjoy the security of tenure until retirement. Salaries compare reasonably well with those of many professional groups and government employees, and are adjusted regularly to take account of inflation; there are liberal study or sabbatical leave provisions. Within the society, many of them serve on government committees or inquiries, take leading parts in the life of professional and cultural associations, and play prominent roles in public affairs. Many also participate actively in political life. In the last three very lively federal general election campaigns, considerable numbers of academics entered openly into the fray, addressing public meetings, writing letters to the press, and participating in the battle of words over inflation and other economic questions.

This paper, however, is not concerned with Australian academics in general, nor with the roles of academics in Australian society and public life. These matters have been discussed to some extent elsewhere (Partridge 1968; Buckley 1962; Browne 1970; Harman and Selby Smith 1972; Harman 1975; Anderson et al. 1975), though no one yet has attempted any detailed or comprehensive study of Australian academics in both universities and colleges

---

Note: The figures for student enrollments and staff numbers are from publications of the Australian Bureau of Statistics, the Universities Commission and the Commission on Advanced Education.

of advanced education. Rather, this paper is concerned with academics only in colleges of advanced education, and only in relation to a phenomenon that has been referred to in the literature as academic drift.

Academic drift is defined here as a process whereby nonuniversity institutions aspire and work to become more like universities. The Australian colleges of advanced education illustrate this process well. They were created to offer tertiary-level, vocational courses, distinct from university courses. But almost from the start, most of the colleges took the universities as their reference point and strove to model themselves on universities. As a result, the colleges have become increasingly like universities. Their academic staffs, without doubt, have contributed to this process of academic drift, although they have been by no means the sole cause of the changes. Academic drift, in turn, has produced important changes in key characteristics of college academics, particularly in the level of formal qualifications, varieties of past experience, interest in and emphasis given to research and publications, and attitudes and orientations. In this paper we will explore some of these changes and discuss some of the consequent problems facing the college of advanced education as future development is planned.

Unfortunately, there is a lack of adequate data for a detailed and extensive documentation of the changes that have taken place in a little over a decade with respect to those particular characteristics considered here. In particular, there is a lack of information concerning many of the characteristics of college academics before 1973. In the dicussion that follows data from documentary and other sources are used, but the main single source is data from a 1973 national survey of college of advanced education academic staff conducted by the author, as part of the Regional Colleges Project. This project was a major multi-disciplinary team study carried out over the period 1973 to 1975 by members of the Education Research Unit, Research School of Social Sciences, Australian National University for the Commission on Advanced Education, the federal government's coordinating agency for the college of advanced education sector. The results of the study are reported in Anderson et al. (1975), while the survey instruments used have been published separately (Beswick and Harman 1975). There are two samples from the 1973 academic staff survey, one of 263 staff members from 14 regional or nonmetropolitan colleges and the other of 169 staff members from 7 metropolitan colleges. The colleges used in the survey included multi-school colleges as well as single-school agricultural and teachers' colleges. In the regional and smaller metropolitan colleges a random sample of one in every three staff members was selected, while in the larger metropolitan institutions the sample was one in six. Questionnaires were delivered personally by members of the project team to each prospective respondent, who was asked to return the completed questionnaire by mail. The response rate was 86 percent for the regional sample and 75 percent for the metropolitan sample.

# THE STRUCTURE OF AUSTRALIAN HIGHER EDUCATION: THE UNIVERSITY-CAE DICHOTOMY

The Australian system of higher education today consists of two groups of institutions, universities and colleges of advanced education (CAEs).

The origins of both sectors go back quite a long way for a country with a relatively short history. The first universities were established in Sydney and Melbourne in the 1850s, while the college of advanced education sector can trace its antecedents back to the mechanics institutes and technical colleges which flourished in a number of colonies in the second half of last century and to early teacher training schools. But it is only since World War II, and especially since the 1960s, that the main expansion of higher education has taken place and that the present patterns have emerged. In these developments the single most important source of initiative has been the federal government. Constitutionally, the federal government has no direct responsibility for education outside federal territories, and today all the universities, with the exception of the Australian National University and almost all the colleges of advanced education, are state government creations, established under state legislation and responsible to a state minister.

After World War II the federal government gradually became increasingly involved with the financing of higher education, first of the universities and later of the colleges. For a number of years federal and state authorities provided matching grants to finance higher education (dollar for dollar for capital expenditure, and a $1.85 from state sources to each Commonwealth dollar for recurrent expenditure), but on January 1, 1974 the federal government assumed full responsibility for all costs, both recurrent and capital, for universities and colleges of advanced education. Under the new funding arrangement, tuition and other compulsory fees were abolished and the federal government established a new scheme of providing living allowances on a means-tested moncompetitive basis to all full-time students.

Today there are 19 universities. Of these, thirteen are located in state capitals, one is in Canberra, the federal capital, and the remaining five are in provincial centers in the three eastern states. By North American standards, Australian universities are not large institutions: in 1975 only four had total enrollments of more than 15,000 students (the largest, the University of New South Wales in Sydney, had 18,128 students), while seven had less than 5,000 students. Total university enrollments in 1976 slightly exceeded 153,000 students: 62 percent were full-time students, 30 percent were part-time "internal" students, and 8 percent were "external" students (major external studies, or off-campus programs, have been offered by three universities for a number of years). Each university offers degrees at bachelor's, master's, and doctoral levels.

The Australian universities are all public or state institutions, there is no tradition of private institutions, as in the United States; yet, they are relatively autonomous, being governed by their own councils or senates made up of government and parliamentary nominees, and representatives of academic staff, present students, and past students. Among academic staff there is a strong tradition of university autonomy and academic independence, derived mainly from British precedents and connections.

The British influence has always been strong in Australian universities and it continues to be so. The Australian universities were modeled on English and Scottish institutions, and for many years the relative isolation of each of the six state universities from one another tended to reinforce their connections with Britain. As one Australian scholar (Partridge 1968, pp. 120–21) has remarked,

> Many of the staff were recruited from universities in the United Kingdom . . . ; most of the native Australian teachers would have done their postgraduate training in a British university; and they usually returned to Britain when their year of sabbatical leave came round. Collectively the universities were dominated by British traditions and practices; they judged themselves by British standards and sought British recognition.

Of course, in recent years the extent of overseas influence has declined, and for the last decade or so Australian higher education has been influenced increasingly by North American, as well as British, ideas and practices. The latter are still a dominant characteristic of the Australian university scene. Australian academics still look for overseas recognition, and many universities favor applicants for academic posts with overseas qualifications; in 1976 almost 65 percent of the academic staff of the Australian National University held a degree or degrees from an overseas university. Australian universities still provide study or sabbatical leave conditions superior to any in the world (twelve months leave on full salary plus a travel allowance after each six years of service, or six months leave after every three years service), since it is held to be of vital importance that staff keep in touch with overseas developments.

The college of advanced education sector is relatively new, springing from recommendations made in 1964 by a federal government committee appointed to advise on the future development of tertiary education. This committee suggested that a major expansion and diversification of higher education was desirable, and recommended the establishment throughout Australia of tertiary colleges having a strong technological and vocational orientation. It envisaged these colleges as offering courses mainly at a lower academic level than university work, and leading to a diploma or certificate, rather than a degree. In each state existing technical colleges, institutes of technology, agricultural colleges, and other institutions involved with nonuniversity tertiary courses soon secured recognition by the federal government as colleges of advanced education, thus qualifying for federal financial assistance. In time, a number of completely new colleges were established (such as the Canberra College of Advanced Education), while institutions such as teachers colleges were used as the bases of new, multi-school colleges of advanced education. In mid-1973 the federal government agreed to recognize state government teachers' colleges and a number of nongovernment preschool and nursery teachers' colleges as colleges of advanced education. In the following year six nongovernment teachers' colleges came into the CAE sector.

As a result of these developments the CAE sector today is a large and rapidly growing one. In late 1965 the federal government was providing funds for 26 colleges with a total enrollment of 24,300 students. In 1976 there were almost 80 colleges, scattered over all six Australian states and the Australian Capital Territory, with a total enrollment of over 134,000 students. In terms of student enrollments, the CAE sector will soon be comparable in size to the university sector. Unlike the Australian universities, however, which display a surprising degree of uniformity and similarity, the college sector is marked by diversity. Some colleges, like the Royal Melbourne Institute of Technology or the Western Australian Institute of Technology, are major institutions with over 10,000 students, far larger than many Australian universities; others have a few hundred students, or ever fewer. Some are multi-school in structure, offering a wide variety of undergraduate and postgraduate programs in the physical and biological sciences, technology, social sciences and humanities, business, fine arts, and education; others are single-school, preparing students for a single profession or group of closely related professions. Rather confusingly, CAEs go by a wide variety of titles: institute of technology, institute of advanced education, college of advanced education, teachers' college, pharmacy college, college of nursing, agricultural college, and conservatorium of music are merely some examples.

Colleges now offer a range of undergraduate and postgraduate courses ranging from one-year undergraduate certificates to master's degrees. In spite of a fair measure of independence, they are subject to much closer scrutiny by federal and state coordinating agencies than are universities, especially with regard to financial matters and the introduction of new courses. Although many of the values and traditions of the university sector have been adopted by colleges, the latter are far less influenced by British university traditions.


## THE ACADEMIC PROFESSION IN AUSTRALIA

The structure of the academic profession in Australia has changed to a marked degree in recent years, reflecting the expansion and diversification of higher education.

## The Expansion of Academic Staff

Perhaps the most dramatic change has been in the size of the profession. This change has resulted from two factors: rapid growth in universities and the development of the CAEs as a recognized part of higher education. The expansion of university staffs has been impressive—in the last ten years the number of full-time university teachers and researchers has increased from just over 5,000 to almost 12,000.

The acceptance of the CAEs within higher education and their development have had greater impact. Before the CAEs were developed lecturers in teachers' colleges, agricultural colleges, and institutes of technology were not widely recognized as parts of the academic profession. Admittedly, a few leading college lecturers were sometimes recognized by particular university academics as specialists within their disciplines, but most of them occupied a twilight zone on the edge of the academic world. There were many reasons for this: often college lecturers had much lower formal qualifications than university staff members, college salary scales were appreciably lower, and the highest awards their colleges could give were certificates or diplomas, not degrees. Moreover, most of these earlier colleges were controlled by state government departments and lecturers had the status of public servants. This situation, however, has now changed, and today CAE staffs are now widely accepted by their university colleagues as being members of a common academic profession.

Of course, a considerable degree of jealousy, and sometimes mistrust, remains between the two sectors. Some university people still look on colleges as second-class institutions and consider that college courses are generally less demanding intellectually than university courses, while college academics are sometimes critical of the conservatism, snobbery, and poor teaching techniques of their university counterparts. But gradually the barriers between staff in the two sectors are becoming less important, and, more and more staff members from both groups of institutions are working together in professional and learned associations.

In 1976 university academics still outnumbered college academics, but within a decade college academics will probably constitute the larger group. Over the previous decade the rate of growth of academic staff in the college sector was dramatic. In late 1965 there were 1,200 full-time college staff members: by 1976 there were almost 8,500. Of course, not all this growth came from the establishment and filling of new teaching positions—part resulted from the transfer of entire colleges and their staffs into the college sector. Still, the rate of new recruitment was dramatic. In the 1967-73 period, it is estimated that 4,000 new academic positions were established and filled in CAEs and in state government teachers' colleges that became CAEs in 1973.

The expansion of the academic profession had many effects on the profession itself, some highly desirable and others less so. In the first place, the rapid rate of expansion in both sectors provided many attractive opportunities for both promotion and participation in the planning of new courses, programs, and even new institutions. In the university sector, it facilitated a marked growth in specialization and the development of stronger research and graduate studies programs. With considerably more scholars in each of the major disciplines, it became possible to develop active learned societies at local, state, and national levels. The national societies have brought academics from the various states into close contact with one another; gone, to a large measure, are the isolation and parochialism that for so long characterized academic staff in each of the state capitals. On the other hand, for at least a decade recruitment of well-qualified and experienced staff was difficult. Then there were often strains because of the large numbers of new staff that had been recruited quickly so that new programs could be launched. In our 1973 survey of academic staff in colleges we found that seven out of ten respondents in regional colleges had been with their college less than five years.

Part-time staff have always played an important part in Australian higher education. Even with the expansion of the last decade in the numbers of full-time staff, universities and colleges still employ large numbers of part-time lecturers and tutors. In 1973 in one large metropolitan institute of technology two out of five staff members were part-time employees. While large numbers of part-time staff are employed, however, in both sectors part-time staff take on only approximately 11 percent of the teaching load.

In terms of age and sex distribution, there is a close similarity between the two sectors. In both staff are reasonably young, though not as young as British university staffs were in 1964-65 and 1968 (Halsey and Trow 1971, pp. 9, 71, 158). In our 1973 survey we found that 63 percent of respondents in regional colleges, and 53 percent in metropolitan colleges, were under 40 years of age. As in most countries, the Australian academic profession is male-dominated. Only 15 percent of full-time university academics are female, while in the colleges the figure is 12 percent. In both sectors women are concentrated in the lowest academic grades and in fields such as education, paramedical studies, the humanities, and social sciences.

## Rank Within the Profession

The academic profession is also divided by academic rank and by subject or field of specialization. In both sectors the grade structure of academic rank is a five-level hierarchy. Details of these levels, together with salary levels and proportional distribution in each are shown in Table 4.1. At the bottom of the university hierarchy is the grade of tutor or senior tutor, which is usually

## TABLE 4.1

Rank and Salary Scales for Academic Staff in Australian
Universities and Colleges of Advanced Education

| Rank | Percent in Each Rank | Salary Scale, May 1976 (in Australian dollars) |
|------|----------------------|------------------------------------------------|
| Universities | | |
| Professor | 9 | 25,955 |
| Associate Professor or Reader | 9 | 22,247 |
| Senior Lecturer | 24 | 17,569 |
| Lecturer | 25 | 12,835 |
| Senior Tutor/Tutor/ Demonstrator | 33 | 9,127 |
| | | |
| Colleges of Advanced Education | | |
| Dean or Head of School | -- | -- |
| Principal Lecturer or Head of Department | -- | -- |
| Senior Lecturer | 24 | 20,421 |
| Lecturer | 58 | 17,729 |
| Assistant Lecturer or Tutor | 12 | 12,835 |

*Note:* On May 1, 1976 Australian $1.00 = U.S. $1.23.

reserved for new recruits without a doctoral degree—often it is used by recent graduates proceeding to a masters' or doctoral degree by part-time study. Next comes the rank of lecturer, to which most new recruits with a Ph.D. would be appointed. Usually after a period of probation lecturers are given a permanent appointment with tenure; more senior posts carry all tenure. Promotion to senior posts is on the basis of merit and is by no means automatic. At the top of the hierarchy is the exalted rank of professor. The proportion of full professors is comparable to that in the United Kingdom, but considerably lower than that in the United States and Canada.

The college sector has developed equivalent grades with identical salary scales. At the bottom is the rank of assistant lecturer or tutor, which is usually used for short-term, nontenured appointments. Appointments at other grades generally carry tenure after a short probationary period. One notable difference between the two sectors is that the proportions of college staff in the two highest and the lowest grades are much smaller than for university staff. To date no college has used the title of professor for the highest grade, though one metropolitan institute of technology refers to posts of the highest grade as chairs. To date there is parity of salaries between the two sections, and salary scales are determined nationally by the Academic Salaries Tribunal that reports its findings directly to the federal parliament.

The division into subject fields differs between the sectors. The myth still lingers on that the college sector is dominated by staff in applied science, engineering, and technology; however, in 1975 almost half (47 percent) of the full-time college academics were in education. Next in rank order came science and mathematics (12 percent), engineering and technology (9 percent), humanities and social sciences (8 percent), with other fields being numerically unimportant. In the university sector, no one field dominates to such an extent. Science and mathematics constitutes the largest group (29 percent), followed in order by the humanities and social sciences (20 percent), economics and commerce (12 percent), medicine and chemistry (11 percent), and engineering and technology (10 percent). In the more traditional universities, staff from particular subject fields or groups of subject fields are arranged in faculties, each headed by an elected dean. Within the faculties are departments with appointed professorial heads. Many of the newer universities, however, have experimented with schools in place of faculties, while in a number of universities there has been a move towards rotation of department heads. The colleges generally use schools, faculties, or divisions as their major administrative units, often with departments within these. Heads of schools and departments are usually appointed permanently.

Most Australian academics spend little time thinking about their profession as a whole. Admittedly, a few bemoan the lack of real intellectual life in Australian colleges and universities (these are mainly in the humanities, and many of them would like to create something like an Oxbridge collegiate style of academic life), or their essentially utilitarian or vocational spirit; most are concerned about their disciplines, their teaching, their research, their salaries, and making the most of their private lives.

## ACADEMIC DRIFT

In higher education academic drift refers to a process whereby nonuniversity institutions aspire to become more like universities. This usually involves the upgrading of courses, an increased emphasis on higher-level, rather than lower-level, work (that is, degree rather than diploma, and postgraduate rather than undergraduate), an increase in academic or theoretical emphasis in courses, and the development of research and publication functions.

Academic drift has been a common phenomemon in a number of Western countries. In the United States, for instance, there are many examples of institutions being upgraded: in some cases a single institution has, over a few decades, moved from a normal school to a teachers' college, to a state college, to a state university. In Britain there is just as long and as strong a tradition of this phenomenon. Pratt and Burgess (1974, p. 23) write in their book on the British polytechnics:

> For more than a century colleges founded in the technical college tradition have gradually changed it for that of the universities. They have aspired to an increasing level of work, to a narrowing of student intake, to a rationalisation of course structure, to a more academic course content. This has inevitably led to a neglect of local needs, demands and the education of the people for whom the colleges were founded. Other colleges then had to take over their responsibilities for further education, and they too suffered the same pressures.

They go on to document these changes; the attempts of the early nineteenth century colleges to model themselves on universities; the aspiration of many colleges created in the second half of the nineteenth century, such as Owens College at Manchester, to be university status, and how a number grew into civic universities; the elevation, after the World War II, of some technical colleges to colleges of advanced technology and the achievement of university status by some of the CAEs; and the efforts by many polytechnics today to model themselves on universities.

Academic drift is not a new phenomenon in Australia, though it appears to have a much shorter tradition than that in the United Kingdom. One notable example was in Sydney after World War II, when part of Sydney Technical College was upgraded to become a special university of technology. The new university soon shed lower-level courses in order to concentrate on degree and postgraduate work, and branched out into nontechnological fields. Within a decade it had changed its name to the University of New South Wales and was little different from other Australian universities. One result was that soon there was a serious gap in course offerings in technologies in Sydney, and in the early 1960s the New South Wales government had to create a new institute of technology to concentrate on nondegree work.

The best example of academic drift is the current CAE sector. As we have already noted, CAEs were created to train middle-level manpower. Their courses were to be vocational and technical in orientation, at a lower academic level than those in universities, and they were to lead to the award of diplomas or certificates rather than degrees. Moreover, they were to be teaching rather than research institutions, with experienced staff drawn mainly from industry and business. The colleges were established on these lines, but in a little over a decade they became decidedly more like universities. In most colleges there

has been a determined upward push with regard to the academic program—
seeking to expand degree-level, in relation to diploma and subdiploma, teaching, and postgraduate, in relation to undergraduate, work.

It is not easy to get statistical data to illustrate this trend. Unfortunately,
the Australian Bureau of Statistics has only collected and published statistics
on student enrollments by level of courses since 1973. Even for the two-year
period 1973-75, however, postgraduate and bachelor degree enrollments increased from 33 to 38 percent of the total, while enrollments in diploma and
associate diploma courses dropped from 67 to 62 percent. The only other
figures readily available to demonstrate the upward drift of courses are those
for enrollment by level in particular institutions. For example, in 1967 diploma
and subdiploma enrollments at the South Australian Institute of Technology
constituted 95 percent of total enrollments, while bachelor degree and postgraduate enrollments constituted 5 percent; by 1976, the proportions were:
diploma and subdiploma, 61 percent; bachelor degree and postgraduate, 39
percent. Over almost the same period bachelor degree and postgraduate enrollments at the Royal Melbourne Institute of Technology increased from 25
percent to almost 50 percent of total enrollments.

Changes in the level of courses, however, have not been the only changes
of importance. In many cases courses have become more academic and entrance requirements more demanding. The colleges still have a strong technical
and vocational emphasis, though now there are many courses in various nontechnological fields; some colleges have been allowed to offer even unashamedly nonvocational B.A. degrees. While the colleges are primarily
teaching institutions, research has developed to a significant degree. Finally,
as already indicated, there have been marked changes in college academic staff,
some of which will be explored shortly.

The fact of academic drift in Australian CAEs is now quite widely recognized, not only by college personnel but also by government agencies, government committees, and researchers. A recent committee of inquiry into
postsecondary education in the state of Western Australia (Committee on
Post-Secondary Education 1976, p. 22), for example, reported that

> a controversial question that has arisen with regard to colleges of advanced
> education concerns what has been called "upward drift"—that is the ten-
> dency of some colleges to expand degree-level in relation to diploma-level
> teaching, postgraduate in relation to undergraduate teaching, and to
> strengthen their investment in research.

To take another example, in reporting on a case study of one multi-school
regional college in Queensland a team of researchers (Anderson et al. 1975,
vol. 3, p. 163) summed up their findings with regard to academic drift as
follows.

The Institute was designed to have a very different emphasis from that of a university. Its prime objectives were to give priority to the teaching-learning process in high level vocationally oriented courses, and to develop community orientation. However, these directions are shifted by the push for academic status. . . . Emphasis is placed [for academic staff] on academic qualifications when matters such as course accreditation and promotions are considered. There is also a push to upgrade all courses, and to do away with lower level certificate courses, which are to become associate diplomas. The diplomas have become degrees . . . and all schools are applying to offer master's courses.

It is clear that academic staff in colleges have contributed in a marked degree to this upward push. Many senior appointees in CAEs set their sights firmly on the university, and they often deliberately sought to recruit other staff with a university-type orientation and with interest in teaching advanced work. They also held out to new appointees the possibility of developing and partic-ipating in bachelor's degree and postgraduate courses. Thus many persons came to their appointments in colleges with high hopes of being able to upgrade courses and teach mainly at bachelor's and postgraduate levels. Apart from this, many staff in colleges quite naturally aspired to the status enjoyed by university academics, and to university salary scales, working conditions, and fringe benefits, especially study leave. Of course, not all college academics have set their sights on the university model. In fact, many have strongly urged that colleges keep out of all degree work and become more like American community colleges; these have never constituted more than a small, some-times vocal, minority.

At the same time it needs to be emphasized that academics have not constituted the sole stimulus for academic drift in colleges; rather, govern-ments, government committees, college administrators, college councils, col-lege students, and professional bodies have often deliberately encouraged and sought to facilitate the upward academic quest of the college sector as a whole and of particular colleges. For instance, in the late 1960s, on the recommenda-tions of two special committees appointed by the federal minister for educa-tion, federal and state governments agreed that, under certain restrictions, colleges should be able to award bachelor's and master's degrees and that there should be university salary scales in the college sector. College council mem-bers, college students, and professional bodies have often supported the devel-opment of degree courses, since in Australia the degree has a special prestige seldom found in the United States and Canada, while many college principals have had a secret (and sometimes not so secret) yearning to turn their institu-tion into universities and to be a university vice-chancellor, with all the high status associated with that role.

Of course, governments and others have sometimes followed seemingly contradictory policies with regard to academic drift. Within a short time of the federal government's agreeing to the idea of colleges awarding degrees and college academic staff being paid at university rates, for instance, its advisory commission on advanced education was warning colleges about "the temptations to follow certain overseas institutions along the path of 'academic respectability' " (Commission on Advanced Education 1972, p. 3).

Apart from deliberate encouragement, governments and colleges have also indirectly and sometimes unknowingly stimulated or facilitated academic drift. A particularly important factor has been the failure of federal and state governments to spell out clearly the objectives of colleges, the precise levels at which they will teach, and the emphasis to be given to work at each level. Then too, state coordinating agencies have often operated accreditation systems in such a way as to emphasize the university model; members of accreditation committees have been drawn largely from universities, and have understandably tended to use university frames of reference and standards. Further, college academic staff promotion systems have placed increasing emphasis on formal academic qualifications and publications, rather than on teaching and college contribution alone. Apart from all these factors, the upward drift without doubt has been facilitated by the rapid pace of the expansion in student numbers—in a steady state situation academic drift would have been much more difficult.

## ACADEMIC EMPLOYMENT QUALIFICATIONS

### Formal Academic Qualifications

We now turn to look in detail at some particular changes in CAE academic staff. Perhaps the most dramatic change relates to formal academic qualifications—the emphasis placed by government coordinating agencies on academic qualifications, to particular qualifications sought by colleges in recruiting new staff, the actual qualifications held by college academics, and changing college attitudes towards study for further qualifications.

Official views concerning desirable qualities for college academic staff have changed significantly since 1965, reflecting the upward academic movement that has taken place in most colleges. These changes can be well illustrated by reference to statements made by the federal government's coordinating agency for colleges (first the Advisory Committee on Advanced Education, and later the Commission on Advanced Education) in triennial reports. In its 1966 report, the Advisory Committee set out its blueprint for colleges. Just as college courses were to be distinct from university courses, so college academics were to be distinct from university academics. They were to be specialists in the application of knowledge, rather than in discovery; to be good teachers, rather than great scholars. The committee placed little emphasis on the high formal qualifications required by universities; in fact, it stated categorically that "in many fields appropriate experience will rank higher than formal post-graduate studies" (Commonwealth Advisory Committee 1966, p. 31). By 1969 there had been some softening of this policy. It was stated that one legitimate purpose of study leave was to enable staff to secure "relevant higher qualifications" (Commonwealth Advisory Committee 1969, p. 43). Furthermore, the previous statements with regard to formal postgraduate studies were not repeated; in fact, no reference at all was made to formal qualifications, except in regard to study leave. Even greater changes followed in the next two reports: in 1972, academic excellence was recognized as one important criteria in staff selection, while three years later the commission emphasized that all staff should be "academically well-equipped" and recommended that the federal government make special funds available to assist college staff wishing to pursue postgraduate studies.

These changes have been important. But even more dramatic are the changes in the statements about qualifications made by colleges in their press advertisements for new staff. In Australia there is a long-standing and firm tradition that academic vacancies in universities are filled by seeking formal applications through public advertisement in the press, and the colleges have followed this tradition. For the first three or four years colleges usually placed strong emphasis on professional experience in their advertisements, but said very little about formal academic qualifications. Sometimes it was stated that an appropriate degree was necessary, sometimes that a degree or diploma was desired, and sometimes there was no statement at all about formal qualifications being necessary or desired. Now, however, most colleges stress that a higher degree or an honors bachelor's degree is essential for appointment, and often the primary emphasis is given to formal qualifications rather than to professional or teaching experience. Consider, for example, the wording below from a recent press advertisement for a principal or senior lecturer in accounting at a new multi-school college in Sydney, "Applicants should possess a higher degree, be qualified for membership of A.S.A. and have lecturing experience in accounting. Relevant experience in business/industry desirable."

We do not have data on changes in the formal qualifications of college academics across the whole college system over time; however, by 1973 certainly a sizable proportion of college staff members had more than an ordinary or pass bachelor's degree—that is, an honors bachelor's degree or some postgraduate qualification. Table 4.2 summarizes information on the highest formal academic qualifications of respondents in both samples of 1973 survey by Anderson et al. It will be remembered that in 1973 all state government teachers' colleges and some private preschool teachers' colleges were absorbed into the CAE sector. Note that in colleges other than teachers' colleges approximately 40 percent of staff had a postgraduate degree, while another 25-30 percent had a postgraduate diploma or an honors degree (in Australia, to

## TABLE 4.2

Highest Formal Academic Qualifications of Academic Staff in
Colleges of Advanced Education, 1973 (percent)

| | Regional | | | Metropolitan | | |
|---|---|---|---|---|---|---|
| | Teachers' Colleges | Other CAEs | Total | Teachers' Colleges | Other CAEs | Total |
| N= | 55 | 202 | 257 | 48 | 116 | 164 |
| Doctorate | 4 | 15 | 12 | 2 | 2 | 9 |
| Master's degree | 20 | 22 | 21 | 25 | 25 | 21 |
| Postgraduate bachelor's (for example, B.Ed., B.D.) | 20 | 4 | 8 | 15 | 15 | 8 |
| Postgraduate diploma (e.g. Dip.Ed.) | 20 | 24 | 24 | 29 | 29 | 15 |
| Bachelor's degree with honors | -- | 10 | 8 | 8 | 8 | 10 |
| Bachelor's degree | 14 | 15 | 15 | 8 | 8 | 18 |
| Diploma, 3 or 4 years | 13 | 5 | 7 | 7 | 7 | 15 |
| Diploma, 2 years or certificate | 7 | 5 | 5 | 6 | 6 | 4 |

*Source:* Anderson et al. 1975.

graduate with an honors bachelor's degree requires a full additional year of study). Admittedly, even in these colleges staff were not as well qualified as staff in Australian universities—37 percent had master's degrees or doctorates, compared with 70 to 80 percent in universities (see Anderson et al. 1975, vol. 2, p. 96).

While we do not have survey evidence to demonstrate that the level of qualifications rose significantly across the college sector over time, it is comparatively easy to secure convincing evidence for a number of individual colleges, for example, the Royal Melbourne Institute of Technology, the largest CAE. In 1968 only 10 percent of its staff had doctorates or master's degrees, another 44 percent had as their highest qualification a bachelor's degree, a postgraduate diploma, or a postgraduate bachelor's degree, while 46 percent had less than a bachelor's degree. Six years later the proportions were: master's and doctorates, 28 percent; bachelor's degrees, postgraduates diplomas, and postgraduate bachelor's degrees, 40 percent; less than a bachelor's degree, 32 percent.

The growing emphasis of colleges on high formal qualifications is also reflected in the attitudes and habits of staff towards further formal study. In our 1973 survey we asked respondents whether they felt under pressure to earn a higher degree. Almost 60 percent in the regional sample, and almost 70 percent in the metropolitan sample, said that they certainly felt under pressure. One respondent in a multi-school country college explained crisply, "No promotion without master's as a minimum." Another, at an agricultural college, wrote, "Further promotion is dependent on a higher qualification." Some who said they felt strong institutional pressure on them indicated some doubt about the value of higher degrees, particularly the Ph.D., for college teaching. "These higher degrees," wrote one senior lecturer in English at a country teachers' college, "seem to be the only qualifications given any recognition." A colleague in geography at the same institution commented, "Have already done research for a higher degree which has been accepted for publication. Nonetheless blind adherence to the magic letters Ph.D. by institutions makes the doing of one highly advisable." In our survey we also found that almost 40 percent of respondents were actually enrolled and studying for a further degree or diploma. Of these, almost half were enrolled in master's degree courses.

## Previous Experience and Sources of Recruitment

The federal government's plans for colleges, with regard to the main sources of academic staff recruitment and the kinds of previous experience to be sought when recruiting new staff, did not work out as planned. This was largely because the colleges gradually placed increasing emphasis on formal academic qualifications in staff selection.

The federal government's advisory committee in 1966 envisaged that the bulk of staff for the new colleges would come from industry, commerce, and the professions, and that there would be a regular movement of staff between industry and commerce, on the one hand, and colleges on the other. It stated its guidelines as follows (Commonwealth Advisory Committee 1966, p. 31): "The closest possible contact with the business world is therefore necessary. So it is hoped that many members of staff will be recruited after service in industry, in commerce, or in community services. Likewise there will be some staff members who move out, possibly to return later."

For the first few years colleges followed these guidelines fairly closely; in 1969 the Advisory Committee on Advanced Education was able to report that a survey conducted in September 1968 within six of the major colleges in five different states revealed that 69 percent of full-time staff had industrial or commercial experience, and that 41 percent had been recruited directly from industry or commerce. From the late 1960s on, however, it appears that colleges moved fairly quickly away from the guidelines.

How far they had moved by 1973 is indicated by data from our survey. In the first place, as indicated in Table 4.3, comparatively few staff—even in colleges other than teachers' colleges, most of which had been in the college sector for some years—had been recruited from industry and commerce. Rather, most had come from the academic world (from another college or a university) or from education (school teaching). Admittedly, these figures

## TABLE 4.3

### Sector in which Last Appointment before Current Appointment Held, Staff in Colleges of Advanced Education, 1973 (percent)

| Sector of Last Appointment | Regional | | | Metropolitan | | |
| --- | --- | --- | --- | --- | --- | --- |
| | Teachers' Colleges | Other CAEs | Total | Teachers' Colleges | Other CAEs | Total |
| N= | 55 | 188 | 243 | 46 | 108 | 154 |
| No appointment | -- | 9 | 7 | 4 | 10 | 8 |
| College | 91 | 35 | 47 | 67 | 33 | 43 |
| University | 4 | 15 | 13 | 2 | 14 | 11 |
| School teaching | 4 | 21 | 18 | 23 | 12 | 16 |
| Industry or commerce | 1 | 10 | 8 | -- | 17 | 12 |
| Public service | -- | 8 | 6 | -- | 8 | 5 |
| Other | -- | 2 | 1 | 4 | 6 | 5 |

Source: Anderson et al. 1975.

include some who in 1973 had been recruited to their present position from a post within the same college, but if we take only those respondents who came directly to their posts from posts outside their present college, the results are still broadly the same. In the case of the colleges other than teachers' colleges, 25-35 percent came from college or university teaching, 20-30 percent from school teaching, while less than 20 percent came from industry and commerce and only about 10 percent from the public service (that is, government employ-ment). The proportion of staff having had experience at some point in their careers within industry or commerce had also fallen. In 1968, according to the survey mentioned above, 69 percent had industrial or commercial experience; among our 1973 respondents we found that only 25 percent for the total regional sample and 30 percent for the total metropolitan sample had this type of experience. Moreover, even if we look at staff in colleges other than teachers' colleges the results are not greatly different: only 30 percent in the regional sample and 38 percent in the metropolitan sample reported experience in industry or commerce.

By 1975 the Commission on Advanced Education had recognized that the hopes of its predecessor were unlikely to be realized. In discussing criteria for staff appointments in its triennial report (Commission on Advanced Education 1975, p. 31) it merely said that "successful professional experience" and aca-demic competence were desirable attributes for staff.

## Research and Publications

The changing situation since 1965 with regard to research and publication in colleges can also be well illustrated by the views expressed in triennial reports.

In its key 1966 report, the Advisory Committee on Advanced Education made it clear that the colleges were to be teaching and not research institutions, and that university-type research would be discouraged. It emphasized that there would be little scope for research in colleges and that research would "rarely play a leading part in the work of the colleges" (Commonwealth Advisory Committee 1966, p. 31). However, it did say that some staff members could possibly engage in investigations that had a direct application to indus-try.

By 1969 there had been some modifications in this policy. "Investigational work" for industry was not to be merely tolerated but encouraged, and colleges were to be allowed to acquire some facilities for research, provided such research was clearly related to industry. Much greater shifts took place in 1972 and 1973. In 1972 the Commission on Advanced Education announced that it recognized that research had an important role in colleges. "The Commis-sion recognizes," it stated, "that staff in colleges of advanced education will wish to undertake some measure of research activity, both for intellectual stimulation and as a means of maintaining familiarity with advances in the disciplines of concern to them" (Commission on Advanced Education 1975, p. 112). It went on to say that it was legitimate to teach research techniques to students in courses and for college staff to undertake both commissioned research for industry or government and research projects funded by outside bodies. Yet, it warned against colleges emphasizing research at the expense of teaching, and against attempts to duplicate the extensive postgraduate research activities of universities. It expressed the hope that most research would be of an applied character, though it did recognize the difficulty in distinguishing between pure and applied research. Three years later the commission went even further: colleges could fund a small amount of staff research from normal college budgets. Admittedly, the commission again warned about the dangers of too much emphasis being placed on research at the expense of teaching, and that most of the research should be applied research.

While there has been a fundamental shift in government policy on research, we found in our 1973 survey that college academics still had rather poor publication records, certainly worse than those of their counterparts in Australian universities. Some 60 percent had never published an article at all, while only about 17 percent had published five or more articles. Browne (1970, p. 139) found in a survey conducted in late 1967 that of academic staff appointed to the University of Queensland over the period from the beginning of 1964 to mid-1967, the proportions who had written or presented a scholarly paper during the past two years, in three broad fields of specialization, were as follows: arts, 39 percent, science, 65 percent; and professional schools, 54 percent. In our survey (Anderson et al. 1975) we asked for numbers of scholarly or scientific papers published, not scholarly papers written or presented; making allowances for conference papers and for papers written but not accepted for publication, the figures in our samples clearly point to poorer publication records. For the regional sample, 23 percent of respondents had published an article in the previous two years, while the figure for the metropolitan sample was 22 percent. For the two samples combined, the figures for liberal studies and applied science that correspond to Browne's categories of arts and science are, respectively, 30 and 24 percent.

In many respects it is not surprising that in 1973 many college academics had poor publication records. Some were appointed when colleges were not supposed to do research, less than 30 percent had a research degree, and most were heavily involved in teaching and developing new courses. Almost 50 percent of respondents said they spent no time at all during term time in research and writing. Yet respondents clearly showed an interest in research. We asked them to rate on a five-point scale their degree of interest in each of three key work activities: administration and committee work, teaching, and research and writing (See Table 4.4). Teaching was rated as by far the most

## TABLE 4.4

Ratings of Three Different Work Activities as
Extremely Interesting or Interesting (percent)

| Institution | Administration and Committee Work | Teaching | Research and Writing |
|---|---|---|---|
| Regional | | | |
| Teachers' colleges | 32 | 96 | 60 |
| Other colleges of education | 25 | 91 | 69 |
| Total | 26 | 92 | 67 |
| N= | 55 | 205 | 260 |
| Metropolitan | | | |
| Teachers' colleges | 29 | 94 | 54 |
| Other colleges of education | 25 | 92 | 66 |
| Total | 26 | 93 | 62 |
| N= | 48 | 121 | 169 |

*Source:* Anderson et al. 1975.

interesting—over 90 percent in each sample said they found it extremely interesting or interesting. Research came next, with 67 percent in the regional and 62 percent in the metropolitan sample saying they find it extremely interesting or interesting, while only 26 percent in both samples said administration and committee work was extremely interesting or interesting.

## ATTITUDES AND ORIENTATIONS

There is little data available to demonstrate what shifts in attitudes and orientations have taken place among college academics over the past decade. It is widely believed, however, that staff have become decidedly more university-orientated, and we certainly found a strong university orientation among staff we surveyed and talked with in 1973.

In conversations academic staff make frequent use of the university as a reference point. The standard of entering students is compared to that of a university, course standards are compared to those of university courses, and facilities and working conditions are compared to those in the well-established universities. Many openly admit their hope that their institution will become a university. From our survey results it is clear that college academics share most of the distinguishing beliefs and values held strongly by university academics—beliefs about the purposes of higher education, the academic community, and academic work. They think young people should go to college to develop their talents and creative abilities and to study subjects that really interest them, as well as to acquire professional training or occupational skills. They think a college should be run as a community of scholars, not as a business or government department. Overwhelmingly, they see academic freedom as being essential in any form of higher education. Like university academics, college academics are more inclined to a left-wing political position than the Australian electorate as a whole, and they are even more inclined to the left in comparison with the upper-middle-class groups to which they belong in terms of income (Harman 1975). Most upper-middle-class groups support the conservative Liberal Party and Country Party, whereas both university and college academics prefer the socialist Labor Party.

Most revealing of all, in some respects, were the responses of college academics to a survey question about career plans. We asked respondents to rate on a five-point scale how attractive they would find appointments in four different kinds of institutional settings (city college, country college, university, industry or public service) at three different salary levels for each (same salary, higher salary, lower salary). Overall respondents found a university appointment the most attractive, 35-38 percent said it would be attractive at the same salary, and 10 percent said it would even be attractive to them at a lower salary.

## SUMMARY AND DISCUSSION

Our argument in this paper has been that academics in the colleges of advanced education have contributed to an upward academic push in colleges, and that, in turn, academic drift has produced marked effects on the composition of college academic staff, on their attitudes and orientations, and on their work roles and interests.

Some hint has already been given that a number of practical problems have emerged as a result of the changes here described. It is clear that academic drift has created various problems for individual colleges, for the college sector as a whole, and for the system of higher education. Perhaps one of the most serious problems is that the range of choice in tertiary courses is being restricted rather than diversified. Associated with this is a gap that is developing between the course offerings of technical colleges (which work mainly at subtertiary levels) and the colleges of advanced education, a gap the CAEs were designed to fill.

Academic drift has also created problems for academic staff in colleges. These have been particularly severe for staff without postgraduate qualifications and research experience, many of whom were recruited when the role of colleges was different. These staff feel under strong pressure to secure higher degrees and to begin research, but often they find barriers in their way. Many Australian universities require more than a bachelor's degree at pass level for entry to graduate programs, Ph.D. programs usually require full-time attendance, and research is a difficult activity for a person without appropriate skills, facilities, and counseling. In some cases the upward drift has created a marked sense of uncertainty and tension. "It's OK when you offer diplomas," one staff member in a country college told a member of the Regional Colleges Project team, "but when you offer degrees you start by identifying with a university, and cut out the lower students. We don't know where we are" (Anderson et al. 1975, vol. 3, p. 164). Moreover, staff in many colleges are often discontented when moves to acquire more of the desired features of the university are denied. This is particularly felt by young staff with high qualifications, who often were promised university-type conditions and work at recruitment.

In many respects it appears likely that the extent of these problems for academic staff will increase rather than decrease in the next few years. Since August 1975 the federal government has cut back on its expenditures for higher education, and there are now moves to achieve greater rationalization of institutions. One suggestion being canvassed is that some of the smaller colleges, especially those in country areas, should develop in the subtertiary area, possibly dropping some (or even all) degree programs. This proposal is, understandably, opposed by university-type staff in these colleges who wish to teach at degree level and to make their colleges more like universities.

This chapter suggests a number of important questions and points to possible further research. One important question raised is about the relative influence of academics, compared to other groups and factors, in stimulating academic drift in the colleges. There is some evidence to suggest that academics have constituted the single most important influence. Another question relates to the effects of academic drift on systems of higher education generally.

Is academic drift always dysfunctional, and has it been dysfunctional in the case of the Australian CAE? We have noted some of the problems it has created, but this does not necessarily mean that its overall effects have been adverse; clearly, academic drift has produced many desirable effects. For example, it has made CAEs intellectually more stimulating, it has helped increase the number of degree program available to students, and, through enabling colleges to offer some programs at the same level as universities, it has provided competition and sometimes a challenge to the very conservative universities. Still another question is whether it is possible for governments and planners to avoid academic drift in any set of nonuniversity institutions, and, if so, what particular conditions or safeguards are necessary.

## REFERENCES

Anderson, D. S.; Batt, K.J.; Beswick, D. G.; Harman, G. S.; and Selby Smith, C., eds. 1975 . *Regional Colleges: A Study of Non-Metropolitan Colleges of Advanced Education in Australia.* 3 vols. Canberra: Education Research Unit, Research School of Social Sciences, Australian National University.

Beswick, D. G. and Harman, G. S., eds. 1975. *Survey Instruments in the Study of Regional Colleges.* Canberra: Education Research Unit. Research School of Social Sciences, Australian National University.

Browne, R. K. 1970. "Academic Recruitment in an Australian University: An Analysis of Selection Practices and their Consequences." Ph.D. dissertation, University of New England.

Buckley, Vincent. 1962. "Intellectuals." In Peter Coleman, ed., *Australian Civilization.* Melbourne: Cheshire.

Commission on Advanced Education. 1972. *Third Report on Advanced Education.* Canberra: Australian Government Publishing Service.

————. 1975. *Fourth Report on Advanced Education.* Canberra: Australian Government Publishing Service.

Committee on Post-Secondary Education, appointed by the Minister for Education in Western Australia, under the Chairmanship of Professor P. H. Partridge. 1976. *Post-Secondary Education in Western Australia.* Perth: Government Printer.

Commonwealth Advisory Committee on Advanced Education. 1966. *Colleges of Advanced Education, 1967-69.* Canberra: Government Printer.

————. 1969. *Second Report, 1970–1972.* Canberra: Government Printer.

Halsey, A. H. and Trow, M. A. 1971. *The British Academics.* London: Faber.

Harman, Grant S. 1975. "Political Orientations of Academic Staff in Colleges of Advanced Education." *The Australian Quarterly* 47: 26–44.

———— and Selby Smith, C., eds. 1972. *Australian Higher Education: Problems in a Developing System.* Sydney: Angus and Robertson.

Partridge, P. H. 1968. *Society, Schools and Progress in Australia.* Oxford: Pergamon.

Pratt, John and Burgess, Tyrell. 1974. *Polytechnics: A Report.* London: Pitman.

# 5

# Notes on the Canadian Professoriate
## Janet Scarfe & Edward Sheffield

### CHARACTERISTICS OF THE PROFESSORIATE

For 20 years, Statistics Canada has compiled and published basic data on university teachers (Canada 1956–57 et seq.) The most striking fact about the professoriate since 1960 is its expansion, paralleling the growth in student numbers, as can be seen in table 5.1.

Over these years, the overall ratio of full-time teachers to full-time students improved until 1973–74 and then worsened. The ratio is more favorable in some fields than others and, of course, at the graduate and senior undergraduate levels. It seems likely that the ratio will continue to worsen in the remaining years of the 1970s.

Rapid growth in the 1960s and leveling off in the early 1970s are reflected in the age distribution of Canadian academics. In the 1960s, the continual addition of young teachers reduced the median age of the academic community —from 39 in 1960–61 to 38 in 1965–66, and to 37 in 1970–71. The figure for 1972–73 was 38.4 and, with the stabilization of hiring, the tide appeared to have turned in the direction of a gradually aging professoriate. As Jeffrey Holmes, in a gloomy article in *University Affairs* (1974), wrote: "The spectacular growth of the 60s has left the universities with a block of young professors, some with advanced promotion and the majority with tenure. This group, gradually aging, will dominate the university for many years to come . . . the future for an ambitious 25-year-old is far less bright than in the heady 60s."

Using Holmes's figures, Tepperman (1975) predicted a professoriate with a median age of 46.7 years in 1982–83, a situation which obviously means seriously reduced mobility in the university. Holmes found the statistics depressing. Unconvinced that age brings wisdom, he argued that it is more likely to mean "increased conservatism, and . . . attitudes of die-hard reaction." He

## TABLE 5.1

### Full-Time Teachers and Students in Canadian Universities

| Academic Year | Full-Time Teachers | Full-Time Students | Full-Time Teachers: Full-Time Students |
|---|---|---|---|
| 1960-61 | 7,760 | 113,729 | 1:14.6 |
| 1965-66 | 14,370 | 205,888 | 1:14.3 |
| 1970-71 | 24,733 | 309,469 | 1:12.5 |
| 1971-72 | 26,318 | 323,026 | 1:12.3 |
| 1972-73 | 26,926 | 322,404 | 1:12.0 |
| 1973-74 | 28,912[a] | 332,124[a] | 1:11.5 |
| 1974-75 | 29,915[a] | 347,061[a] | 1:11.6 |
| 1975-76 | 30,740[a] | 369,900[a] | 1:12.0 |
| 1976-77 | 31,870[b] | 385,090[b] | 1:12.1 |

[a] = preliminary.
[b] = estimate.

regarded this trend as placing teaching, research, salary scales, and the attraction of young faculty in severe jeopardy. Deploring the lack of evidence from which to plan, he urged universities to draw up faculty profiles for the next decade.

Not unexpectedly, the number of women in the Canadian academic community has recently become the subject of attention, although Statistics Canada analyses (Canada 1956–57 et seq.) have included comment on the sex imbalance for nearly 20 years. In 1961, the Canadian Association of University Teachers (CAUT) adopted a policy statement on equal opportunity for women faculty, which was subsequently endorsed by 23 of Canada's 47 universities. In 1974, however, the Canadian Federation of University Women (CFUW 1975) surveyed 52 of the then 66 institutions and discovered that, despite an abundance of reports and studies, the picture was still discouraging: "small

| Academic Year | Percent Male Teachers | Percent Female Teachers |
|---|---|---|
| 1960–61 | 88.6 | 11.4 |
| 1965–66 | 87.3 | 12.7 |
| 1970–71 | 87.2 | 12.8 |
| 1974–75 | 86.1 | 13.9 |

numbers of women on the academic staff, smaller salaries than for males, lower rank, and dissatisfaction of the women with unequal fringe benefits and working conditions."

One of the thorniest issues concerning the professoriate in recent years has been the so-called Canadianization issue. The fracas sparked off by Robin Mathews and James Steele (1969) with their dossier, *The Struggle for Canadian Universities*, has continued almost unabated.

In 1969–70, Statistics Canada first sought information on the citizenship of academics in Canada. As the figures in Table 5.2 show, the situation changed noticeably between 1970–71 and 1974–75. The controversy has continued even though the percentage of full-time staff who are Canadian citizens has increased, largely because the percentage of foreign professors is still high in such sensitive fields as the social sciences (Alberta 1972; AUCC 1975; Ontario 1975; Parrott 1976).

Perhaps because the presence in the academic community of two principal language groups is taken for granted, the decennial census of Canada is the only source of data on the languages spoken by teachers, and there are no compilations showing the language that university professors use in teaching. We would estimate that one in four teach in French, the others in English.

Also, relatively little is known about the social origins and personal characteristics of professors. One study of the characteristics of effective teaching (Sheffield 1974) suggests, however, that these vary enormously.

## Recruitment and Selection

Recruitment for Canadian universities has always been on an international scale, but the spectacular expansion of the 1960s made the reliance on

TABLE 5.2

Citizenship of the Canadian Professoriate (percent)

| Academic Year | Canadian | U.S. | U.K. | Other |
|---|---|---|---|---|
| 1970-71 | 62.6 | 10.2 | 15.2 | 12.0 |
| 1974-75 | 67.5 | 14.4 | 7.9 | 10.2 |

*Note:* Figures for non-Canadian citizens include "landed immigrants" who could qualify for Canadian citizenship after five years of residence.

foreign scholars even more necessary; until recently, Canadian graduate schools were unable to provide the required number of teachers. In addition, Canadian undergraduates showed little interest in the academic profession, at least in the early 1960s. In a study of undergraduate perceptions of the academic career, R. A. Robson (1966) found that although 25 percent of his sample had considered it with some seriousness, only 6 percent actually chose it. The academic profession was, he noted, an invisible one, involving a late career choice. Moreover, the job was not perceived as particularly attractive: it was regarded as "pleasant, steady and safe, but not particularly challenging or exciting." Robson's data were gathered before the phenomenal expansion of Canadian universities in the late 1960s, but it remains the only study of its kind in Canada.

Information on the public perception of the academic profession is no less scanty, and is extremely difficult to gauge accurately. Robson's conclusion that it was not high in the estimation of undergraduates contrasts with the findings of P. C. Pineo and John Porter (1967) in their study of occupational prestige in Canada. They found that in terms of prestige the academics were surpassed in the eyes of the general public only by provincial premiers and physicians.

Before pressure in the late 1960s made recruitment procedures more open, new staff members were sought among former students or by seeking recommendations from colleagues in the academic community. In the past few years, however, the "old boy network" has been much derided. Economic exigencies and the desire to employ qualified Canadians have obliged universities to examine and make known their hiring policies. Operation Retrieval, a program begun in 1966 that was designed to attract Canadian graduate students studying abroad, especially in the United States and the United Kingdom, to vacant academic positions at home, also assisted in this reevaluation (Sheffield and McGrail 1966). Since 1960, the Association of Universities and Colleges of Canada (AUCC) has undertaken the advertising of university positions. The relative infrequency of publication of the lists of posts was, for a time, a severe limitation—only 3 times a year until 1968 and 9 times a year since mid-1969. At that time it was estimated that only 25 percent of academic vacancies were advertised in the AUCC's periodical bulletin, *University Affairs* (Holmes 1969), but there has been no estimate of the percentage of vacancies appearing in more recent years. The CAUT has long been active, even aggressive, about advertising academic vacancies. In 1971, its executive urged that the senior academic body of every university make compulsory the advertising of vacancies, preferably in *University Affairs* (CAUT 1973).

Recently, several universities have made statements about their hiring policies, always emphatic about the openness of their procedures. A task force of the University of Toronto, for example, in 1973 proposed wider advertising in *University Affairs* and the *C.A.U.T. Bulletin*, in national and international journals in the discipline, and in other appropriate periodicals. The intention was clearly to attract the best candidates (though not all are agreed on the interpretation of "best"). The report of the Select Committee on Economic and Cultural Nationalism (Ontario 1975) also contained a number of references to recruitment. There the concern was undoubtedly with openness to *Canadians,* and it strongly recommended that advertisements be placed in "at least the two periodicals which are most likely to reach the widest audience among prospective Canadian candidates." In 1976, the CAUT responded to criticism of university hiring policies by amending its guidelines on Canadianization— urging that every vacancy be widely advertised and that in each case appoint- ment be offered to the best qualified Canadian unless a university-wide review committee is persuaded that appointment of a non-Canadian is justified.

Selection of faculty members continues to vary from university to univer- sity, but the 1960s saw a trend away from closet decisions by deans and department chairmen to selection or search committees comprised of elected or appointed members of the department or division in which the appointment was to be made.

## Preparation for the Professorial Role

As in other countries, the normal requirement for admission to the Cana- dian professoriate is anomalous. The Ph.D., that is, training in research, is the most desired qualification even though it is for a role that involves at least as much teaching as it does research. If measured by the bald statistic of the number of faculty with a Ph.D. degree, the trend of recent years has been encouraging. Statistics Canada figures indicate a considerable increase in the proportion of faculty with the doctorate as the highest earned degree—from 43 percent in 1960–61 to 57 percent in 1974–75—for all of Canada, though the percentages are higher for the affluent province of Ontario and lower for the Atlantic provinces.

Some of the improvement is undoubtedly due to faculty up-grading their qualifications (by completing their dissertations, for example), but the most significant factor was the influx of new, young teachers in the 1960s. It must be noted, too, that the possession of the doctorate varies considerably across fields and disciplines (Von Zür-Muehlen 1971); for example, in such areas as nursing, physical and health education, and business administration the per- centage of faculty with doctorates is below average. Nevertheless, the Ph.D. degree or its equivalent is in many, if not most, cases essential for appointment as an assistant professor, the normal starting point of an academic career.

That the ability to teach is subtly and mysteriously inculcated by the acquisition of a Ph.D. degree is a popular assumption, though it is now being questioned. The University of Toronto attempted an innovation in the mid- 1960s with the introduction of the Master of Philosophy (Phil.M.) degree, designed for would-be university teachers. It attempted to overcome problems of the heavy research component and long gestation period associated with the Ph.D. It remains in the university calendar, but is no competitor to the Ph.D.: only two Phil.M. degrees were awarded at Toronto in 1976.

In-service training, faculty development, and the use of pedogogical services are recent arrivals in Canada. Their inauguration on a systematic basis can be dated to the formation of the Center for Learning and Development and McGill University in 1969 and the establishment of the CAUT Committee on Professional Orientation in 1970. This committee was to consider the timing of training for would-be or established university teachers, but to date its most public activity has been a report on the evaluation of teaching by students (CAUT 1973, pp. 104–13). By 1976, there were units offering what could be described as pedagogical services in at least 17 universities (Donald and Shore 1976). Figures are not available for the participation of faculty in these programs, but there is no evidence that professors are clamoring for them. Academics in Canadian universities are not required to participate in teacher training courses and it seems unlikely that either pre-service or in-service instructional development programs will involve large numbers (Shore 1974; Good 1975).

## SALARIES AND FRINGE BENEFITS

Robin Harris's article on the universities of Canada for the 1975 edition of the *Commonwealth Universities Yearbook* contains a good deal of compact information on the general characteristics of the Canadian professoriate. In the area of salary and fringe benefits it gives an indication of the main developments and policies.

> Salaries, which are a matter which each university itself decides—there are neither national nor provincial scales—are tied to rank. At each university there are minimum scales for all ranks ... Salary scales in 1973–74 were highest at the University of Alberta where the minimum for full professors was $21,827. In that year, there were 13 universities at which teachers in that rank were paid at least $20,000. The median salary for all university teachers in 1972–73 was $15,000. Salaries increased substantially during the 1960s (in 1960–61 the median was $8,151) but in the 1970s the increases have tended not greatly to exceed the cost-of-living factor. ...
>
> Among the more mundane but nonetheless important developments of the 1960s was the general adoption of satisfactory pension plans and the establishment of other "fringe" benefits such as medical and group life insurance. A relatively small number of universities provide reduction in fees for the children of staff members other than presidents, but all have housing offices which offer assistance and some will guarantee housing loans. Sabbati-

cal leave is never granted automatically but can normally be applied for after about five years of service. The usual arrangement is six months' leave of absence on full salary or a full year on half salary but increasingly the full year sabbatical is being offered with 60 to 75 percent of full salary. The person receiving a full sabbatical is expected to return to the university which grants it for at least another full year (Harris 1975, p.810).

Since the above was written, salary data for 1974–75 have become available. Scales were highest at the University of Calgary, where the minimum for full professors was $26,775. The median salary for all university teachers in 1974–75 was $19,030. Also, a new development arising out of collective bargaining is that at one university (Carleton) sabbatical leave is now a right.

The Canadian Association of University Teachers has always devoted much energy to improving the salaries and fringe benefits of its members; indeed, as Donald Savage (executive secretary, 1973–76) has emphasised on a number of occasions, the motives behind the formation of the association were principally economic, and such issues still receive high priority (Savage 1973). Considerable effort has been expended in gathering information about salaries and benefits and presenting it in briefs to provincial governments. Nevertheless, these efforts have been inadequate to buffer the effects of the economic recession of the 1970s and, undoubtedly, professional concern about a decline in economic status has contributed to the recent spread of collective bargaining among Canadian universities.

R. A. Robson and Mireille Lapointe (1970), in a paper for the Royal Commission on the Status of Women in Canada, examined Statistics Canada data for 1965–66 concerning salaries, promotions, hiring policies, retirement schemes, and insurance plans in universities across Canada and found considerable differences in both the salaries and fringe benefits of male and female professors. They concluded that slightly more than half of that year's $2,262 discrepancy between men's and women's average salaries resulted directly from the sex difference and, moreover, that the discrepancy in salary had significant effects on fringe benefits, especially in pension plans and life insurance. Despite vocal protests from women academics and greater general awareness of discrimination against women in society, the situation has not improved. In its background paper for the 1975 conference of the AUCC, the Canadian Federation of University Women summarized the various studies on the status of women academics as follows.

> The findings of all studies on the status of women academics have been strikingly similar: they ... have shown that Canadian women with solid academic credentials are not as likely as men to obtain university teaching-/research positions, that they can expect to earn less when they do, that they progress more slowly through the ranks, or are more likely to "plateau" at the lower ranks of lecturer/instructor, and that the whole system discourages women in dozens of subtle ways as well.

## RANK, PROMOTION, AND TENURE

For a general view of the progress through the ranks in Canadian universities, we again draw on the Harris article:

Since the turn of the century there have been four professional grades in the Canadian universities: lecturer, assistant professor, associate professor, professor. Prior to 1960, a person more often than not spent four to six years as a lecturer and as an assistant professor, and six to eight as an associate professor before being promoted to the next rank, with tenure normally being obtained at the associate professorship level. Today there is great variation from university to university in the procedure for obtaining tenure although in all cases it is carefully spelt out. It may be granted at any of the professorial ranks and even at the lecturer level but except in the case of persons appointed initially as full professors, where a one year probationary period is the general rule, seldom until the individual has been a member of staff for three to five years. The granting of tenure is almost invariably made on the recommendation of a committee appointed for the purpose and at a few institutions the committee can or must include a student. Progression through the ranks has accelerated, the full professorship now being obtained in about twelve years. It has not in this century been the practice to limit the professorship to a single person in charge of the department, and there are departments with as many as twenty full professors. Promotion is not, however, automatic; the recommendation of the department chairman, director or dean is now usually based on that of a committee consisting of persons both inside and outside the department or faculty concerned. The claims of students to be included on such committees have to date been resisted at most institutions but at a small number they have been recognized (1975, p.810).

Tenure (short for permanent tenure) is a concept about which there has been considerable controversy in recent years, for several reasons. In certain circles, for example, tenure has been criticized as providing shelter for stale, incompetent, or uninterested professors. The Worth commission in Alberta roundly condemned the concept in its report, *A Choice of Futures*:

Unlike academic freedom, tenure is not crucial to the idea of the university
. . . it is an individual privilege.
It is also difficult to view tenure as any great benefactor of the learning transaction—tenure is a recognition and a reward of advanced professionalization . . . As such, it helps to perpetuate the idolatry of conventional subject matter, scholarly respectability, and the institutional mode of program operation. Indeed, cynics might say that tenure is a life-time guarantee against having to respond to learners' needs. Consequently, the Commission recommends that tenure be abolished and that it be replaced by limited term renewable appointments (Alberta 1972, p.250).

CAUT policy represents the opposite view. In its *Handbook*, it portrays tenure as essential to "protect free criticism and independent judgment in the interest of the university community and of society at large" (1973, p.34). The *Handbook* provides a catechism of 27 questions and answers depicting tenure as an essential and integral part of the academic career. The former chairman of the CAUT Committee on Academic Freedom and Tenure, A. E. Malloch, was always emphatic, however, that tenure is not unbridled academic license, and under his guidance the committee was at pains to demonstrate that "tenure for a university faculty member is not a freehold," rather that it refers to *particular procedural guarantees* against dismissal (Malloch 1972). Debates about tenure appear in virtually every issue of the *C.A.U.T. Bulletin* and frequently in *University Affairs*. Among the profusion of letters, speeches, and articles was an interesting comment on the public's perception of tenure from a professor of philosophy at Dalhousie: "The most serious complaint that the public has against professors in the matter of tenure is not that professors should not have it, but that having it they do not use their special freedom more frequently and more vigorously" (Braybrooke 1972).

## TEACHING, RESEARCH, AND COMMUNITY SERVICE

Canadian professors, like their counterparts elsewhere, are the manpower resources for sustaining the three traditional functions of universities—teaching, research, and community service. Beneath that blanket statement lie a multitude of complex and demanding issues—the preferences of the individual professor and potentially conflicting demands of his department and institution, differences between disciplines, possible differences between work habits of tenured and untenured faculty and, not least, community expectations about the social responsibilities of a university.

There is considerable difficulty in discovering how individual professors do in fact spend their time. According to Robin Harris,

> the normal teaching load in the Canadian university is nine hours per week, the equivalent of three full courses meeting three times a week for lectures, seminars or tutorials. In some of the smaller institutions where graduate work is not offered the load is more often twelve hours, and in some departments in those which emphasize graduate work the load may be as little as six. All full-time teachers are expected as a part of their normal duties to serve on departmental, faculty and university committees, but the administrative duties of the chairman, associate chairmen and secretaries of departments are recognized by a reduction in their teaching load (1975, p.810).

Formal, published studies of faculty work loads in Canada have been few. Indeed, only one has been widely circulated—that undertaken at the University of Toronto in 1967 and published under the title "The Ten O'Clock Scholar? What a Professor Does for His Pay" (Trotter, McQueen, and Hansen 1973). That study revealed that during the 1966–67 academic year (September till May) a University of Toronto professor's working week was likely to exceed 50 hours, while over a 12-month period the average working week was 40 hours. The percentage distribution of time was as shown below:

Trotter, McQueen, and Hansen were emphatic that rigid formulae were quite inappropriate in the planning of faculty activity and staff-student ratios, arguing rather that each university should determine its own priorities in resource and manpower allocation.

One particularly interesting comment on faculty activity appeared in the brief submitted by the Committee of Presidents of Universities of Ontario (CPUO, now the Council of Ontario Universities) to the Commission on Post-Secondary Education in Ontario. It predicted that the traditional professor-scholar would become less typical and, moreover, that attention would be paid to teaching interests and ability in selection and promotion. In particular, the currently anomalous position of the professor within his department, institution, and society at large must, the report insisted, be resolved:

> The important thing that should be done is to define more accurately the role of the university professor, to spell out what in fact is expected of him.
> There may be a need to rethink the whole concept of the university teacher, not simply in relation to teaching, research and administration in the university, but as well in the context of society as it is developing (Porter et al. 1971, pp. 36–37).

The CPUO brief spoke of "publication pollution," lamenting not least the emphasis on publication in the awarding of tenure. It is difficult to estimate the average Canadian academic's attitude towards publication. One study of journal abstracts in the physical and natural sciences, social sciences, and humanities for 1966–67 (Nelson and Poley 1971) revealed that during that academic year the average number of abstracted publications per scholar in the physical and natural sciences (biology, chemistry, mathematics, and physics) was about 1.5 times that in the social sciences and humanities (history, political science, psychology, and sociology). Figures for scholars in ten major Canadian psychology departments showed a steady rise in the annual average of publications per individual, from 0.4 in 1961 to 1.1 in 1965, but then a decline

| Function | September to May | Year Round |
|---|---|---|
| Teaching activities | 40 | 40 |
| Research and scholarship | 33 | 40 |
| Administration activities | 22 | 15 |
| Professional activities | 5 | 5 |

to 1.0 in 1967. The averages for physics and psychology were similar in 1967 (0.7), but for history in 1966 the abstracted publication rate was 0.03. It is perhaps significant that criticism of the publication mania has come from a number of university circles since the period referred to by the data, as this may have modified academics' behavior. On the other hand, the current surplus of Ph.D. graduates and the intense competition for tenured positions may well have produced a greater enthusiasm for publication.

More controversial than teaching and publication have been the professors' research and community service activities, which are often found in combination. Even a rapid perusal of the "activities" section of any issue of *University Affairs* indicates that Canadian professors usually extend their interests outside the immediate university confines: they chair commissions, head committees and councils, and contribute to international agencies. However, the importance of such activities has been questioned. R. N. Scott of the University of New Brunswick alluded in an article in *University Affairs* to the familiar argument about the professor's conflicting interests when involved in community service: "frequently, these activities are not recognized by the public. More serious, however, is the fact that they are not understood within the university ... These activities are part of the proper function of the university, not an avocation for university faculty" (Scott 1972).

## PROFESSORIAL ASSOCIATIONS

Professors associate with each other in discipline groups, in professional associations or unions, and (along with others) in university governing bodies. Their associations are, therefore, both institutional and interinstitutional, local and national.

Almost every discipline and field has a national association and these societies, scholarly and professional, usually publish a journal and convene at least annually. Although the list of the societies is long and the interests to which they cater diverse, it is difficult to gauge the extent of participation by members of the academic community. There is some evidence that a considerable number of these societies are small, suffering from financial difficulties and a lack of interest from members. A. S. West, in a study of Canadian national societies of science (1972), uncovered 119 organizations and examined their membership and activities. He concluded that "most are young, small, and in competition with larger American counterparts. They have low fees, small incomes and difficulties in supporting secretarial staff and journalism. Bilingualism is expensive. Young scientists are too little involved and the social conscience of many of them is poorly developed." Many of these associations are at least partly devoted to professional licensing issues that compete for attention with more scholarly pursuits.

As with so many other areas related to the Canadian professoriate, information and research on the learned societies are limited. There has been no study of the associations of academics in the humanities and social sciences, although it seems likely that they would suffer equally from the problems that plague the scientific societies—the extent of Canadian geography, the necessity of coping with two languages (English and French), competition from American associations, and lack of interest.

Faculty associations in Canada are organized on individual campuses and membership in them is voluntary. They are grouped provincially, but the Canadian Association of University Teachers, a federation of local associations, indirectly represents between 70 and 75 percent of all eligible faculty members of the universities.

The CAUT has always been unashamedly an interest group: "The objects of the Association are to promote the interests of the teachers and researchers in Canadian universities and colleges, to advance the standards of their profession, and to seek to improve the quality of higher education in Canada" (CAUT 1973, p. 9). Formed in 1951, the association's original emphasis was on salary issues, then academic freedom, and more recently on tenure and collective bargaining. The *C.A.U.T. Handbook* (CAUT 1973) contains the current guidelines and policy statements that absorb the associations's energy: academic freedom and tenure, economic benefits, internal university and professional affairs, and relations of the university to government. The *C.A.U.T. Bulletin*, published six times a year, is devoted to short articles on these matters and also includes a list of vacant academic posts.

The attitude of the Canadian university teachers to their association is extremely difficult to determine. Undoubtedly, CAUT contains a broad spectrum within its ranks, ranging from those who are quite apathetic or oblivious to the association to those deeply committed to its crusade for improved salary and working conditions. Henry Mayo, in a paper for the Commission on the Relations Between Universities and Governments, described both the strengths and failings of the local and federated associations since their emergence in the early 1950s:

> These were formed in desperation and self-defence, primarily to serve the interest of faculty with respect to salaries, fringe benefits and other personnel matters. Many of these Associations are still weak, timid and deferential . . . But despite their faults they have managed to introduce more rationality into salary schedules, and in many places to inject "due process" into a formerly arbitrary power structure. The Associations are in fact one of the few democratic elements in the university system (Mayo 1970, pp. 551–52).

Criticisms can be leveled at the CAUT and its members for absorption in affairs relating to the well-being of its membership and the restricted, narrow view of the university such self-interest encourages. Again, assessment is extremely difficult. It is significant, however, that the *Report* of the Task Force on Post-Secondary Education in Manitoba referred in some detail to this issue. Commenting on the briefs and meetings with the faculties at the three universities in Manitoba, the writers of the report were critical of their general tenor:

> University faculties viewed themselves as professionals: their concerns centred on the participation of faculty in university government, faculty work loads, the value of tenure, unionization, academic freedom. Only tangentially did any of the faculty associations touch on the problems faced by undergraduate students, or on the problems of curricula and of combining teaching and research. In one eight-page faculty brief, for example, seven pages were devoted to faculty concerns and approximately one page dealt with teaching methods and the problems of teaching-research (Manitoba 1973, p. 181).

The question of faculty members being professionals has recently come to the fore among faculty in some universities with the sudden popularity of collective bargaining as a means of negotiating for salaries and working conditions. The first faculty associations were certified as official bargaining agents in 1970. In mid-1976, it was estimated that approximately one-third of all Canadian faculty members were either in or about to enter collective bargaining units (University of Toronto Faculty Association, 1976). The issues involved are extraordinarily complex (Adell and Carter 1972; Adell 1975), but several aspects deserve brief attention; for instance, the reasons for the popularity of collective bargaining as a means for negotiating salaries and benefits. When referring to the CAUT Collective Bargaining Committee in his 1973 annual report to the CAUT, Donald Savage enumerated three basic causes: professors concerned about their declining economic status, faculty reaction to sharing power in the university with administrators and students, and inadequate procedures for hearing faculty grievances (Savage 1973). The matter is one that stirs up many emotions—to some, academics in a trade union seems a contradiction in terms, to others it is the only solution to satisfy their demands—and the relative strength of each position is difficult to ascertain. As A. Monahan wrote in *University Affairs*, most faculty probably occupy the middle ground: "Most faculty concede—where they do not insist on—the right to be a full and equal party to negotiations on matters concerning their professional responsibilities and terms of appointment, although there is a notable uneasiness about the implications of this view for such hallowed values as academic freedom and tenure" (1972).

Faculty members in Canadian universities participate in administration and governance within their own particular university community, at the departmental, faculty and university level. In the 1960s, the pressures for participatory democracy were felt in many universities and at many levels.

Members of the academic community in Canada, concerned about their lack of representation on the boards of governors, pressed successfully for a study of university governance in the early 1960s. The result was the Duff-Berdahl report, *University Government in Canada*, sponsored by the CAUT and the AUCC (Duff and Berdahl 1966). It heralded considerable changes in the administration and decision-making processes of Canadian universities, not least the participation of faculty members on governing bodies (Houwing and Michaud 1972; Houwing and Kristjanson 1975).

The consequences of such changes have not been entirely happy, however. Faculty members concerned with increasing their influence within the university power structure quickly discovered that there were rival claimants to their power. While most universities now have faculty representation on their boards, many also have students as well, for faculty opposition was unable to stop student participation although it did, to some extent, limit it. However, it has been in the relations between academics and university administrators that the most stress and tension has been evident. In 1974, for example, Savage commented that a "good deal of our problems arise from the arrogance of some administrators who insist that they are the university" (Savage 1974). Earlier, Savage (1973) had described the general feeling among academics about the sweeping and supposedly beneficial changes in university governance as a "growing feeling that representation had not brought the gains that the re-formers had desired—that the professors had been co-opted by a powerful mandarinate of presidents, vice-presidents, deans and other funtionaries who really ran the university." This disillusionment, argued Savage, had contributed significantly in some academic circles to the press for collective bargaining and unionization: "Perhaps professors should abandon representation for the formal and legal confrontation of trade unions—abandon the pretence that they were part of the university and opt to be employees just like everybody else" (1973).

The impact of recent changes in university governance were viewed somewhat differently in the report of the Committee on Educational Planning in Alberta, chaired by Walter Worth. It saw the issues as considerably wider than the consequences of a tussle for influence between academics and university administrators:

> In this province, as elsewhere in North America, we appear to be nearing the end of a period of pre-eminent staff power. During the time when there was a short supply of students, staff members consolidated their influence. This consolidation process probably reached its zenith in Alberta with the 1966 revision of the Universities Act which granted general faculty councils responsibility for academic affairs. And as a result of an expansive definition of academe, general faculties' council responsibilites soon included everything that really mattered—even parking.
>
> It is not hard to predict that the governance of higher education will become less staff-dominated over the next decade or two. The demand for

student power has already taken its toll. Further erosion is a likely outcome of the new era of declining market growth for staff. But most of all, staff supremacy will be undercut by the prevalent view that the time has come in higher education ... when the pace of expansion must be slowed down, its direction reassessed, and wiser use made of our resources (Alberta 1972, pp. 129–30).

## THE PROFESSORIATE AND POLITICS

In *The Vertical Mosaic*, John Porter argued that the Canadian academic community or, as he described it, the "clerisy of higher learning" had been conspicuous for its absence from political activities (1965). His analysis of the fellows of the Royal Society of Canada revealed that the cream of the intellectual elite appeared to shun political involvement. He suggested that neither governments nor the wider academic community rewarded political activity with favors or prestige. Engelman and Schwartz (1967), in *Political Parties and the Canadian Social Structure*, argued not that professors regarded politics as tainted, but rather than they have been quite ineffectual as proselytizers for any political system, party, or platform.

For Canadians overtly committed to the Left in their political sympathies, such a condition has been frustrating, an abnegation of the responsibilties of the university to society. For instance, Ian Lumsden, in an essay entitled "Imperialism and Canadian Intellectuals," wrote that "faculty members have become intellectually conservative and loath to engage in controversy that has not been sanctioned by their professional norms. They have ceased to involve themselves in public issues other than as paid "consultants." Thus, Canadian universities are, by and large, devoid of intellectual vitality" (1970, pp. 329–30).

Needless to say, not all Canadian academics have avoided political involvement and not all academics have been cold-shouldered by politicians and parties. Porter's analysis was confined to academics who had been members of the nominated Senate chamber, but professors have held seats in the federal parliament. Pierre Trudeau, now prime minister of Canada, was associate professor of law at the Université de Montréal before being elected to the House of Commons in 1965, and Lester Pearson, an earlier prime minister, had taught history at the University of Toronto.

More typical than the example of professor-turned-prime-minister has been the participation in and influence of Canadian intellectuals, academics, and scholars in political parties, especially in the Leftist Co-operative Commonwealth Federation (CCF) that later became known as the New Democratic Party (NDP). This connection was evident in the 1930s, when scholars at McGill and the University of Toronto formed the League for Social Reconstruction (1931). Among its most noteworthy members were F. R. Scott (law, McGill) and Frank Underhill (history, University of Toronto, and protagonist in a celebrated controversy over academic freedom in 1940–41), who throughout his long career lamented the failure of Canadian intellectuals to provide much needed leadership in public affairs and social criticism (Underhill 1964). These men were also prominent in the formation and policy making of the CCF, and in the publication of a controversial critique of Canadian society, *Social Purpose for Canada* (1935). The NDP has also attracted Canadian intellectuals who have, on a number of occasions, held office in it. Walter Pitman, for instance, president of the Ryerson Polytechnical Institute in 1977, was once a deputy leader of the Ontario wing of the party.

In 1964 a group calling itself the Exchange for Political Ideas in Canada (EPIC), comprised of members of the NDP and the Liberal Party, formed for the purpose of coordinating research, conferences, and the dissemination of information. It was hailed by Engelman and Schwartz (1967) as the "rejection of disengaged intellectual elite as the Canadian model." EPIC has not been a visible force in Canadian intellectual and political life, but the Canadian academic community has not been completely silent. Some political issues have prompted some university teachers and scholars to cast away the shroud of academic detachment. Sporadic protests have come from academic circles over political situations in Vietnam, Greece, Chile, and the Middle East. Around 1967, faculty members at some universities (for example, Queen's and the University of Toronto) organized protests and a few marches against American policies in Vietnam.

Public reaction to the politically noisy professors is hard to estimate. Press reports of the antiwar professors' activities in Toronto were rarely in praise of the academic as social critic. For example, confronted by a list of 350 faculty members, including a solid core of deans and full professors, the editor of the *Toronto Telegram* commented that, while they were "men of stature in the intellectual life of Toronto, . . . when the academicians conclude that the cause of the horror is the U.S. government and call for American withdrawal, they stand with the irresponsible critics who allow emotion to govern reason" (Jan. 6, 1967). The academics themselves were undoubtedly sensitive to public and government criticism and mindful of the dissension over the war and activities of their confreres in the United States. When a number of Canadian academic lawyers pressed for a full investigation of the Song My incident, one spokesman was careful to emphasize that "the Canadian academic community has attempted to create an imaginative, useful document that will point the way . . . It is not a club to beat people over the head with" (*Globe and Mail*, Dec. 5, 1969).

Vietnam has not been the only issue to arouse the political hackles of Canadian professors. The plight of political prisoners in Greece drew protests from some faculty at McGill and Sir George Williams Universities in Montreal in 1967. More recently, in 1974, the recurrent crises in the Middle East prompted the formation of a group describing itself as Canadian Professors for Peace in the Middle East, which attracted support in at least 17 universities. Its first national chairman explained the impetus behind it in these terms: "Academics involved in Middle East studies felt it was becoming impossible to remain professionally neutral and wanted a non-political medium for becoming active" (*Globe and Mail*, November 4, 1974). The group has not been highly visible, rather preferring, it would appear, to confine its activities to study and travel. Academics in Chile, under considerable political pressure since the death of Allende, became the object of an "academic relief movement" in 1974, which attempted to influence both the Chilean government over its intolerance of dissent and also the Canadian government about assisting in the appointment of émigré Chilean professors to academic positions in Canada. Despite lobbying by the AUCC, the CAUT, and the Humanities Research Council, little success was achieved (G. A. 1974).

Lack of research prohibits a final judgment on the present or even the past overt political activities of the Canadian professoriate. The conclusions of Porter and of Engelman and Schwartz may well be dated, for they were concerned with the academic community prior to the Vietnam War protests and the student movement. Research has still to be done on the impact (if any) of the American academics who came to Canada in considerable numbers in the 1960s. The enormous expansion of Canadian universities that increased reliance on foreign talent coincided with the controversies that disrupted so many American institutions where these professors may well have been graduate students or teachers. There has been some suggestion that the effect of the new blood on the academic community in Canada and, in particular, its political persuasions has been less, even the reverse, of what might have been expected. John Margeson (*Globe and Mail*, March 31, 1973), professor of english at the University of Toronto, has proposed that, in fact, the "radical, excited, witty, risk-taking United States professor has been subtly shaped by the Canadian environment into a nice, decent, reticent conservative Canadian." He cited several reasons for such a metamorphosis: the onset of middle age and the quest for respectability, inability to vote in Canadian elections, and the Canadian countryside with its beaver, trout, and cottages. Intriguing as Margeson's hypothesis is, the lack of hard evidence forbids any final conclusion or even an educated guess as to its accuracy.

While examples of political activity by Canadian academics have been difficult to find, it does not necessarily follow that an ostrich, head buried deep in sand, is the appropriate emblem for the academic community. There is considerable evidence to suggest that while academics may find overt political commitment distasteful, they are neither the ostriches nor the eunuchs of the Canadian political scene. They have long provided a major source of expertise on which federal and provincial governments can draw. The channels of communication are many and various: personal contacts, letters, books, articles, and conferences are obvious examples. Royal commissions and government enquiries hold much favored places in the Canadian political scheme of things, and academics frequently sit on them or present briefs on a wide variety of political, social, economic, and legal issues. This predilection for commissions has given members of Canadian universities considerably more than spectator seats in policy- and decision-making circles, both federal and provincial.

The role of academics in Canadian government and political corridors has been well in evidence, when considered from the standpoint of their participation in the civil service in Ottawa. Similarities between so-called academic public servants and university faculty have been analyzed by Z. Kay and J. B. Marshall (1970), in a paper prepared for the Committee on the Relations Between Universities and Governments. They enumerated six such similarities, including background and recruitment, publishing activities and research, and committee work. They also pointed to the informal cooperation and joint appointments between federal organization and universities, particularly in Ottawa, and to the relatively easy transfer possible between university and government employment (facilitated by portable pension schemes). While accurate data on staff mobility are not easily available, Kay and Marshall cited examples of notable academics in government circles, as well as former government employees in influential positions in universities. In his recent book, *The Canadian Establishment*, Peter Newman (1976) scrutinizes the academic pedigrees of a select list of "Ottawa Mandarins," the bureaucratic Establishment between the late 1930s and the late 1960s. Of the 31 entries, 16 held a PH.D. degree or had once had a university appointment. The list includes John Baldwin (lecturer in history, McMaster; Deputy Minister of Transport); John Deutsch (economics, University of British Columbia and Queen's, principal of Queen's; chairman, Economic Council of Canada); Lester Pearson (history, University of Toronto; undersecretary of state for external affairs); Jack Pickersgill (history, University of Manitoba; clerk of the Privy Council); and C. J. Mackenzie (engineering, University of Saskatoon; president, National Research Council).

The interaction between universities and governments clearly requires further study, for it would seem to provide a more accurate estimate of the political influence of Canadian academics than indicators such as protest activities or membership in political parties.

## CONCLUSION

In this chapter we have presented some of the important facts and trends relating to the Canadian academic community: numbers, age, and national origins; the faculty member both inside his university—in teachings, research, administration and governance—and outside— in the wider society. We have attempted to outline the professor's career line, to indicate his scholarly and professional activities and his role as a citizen in the community.

It is difficult to single out any one dominating characteristic of the academic community in Canada. Its rapid growth in the 1960s is probably its most dramatic feature, although it is too soon for the real and lasting impact of the sudden expansion to be assessed. The issues of tenure, Canadianization, collective bargaining, and the greater participation of women dominate the pages of the *C.A.U.T. Bulletin,* but it is next to impossible to estimate the meaning of these debates to an individual faculty member. After reading many issues of the *C.A.U.T. Bulletin* and *University Affairs*, and observing reactions therein to the considerable changes in the majority of Canadian universities in the 1960s and 1970s, a comment from Murray Ross (1973), former president of York University, seems an appropriate conclusion:

> In this critical time one finds the academic staff badly divided about the purposes of the university. They are therefore unable to mount a defence, let alone an offence for the university. In medieval days, masters would occasionally take to the streets with clubs to defend their universities ... Today, we seem immobilized, insecure, impotent, in the face of a movement that would make our universities little more than massive academic cafeterias.

But members of the academic staff are not the only ones who are divided about the purposes of the university. We who "seem immobilized" include members of the administrative staff as well.

## REFERENCES

Adell, B. 1975. "The Legal Framework of Collective Bargaining: Some Short Questions and Some Long Answers." *Canadian Journal of Higher Education* 2: 57–75.

———.and Carter, D. D. 1972. *Collective Bargaining for University Faculty in Canada*. Kingston, Ontario: Queen's University, Industrial Relations Centre. Alberta, Committee on Educational Planning (Walter Worth, commissioner). 1972. *A Choice of Futures*. Edmonton, Alberta: Government Printer.

———.Committee of Inquiry into Non-Canadian Influence in Alberta Post-Secondary Education (A. Moir, chairman). 1972. Report. Edmonton, Alberta: Government Printer.

AUCC, Commission on Canadian Studies (T. H. B. Symons, chairman). 1975. *To Know Ourselves* Vols. 1 and 2. Ottawa: Association of Universities and Colleges of Canada.

Braybrooke, D. 1972. "Tenure-Illusion and Reality." *University Affairs* 13, no. 4: 3.

Canada, Statistics Canada, Education, Science, and Culture Division. 1956–57 et seq. *Salaries and Qualifications of Teachers in Universities and Colleges*. Ottawa: Queen's Printer; Information Canada, annual to 1970–71, thereafter replaced by a series of annual reports covering the same range of data. Cat. Nos.: 81–203 to 1970–71; thereafter 81–241, 81–244, 81–246.

CAUT. 1973. *Handbook*. 2nd ed. William Goede, ed. Ottawa: Canadian Association of University Teachers.

CFUW. 1975. "The Potential Participation of Women in University Affairs." Ottawa: Canadian Federation of University Women. Mimeographed.

Donald, J. G. and Shore, B. M.. 1976. *Annotated Index to Pedagogical Services in Canadian Universities and Colleges*. Montreal: McGill University, Centre for Learning and Development.

Duff, James and Berdahl, R. O. 1966. *University Government in Canada*. Toronto: University of Toronto Press, for the CAUT and the AUCC.

Engelman, F. C. and Schwartz, M. A. 1967. *Political Parties and the Canadian Social Structure*. Scarborough, Ontario: Prentice-Hall.

G[ill], A[udrey]. 1974. "The Plight of the Academic in Chile." *University Affairs* 15, no. 4: 7.

Good, Harold. 1975. "Instructional Development—What? Why? How?" *Canadian Journal of Higher Education* 5, no. 1: 33–51.

Harris, Robin S. "The Universities of Canada." *Commonwealth Universities Yearbook,* 1975. London: Association of Commonwealth Universities, pp. 799–813.

Holmes, Jeffrey. 1969. Letter to the editor, *Globe and Mail,* June 23.

———. 1974. "Demography Affects Employment, Promotion." *University Affairs* 15, no. 4: 2–3.

Houwing, J. F. and Michaud, L. F. 1972. *Changes in the Composition of Governing Bodies of Canadian Universities and Colleges*, 1965–1970. Ottawa: Association of Universities and Colleges of Canada.

Houwing, J. F. and Kristjanson, A. M. 1975. *Composition of Governing Bodies of Canadian Universities and Colleges*, 1975. Ottawa: Association of Universities and Colleges of Canada.

Kay, Z. and Marshall, J. B. 1970. "Academic Public Servants and University Faculty." In R. Hurtubise and D. Rowat, eds., *The University, Society and Government*. Report of the Committee on the Relations Between Universities and Governments, Vol. 2 pp. 281–304. Ottawa: University of Ottawa Press.

Lumsden, Ian. 1970. "Imperialism and Canadian Intellectuals." In Ian Lumsden, ed., *Close to the 49th Parallel: The Americanization of Canada,* pp. 321–46. Toronto: University of Toronto Press.

Malloch, A. E. 1972. "Tenure-Safeguard Not Freehold." *University Affairs* 13, no. 4: 2.

Manitoba, Task Force on Post-Secondary Education in Manitoba (M. Oliver, chairman). 1973. *Report.* Winnipeg: Queen's Printer.

Mathews, Robin and Steele, James, eds. 1969. *The Struggle for Canadian Universities.* Toronto: New Press.

Mayo, Henry. 1970. "Universities and Government: A Preliminary Political Analysis." In R. Hurtubise and D. Rowat, eds., *The University, Society and Government.* Report of the Committee on the Relations Between Universities and Governments, Vol. I, pp. 546–70. Ottawa: University of Ottawa Press.

Monahan, A. 1972. "Collective Bargaining-The Issue for the 70s." *University Affairs* 13, no. 9: 10.

Nelson, T.M. and Poley, W. 1971. "Publication Habits of Psychologists in Canadian Universities." *Canadian Psychologist* 12: 68–76.

Newman, Peter. 1976. *The Canadian Establishment.* Toronto: McClelland and Stewart.

Ontario, Select Committee on Economic and Cultural Nationalism. 1975. *Final Report on Economic Nationalism.* Ontario: Queen's Printer.

Parrott, H. 1976. "Statement to the Legislature on Faculty Citizenship." Ontario: Ministry of Colleges and Universities News Release, April 26, 1976.

Pineo, P. C. and Porter, John. 1967. "Occupational Prestige in Canada." *Canadian Review of Sociology and Anthropology* 4: 24–53.

Porter, John. 1965. *The Vertical Mosaic.* Toronto: University of Toronto Press.

———. et al. 1971. *Towards 2000: The Future of Post-Secondary Education in Ontario.* Toronto: Committee of Presidents of Universities of Ontario.

Robson, R.A. 1966. *Sociological Factors Affecting Recruitment into the Academic Profession.* Staffing the Universities and Colleges of Canada, No. 3. Ottawa: Association of Universities and Colleges of Canada.

———. and Lapointe, Mirielle. 1970. "A Comparison of Men's and Women's Salaries and Employment Fringe Benefits in the Academic Profession." Studies of the Royal Commission on the Status of Women in Canada. Ottawa. Mimeographed.

Ross, Murray. 1973. " 'Higher and Further' Education." *University Affairs* 14 no. 9: 14.

Savage, Donald. 1973. "Professional Societies and Trade Unions: The Canadian Experience in Higher Education." C.A.U.T. *Bulletin* 21, no. 4: 4.

———. 1974. "Report of the Executive Secretary." *C.A.U.T. Bulletin* 22, no. 6:20.

Scott, R. N. 1972. In "Forum," *University Affairs* 13, no. 4:9.

Sheffield, Edward F., ed. 1974. *Teaching in the Universities: No One Way.* Montreal: McGill-Queen's University Press.

————. and McGrail, M. M., eds. 1966. *The Retrieval of Graduate Students from Abroad.* Staffing the Universities and Colleges of Canada, No. 4. Ottawa: Association of Universities and Colleges of Canada.

Shore, B. M. 1974. "Instructional Development in Canadian Higher Education." *STOA: Canadian Journal of Higher Education* 4, no. 2:45–53.

Tepperman, L. 1975. *Social Mobility in Canada.* Toronto: McGraw-Hill Ryerson.

Trotter, B., McQueen, D., and Hansen, B. 1973. "The Ten O'Clock Scholar? What a Professor Does for His Pay." *C.A.U.T. Bulletin* 21:4–10.

Underhill, Frank (1964). "The Scholar: Man Thinking." In G. Whalley, ed., *A Place of Liberty,* pp. 61–71. Toronto: Clark Irwin.

University of Toronto Faculty Association. 1976. *Newsletter,* no. 3. (June).

University of Toronto, Task Force to Review Policy and Procedures at the University of Toronto. 1973. "Report." Mimeographed.

Von Zür-Muehlen, M. 1971. *Business Education and Faculty at Canadian Universities.*

West, A. S. 1972. *National Engineering, Scientific and Technological Societies of Canada.* Special Study, No. 25. Ottawa: Science Council of Canada.

# 6

# Multiple Professional Roles of the Academic: A Canadian Case Study
## Jakov M. Rabkin & Thomas O. Eisemon

In this paper we attempt to analyze networks of professional communication in academic departments. Engineering professors at two Quebec universities are the subject of the paper. While professional communication occurs in various forms, for example, in citations or through such intermediaries as students, we have studied those peer relationships which are direct and long-term in nature, involving a professor's most immediate reference group—departmental colleagues. Our research set out to examine the extent to which segmentation in academic roles is reflected in patterns of professional communication in relation to variations among departments and institutions.

Considerable emphasis has been placed on the issue of role segmentation in academic life. It is widely recognized that different academic roles are competing and complementing at the same time. Research, for instance, may be perceived as a contribution to teaching and as a factor that imposes a constraint on the attention given to instruction. Role segmentation would appear to have a discernible effect on collegial communication in that networks may vary according to different academic roles. In other words, a professor's communication networks may be multiple, each reflecting a particular dimension of his or her academic activities.

Wide variations existing between academic institutions may exacerbate role segmentation. Fulton and Trow (1974) speak of an interinstitutional division of labor, differentiating institutions on the basis of their orientation

The research reported here was supported by the Canada Council and by the Ecole Polytechnique. The authors wish to acknowledge the assistance of Ms. D. Quiniou, Ms. M. Palmer, and Ms. R. Casas in the collection of data.

towards graduate training and research, teaching, and service activities. In so-called research universities, for instance, there is apt to be more pronounced competition than complementariness between research and teaching (Light 1974). In these institutions role segmentation may foster isolation to the extent that recruiting practices giving primacy to research interests result in a diversity of specialities within departments, limiting opportunities for collegial communication in teaching and perhaps in research as well.

Moreover, within academic institutions, communication networks may depend on factors specific to the structure and organization of departments. These factors would include a department's size and its composition in terms of the distribution of academic ranks. Large departments, academic folklore suggests, would be less conducive to collegial interaction than smaller ones. Patterns of professional communication may be influenced by academic status reflecting asymmetrical relationships among professors of different rank. Junior colleagues, in view of their probationary status, would be more likely to seek contact with senior colleagues than vice versa.

Much of the research dealing with academic life has analyzed professors either in terms of their disciplinary specialties or as members of a profession with shared traditions and orientations. Studies that have explored the disciplinary interinstitutional affiliations of academics have sought to identify informal communities (invisible colleges) of scholars sharing similar research paradigms, linked together through complex networks of communication and recognition (Crane 1972). Other researchers have taken the academic profession as their unit of analysis, presuming a common normative structure evidenced by common role preferences (Platt and Parsons 1968). Both modes of analysis stress the primacy of research in academic life.

In contrast to previous studies, our interest is with departments, which are the locus of several dimensions of academic work—teaching, service activities, and research. Departmental affiliation, in our view, functions to integrate individual identification with a discipline and common membership in the academic profession. Peer relationships occurring within departments are instrumental in supporting a range of professional activities. However, our intent is not to delineate the ways in which departments formally organize academic work but to assess factors which influence the informal structure of professional communication.

A note concerning some peculiarities of engineering professors, who constitute our study population, is appropriate here. Inasmuch as engineering is practiced mainly outside systems of higher education, the academic engineer's referents are both the academic community and the practice of engineering in industrial settings. For the engineering professor, different dimensions of academic work—teaching, research, industrial consulting—may be less easily integrated than in other fields because of the different constituencies served (Riesman 1958). Industrial consulting, for instance, may have little pertinence to research activities or to teaching, especially at the graduate level. Moreover, in contrast to the arts and sciences, engineering specialties emerge from the practice of engineering as well as from advances made within the academic profession. Typically, new specialties are added to existing branches of engineering (for example, civil, mechanical, electrical, and chemical), encouraging disciplinary specialization within departments and, thus, little collegial communication. In brief, extensive specialization and the competing constituencies of engineering professors, which narrow the possibilities for shared interests and concerns, may produce weaker networks of departmental communication than in fields that do not have a professional component.

## METHODOLOGY

This paper reports on a study of professors of civil, mechanical, electrical, and chemical engineering affiliated with one English- and one French-language university in Quebec. The two universities are among the oldest, largest, and most prestigious engineering institutions in the province and are well known nationally and internationally. Like many engineering institutions elsewhere in North America, the two began as institutions of applied science, training engineers for employment in public works projects. In the past two decades, the emphasis in engineering education at both institutions shifted from the preparation of first-degree engineers to graduate training and research. This shift, which paralleled changes that were occurring in other university faculties, has brought substantive changes in the objectives of engineering training as well as new definitions of the professional responsibilities of academic engineers—a transition from activities oriented towards the practice of engineering in nonuniversity settings to a concern for the development of basic engineering research. Nevertheless, the transition did not take place simultaneously at the two institutions. At the English-language institution, which, for purposes of anonymity, we shall designate as Alpha University, graduate training and research were developed earlier than at Beta University, the French-language institution.

The study population was limited to professors at the two institutions who held full-time appointments in departments in civil, mechanical, electrical, and chemical engineering; did not occupy administrative positions, except as departmental chairman; and were on campus during the spring term of the 1976 academic year. A total of 124 engineering professors were interviewed and approximately 95 percent of the study population.

Structured interview schedules were used to collect data. The interview instruments solicited information about the professional activities and orientations of faculty. Analysis of the biographical information requested in the interviews (see Table 6.1) indicates that the respondents at the two universities were similar with respect to age and rank. Insofar as level of training is

## TABLE 6.1

Population Characteristics (percent)

| Characteristic | Alpha (N=56) | Beta (N=68) |
|---|---|---|
| Age | | |
| 60 | 7 | 2 |
| 50-59 | 21 | 10 |
| 40-49 | 31 | 31 |
| Under 40 | 41 | 57 |
| Rank | | |
| Assistant professor | 23 | 15 |
| Associate professor | 54 | 54 |
| Professor | 23 | 31 |
| Highest Degree | | |
| B.S. | 2 | 1 |
| M.S. | 11 | 46 |
| Ph.D. | 87 | 53 |

*Note:* Chi squared equals: 6.5, 3 d.f., p.N.S. (age); 1.8, 2 d.f., N.S. (rank); 17.8, 2 d.f., p < .001 (highest degree).

concerned, substantial differences were apparent in the proportion of holders of doctoral degrees: a significantly higher proportion of professors at Alpha University had earned Ph.D.'s (87 percent versus 53 percent). This difference in recruitment patterns reflects, among other things, the fact that Beta University was later in giving attention to graduate training and research.

Variations in professional orientations and activities between respondents at the two institutions have been analyzed elsewhere (Eisemon and Rabkin 1976). To summarize briefly, professors at Alpha University are more active researchers than their colleagues at Beta University who, in turn, are more preoccupied with teaching and somewhat more active as consulting engineers. Despite these differences, it was shown that faculty at the two institutions have similar preferences; for instance, both groups of respondents accord research and graduate training a central place in their definitions of academic work.

The data we are concerned with here deals with networks of departmental communication in teaching, research, and industrial consulting. Respondents were asked to identify departmental colleagues whom they regularly consulted about their courses, with whom they collaborated in research (including co-publication as well as the circulation of manuscripts prior to publication), and with whom they worked on projects initiated by various users of technology (for which they received compensation). This does not exhaust the range of possible faculty activities that would involve collegial collaboration, but these are perhaps among the most important dimensions of an engineering professor's academic work.

## NETWORKS OF PROFESSIONAL COMMUNICATION AMONG ENGINEERING PROFESSORS

Information obtained from questions concerning networks of communication were used to construct Tables 2 to 4 which present sociometric data for the four pairs of engineering departments. In Table 6.2, the number of departmental colleagues contacted with respect to teaching, research, and consulting activities is recorded, as are the ratios to the maximum possible contacts for each activity, by department and institution. Table 6.3 provides information on the number of interactions for various professional activities among engineers of different rank at the two institutions. Table 6.4 depicts the overlap of networks of professional communication by institution, department, and activity. Here the number of professors paired in, say, research has been calculated. Of these pairs, the number who also communicate in teaching and consulting is given.

Comparing the sociometric data for the two institutions in Table 6.2, it is evident that there is more communication among departmental colleagues at Beta University, despite the difference in the number of possible mentions. This holds true for two of the three dimensions of academic work studied, research (1:114 versus 1:51) and consulting (1:280 versus 1:62). The greater amount of collegial communication at Beta University in consulting work, however, may simply reflect the fact that consulting activity is more accepted at this university. Interestingly, the ratios for teaching are virtually identical (1:39 versus 1:38). At both universities, teaching is the most extensive form of collaboration. The patterns of communication that emerge from these data indicate that the department is a force of communication mainly for teaching, particularly in an institution with a more recent emphasis on graduate training.

Insofar as individual departments are concerned, few substantial variations are evident. Possibly the most important variation is that between the Department of Mechanical Engineering at Beta University, with 15 members, and all other departments. More communication takes place here than elsewhere on most dimensions of academic work. This finding, while it may indicate something of the interpersonal dynamics of the mechanical engineering department, is not explicable solely in terms of number of staff, since it is

## TABLE 6.2

Number of Mentions in Teaching,
Research, and Industrial Consulting

|  | Teaching | Research | Consulting |
|---|---|---|---|
| **Alpha University** | | | |
| Civil (N=15, M=210) | 30(1:7) | 10(1:21) | 1(1:210) |
| Electrical (N=16, M=240) | 22(1:11) | 4(1:60) | 1(1:240) |
| Mechanical (N=19, M=342) | 21(1:16) | 12(1:29) | 7(1:49) |
| Chemical (N=6, M=30) | 5(1:6) | 1(1:30) | 2(1:15) |
| Total (N=56, M=3,080) | 78(1:39) | 27(1:114) | 11(1:280) |
| **Beta University** | | | |
| Civil (N=20, M=380) | 30(1:13) | 15(1:25) | 20(1:19) |
| Electrical (N=21, M=420) | 40(1:11) | 26(1:16) | 25(1:17) |
| Mechanical (N=15, M=210) | 26(1:8) | 33(1:6) | 24(1:9) |
| Chemical (N=12, M=132) | 23(1:6) | 15(1:9) | 5(1:26) |
| Total (N=68, M=4,556) | 119(1:38) | 89(1:51) | 74(1:62) |

*Notes:* N = number of members of the department. M = N (N − 1) is the number of possible mentions. Numbers in parentheses express the ratio of number of mentions to number of possible mentions.

a medium-sized department; however, the chemical engineering departments, the two smallest departments, exhibit stronger patterns of communication in teaching and consulting compared to most other departments, as predicted.

Turning to networks of communication within departments, Table 6.3 displays asymmetrical relationships influenced by academic rank. Full professors contact assistant professors, for example, less frequently in teaching, research, and consulting than they contact those of higher ranks at both institutions. Among assistants, most communication is with professors of higher rank, particularly associates. Such asymmetry is characteristic of communication in all activities, except for teaching at Alpha University.

Examining the congruence of networks of communication in teaching, research, and consulting work, it is clear that, within departments, different

## TABLE 6.3

### Academic Rank and Patterns of Communication

| Initiator | PERSON CONTACTED | | | | | |
| of Contact | Alpha University | | | Beta University | | |
| | Assistant | Associate | Full | Assistant | Associate | Full |
| **Teaching** | | | | | | |
| Assistant | 6 | 3 | 1 | 1 | 5 | 0 |
| Associate | 2 | 15 | 9 | 7 | 38 | 18 |
| Full | 3 | 18 | 9 | 4 | 20 | 12 |
| **Research** | | | | | | |
| Assistant | 0 | 1 | 0 | 1 | 3 | 2 |
| Associate | 2 | 8 | 2 | 5 | 22 | 11 |
| Full | 2 | 3 | 3 | 1 | 18 | 6 |
| **Consulting** | | | | | | |
| Assistant | 0 | 0 | 1 | 2 | 2 | 0 |
| Associate | 0 | 4 | 3 | 7 | 14 | 4 |
| Full | 1 | 1 | 1 | 3 | 8 | 1 |

*Notes:* Vertical column represents the person who initiates the contact. Horizontal column represents the person who is contacted.

networks exist for each of these activities (see Table 6.4). This is to say that persons consulted about teaching are seldom those with whom one conducts research and carries out industrial consulting. In the civil engineering department of Alpha University, for instance, of 30 colleague pairs in teaching, only five of these also involve collaboration in research and there are no instances of collaboration in consulting. Taking departments at the two universities collectively, somewhat more overlap in colleague networks exists at Beta University. Still, the greater incidence of overlap at Beta University is distorted by the greater number of pairs.

## DISCUSSION AND CONCLUSION

The tables described above suggest, among other things, that the extensive networks of staff communication prevailing at Beta University may, at least to some extent, reflect institutional orientation and patterns of staff recruitment. We have observed that faculty at Beta University, which has only recently emphasized graduate training and research, were more likely to hold

Overlap of Networks of Communication

| Department | Alpha University | | | Beta University | | |
|---|---|---|---|---|---|---|
| | Number of Pairs | Teaching | Research | Number of Pairs | Teaching | Research |
| Civil | | | | | | |
| Teaching | -- | 30 | 10 | -- | 30 | 15 |
| Research | 10 | 5 | -- | 15 | 8 | -- |
| Consulting | 1 | 0 | 0 | 20 | 10 | 6 |
| Electrical | | | | | | |
| Teaching | -- | 22 | 4 | -- | 40 | 26 |
| Research | 4 | 1 | -- | 26 | 8 | -- |
| Consulting | 1 | 1 | 0 | 25 | 6 | 8 |
| Mechanical | | | | | | |
| Teaching | -- | 21 | 12 | -- | 26 | 33 |
| Research | 12 | 4 | -- | 33 | 7 | -- |
| Consulting | 7 | 2 | 4 | 24 | 9 | 6 |
| Chemical | | | | | | |
| Teaching | -- | 5 | 1 | -- | 23 | 15 |
| Research | 1 | 1 | -- | 15 | 5 | -- |
| Consulting | 2 | 1 | 0 | 5 | 1 | 0 |
| All Departments | | | | | | |
| Teaching | -- | 78 | 27 | -- | 119 | 89 |
| Research | 27 | 11 | -- | 89 | 28 | -- |
| Consulting | 11 | 4 | 4 | 74 | 26 | 20 |

master's degrees. We may infer that these individuals possibly have a more holistic conception of their field compared to colleagues with doctoral degrees. The lower degree of disciplinary specialization, in other words, may promote collegial communication in that there would be a greater likelihood of shared professional interest among staff who identified with a branch of engineering (civil, mechanical, and so on) rather than with a narrow specialty within these fields.

The two institutions studied differ in language of instruction and, consequently, in ethnicity of staff. Perhaps the differences in amount of collegial communication could be attributed to these factors but, at least insofar as orientations towards academic work are concerned, we have shown elsewhere that the staff of Alpha and Beta Universities are quite similar (Eisemon and Rabkin 1976).

That the most prevalent networks of communication among departmental colleagues were found to be in the area of teaching requires further comment. Many respondents, when identifying individuals with whom they communicated about course work, added the qualification that these persons were consulted about undergraduate rather than graduate teaching responsibilities. In most of the engineering departments surveyed undergraduate teaching was a departmental responsibility reflecting a consensus of opinion as to what a first-degree civil engineer, for example, should know in order to practice civil engineering. Graduate teaching, respondents explained, was oriented towards staff research interests. It was unusual to consult colleagues about graduate teaching.

Although we had assumed that the number of departmental staff would be inversely related to staff communication, our findings do not present a very strong argument for the importance of departmental size. Colleague networks were only slightly more evident in the two smallest departments and the most communication occurred in a medium-sized department. Size, therefore, may not necessarily be an inhibiting factor where there are similarities in the professional interests and competencies of staff. In discussions of the functioning of academic departments, much importance is given to the role of a critical mass of departmental staff in fostering collegial contact. Our data lend little credence to the necessity of a critical mass for professional communication.

The asymmetrical nature of networks of communication is noteworthy inasmuch as it indicates something of the hierarchical, as opposed to egalitarian, character of academic life. The academic profession, as Blau (1973) has pointed out, is highly stratified, and its organizational characteristics and processes resemble those of any other complex organization. The discrepancy in the frequency of communication between assistant professors and senior staff, and vice versa, is perhaps an indication that collegial status is "earned" after a period of apprenticeship.

Finally, the fact that networks of communication in teaching, research, and industrial consulting do not overlap leads to the conclusion that these aspects of engineering work may be quite unrelated. Networks of communication at the departmental level are one-dimensional in the sense that engineering professors seem to consult those with specific competencies, as opposed to collaborating with colleagues in more than one dimension of academic work. This may, in part, be a function of the wide range of specialties encompassed within the different branches of engineering.

We mentioned at the beginning of this paper that few attempts have been made to study professional communication within universities. Very important insights into the structure of academic influence have been provided by the study of invisible colleges among researchers. Nevertheless, peer communication within institutions in this study turns out to be another significant dimension of academic work. Intrainstitutional collaboration is of growing importance. Departmental communication is acquiring a greater role as a mode of research organization, not only in engineering but also in many other fields where teamwork is promoted by the policies of sponsoring agencies and the institutions where research is carried out. In teaching, collaboration may also become more prevalent in response to several influences, not the least of which is the current financial retrenchment in many North American universities. Intrainstitutional collaboration in service activities is being encouraged as well, particularly among the staff of professional faculties, as we have seen in the case of engineering institutions.

As opportunities for institutional mobility seem to diminish, departmental attachments are likely to become a more salient point of reference for professional activities. Efforts to foster greater collegial communication in research, teaching, and service activities will profit from a better understanding of the factors that shape collegial communication within institutions. It is hoped that this study will stimulate research examining various kinds of networks of professional communication in different fields and at different institutions.

## REFERENCES

Blau, P. 1973. *The Organization of Academic Work.* New York: Wiley.

Crane, D. 1972. *Invisible Colleges.* Chicago: University of Chicago Press.

Eisemon, Thomas and Rabkin, Jakov. 1976. "Academic Engineers in Quebec: The Myth of Linguistic Demarcation." *Proceedings of the Society for Social Study of Science.* Ithaca, N.Y. p. 415.

Fulton, O. and Trow, M. A. 1974. "Research Activity in American Higher Education." *Sociology of Education* 74, pp. 29–73.

Light, D. 1974. "Introduction: The Structure of the Academic Profession." *Sociology of Education* 47, pp. 2–28.

Platt, G. and Parsons, T. 1968. "Decision Making in the Academic System: Influence and Power Exchange." In C. Krutybosch and S. Messinger, eds., *The State of the University,* pp. 133–80. Beverly Hills, Calif.: Sage.

Riesman, D. 1958. "The Academic Procession." In D. Riesman, ed., *Constraint and Variety in American Education,* pp. 25–65. New York: Doubleday.

# 7

# The Latin American Professoriate: Progress and Prospects
Richard Pelczar

Higher education in Latin America has experienced major and often dramatic changes in the period following World War II. Rapid expansion in the number of universities, in student enrollments, and in faculty ranks has been paralleled by structural differentiation and internal academic and administrative reforms (see, for example, Inter-American Development Bank 1967). Reform attempts have endeavored to change the traditional structures and functions of Latin American universities with the hope of trying to free them from the grasp of isolation, elitism, politicization, and incompetence. Most of these efforts, however, have given rise to new problems and conflicts (see, for example, Pelczar 1972). Resistance to many of the changes has been vocal and they were often met by student strikes, counter-reforms and, occasionally, violence.

For the most part, impressive quantitative advances have been well reported and the resultant conflicts have been widely discussed. Not much attention, however, has been devoted to the impact of these changes on the qualitative aspects of academic life. One area that has been greatly neglected is the development of the academic profession. The three factors that have perhaps most influenced the development of the Latin American academic profession in past decades have been the increased number of university professors, the movement towards a full-time professoriate, and the attempt at faculty upgrading by means of advanced foreign training. The discussion that

Although the author is associated with the Inter-American Developmental Bank, the views expressed in this article are his own and do not necessarily represent those of that organization.

follows tries to assess the effects of these factors on three aspects of the academic profession—recruitment patterns, faculty morale, and scholarly productivity.

The analysis is almost entirely based on the findings of recent studies of university professors in Argentina and Colombia. The Argentina study (Socolow 1972) was based on interview and questionnaire data from a sample of professors in four national universities. In Colombia (Pelczar 1973), the study was based on information obtained through personal interviews of a sample of professors from six universities in the city of Medellín. The author's experience with universities in several Latin American countries has also been utilized in the analysis.

## THE TRADITIONAL IMAGE OF THE UNIVERSITY PROFESSOR IN LATIN AMERICA

The professorial role in Latin America has traditionally been filled by part-time academics recruited from among the leading professionals of the community to teach a few hours a week at local universities. Because university professors have been comparatively ignored in the writings on Latin American higher education (for a valuable review of the literature on the topic, see Arnove 1967), not much is known with certainty about the their characteristics and activities. This lack of information and empirical research has contributed to the perpetuation of a generally negative and stereotyped view of the Latin American university professor. Bakke (1964), for example, observed that

the symbolic word as to the inadequacy of instructors is "taxi professor." The content of this concept suggests a lecturer who is a professor in name only, carrying on jobs outside the university, who seeks a bit of additional income and the prestige of a university connection by teaching one or more courses. In the midst of his preoccupation with many concerns he suddenly remembers it is time for his lecture, hops into a taxi, rushes to the university, delivers his lecture, and rushes back to his "real" job. Or he may not, and frequently does not, show up at all. Of course he is delighted when students go on strike, for then he has a good excuse for not coming to class. When he does come, he is poorly prepared. The part-time professor does not inspire confidence in his educational or technical ability but rather in his ability to get ahead in the world outside the university. He of course has no time for students, conferences, or participation in any joint faculty effort to improve the quality of education. His interest in his job is a purely personal one, and he has no time or inclination for building the educational institution. That task he leaves to the one faculty representative on the academic council of the "Faculty" to which he is attached. Research for this kind of a "professor," is no part of his job.

According to this traditional view, motivations for teaching at a university often included an aristocratic sense of *noblesse oblige,* or the desire to use the professorial position as a launching pad to higher posts or higher fees (Atcon 1965; Lipset 1970; ECLA 1968). Obviously this negative view of Latin American academics does not do justice to the many able and dedicated persons who have filled professorial positions in the past. Notwithstanding this qualification, however, the preceding description does lead us to believe that the majority of the individuals who did occupy the role conceived of themselves more as professionals than as professors and narrowly defined their principal function as the preparation of future professionals. The foregoing, combined with their reputations as poor teachers and individuals with little time for research, publication and university affairs, constitute the main elements of the traditional image of the Latin American university professor.

## ATTEMPTS AT CHANGE

Admittedly the traditional image provides an exaggerated portrait of the Latin American academic. Yet, this view has persisted because many U.S. and Latin American writers who have dealt with the subject have often, perhaps unconsciously, referred to the North American university and professorship as the model for their judgments and comparisons. Other scholars (Waggoner 1966; Benjamin 1965; Atcon 1965) have lamented the lack of empirical information on the topic (for other examples of the kind of research that is beginning to be done see McGinn, Davis, and King 1968; King et al. 1971; and Litten 1973) and have simultaneously contended that the development of a committed professoriate is crucial if modernization of higher education is to occur in Latin America. Often overlooked, however, has been the fact that institutionalized expectations in the form of rewards and sanctions for such activities as research, publication, and administration, in the great majority of cases, were not part of the professorial role in Latin America. Concern with these pursuits is growing, but only recently have there been concerted institutional efforts to redefine the professorial system and change the conditions that produced the negative image of the Latin American academic (see, for example, Harrell 1973).

In the last 15 years, reform-minded university executives, national governments interested in improving university instruction, and external technical assistance agencies* have been instrumental in increasing the number of full-

---

*The following have been among the most active agencies: Agency for International Development, Organization of American States, Inter-American Development Bank, Ford Foundation, Rockefeller Foundation, Kellogg Foundation, and UNESCO.

time professors and in promoting faculty upgrading through advanced foreign training. In part, these efforts were also stimulated by the desire to find solutions to the problem of rapidly rising enrollments that characterized the universities of the region in the 1960s. As Table 7.1 indicates, the average annual rate of increase in enrollments between 1960 and 1969 in all Latin America

## TABLE 7.1

### Average Annual Increase in Enrollments and Number of Academic Staff in Latin American Universities

|  | Average Annual Rate of Increase in Enrollments 1960-69 | Number of Professors[a] 1965 or 1966 | Percentage of Full-Time Professors[a] 1966 |
|---|---|---|---|
| Argentina | 5.4 | 17,171 | n.a. |
| Bolivia | 7.4 | 1,706 | 6.1 |
| Brazil | 12.1 | 30,862 | n.a. |
| Chile | 11.7 | 11,220 | 37.5 |
| Colombia | 13.6 | 6,453 | 37.1 |
| Costa Rica | 11.7 | 659 | 17.3 |
| Dominican Republic | 11.4 | 722 | 10.1 |
| Ecuador | 11.0 | 1,417 | 6.2 |
| El Salvador | 8.8 | 352 | 12.7 |
| Guatemala | 10.9 | 593 | 14.5 |
| Haiti | 3.3 | 226 | n.a. |
| Honduras | 7.3 | 308 | 14.2 |
| Mexico | 10.8 | 16,346 | 6.2 |
| Nicaragua | 19.9 | 355 | 15.4 |
| Panama | 11.6 | 260 | 25.0 |
| Paraguay | 11.8 | 945 | 1.1 |
| Peru | 13.6 | 7,125 | 22.3 |
| Uruguay | 5.8 | 2,308 | 7.2 |
| Venezuela | 13.0 | 5,463 | 25.5 |
| Latin America | 9.8 | 104,541 | n.a. |

*Notes:* Academic staff and professors are terms that are used interchangeably in this paper and in the tables. n.a. = not available.

*Source:* Inter-American Development Bank 1967 and 1969.

was 9.8 percent, with differences ranging from 3.3 percent for Haiti to 19.9 percent for Nicaragua. Increases in student enrollments were naturally paralleled by increases in the number of professors, which exceeded 100,000 in the mid-1960s. Simultaneously, there were considerable increases during this period in the absolute number and relative proportion of full-time professors. Starting from minimal proportions in the 1950s, the proportion of full-time faculty grew to over 15 percent in seven of the 16 countries for which there was data available in 1966.

In the two countries, Colombia and Argentina, which presently concern us, the gains were even more impressive. As the total number of professors in Colombia more than doubled (from 3,941 to 8,266), the number of full-time teachers in Colombia universities more than quadrupled from 803 in 1960 to 3,384 in 1970 (ICFES 1971). The percentage of full-time staff also doubled from 20 percent to 41 percent, giving Colombia one of the highest proportions in all Latin America. In Argentina, by comparison, Socolow (1972) estimated that, while the total number of professors increased from 5,000 in 1957 to over 20,000 in 1970, the proportion of full-time faculty grew from almost zero to approximately 30 percent during the same period. Both the Colombian and Argentine studies revealed, however, that there were substantial differences in the proportion of full-time teachers among universities in the two countries and across disciplines.

As the above figures demonstrate, the movement towards a full-time professoriate has probably been one of the most widespread and important changes in Latin American universities (Inter-American Development Bank 1967). Also, in contrast to other reform attempts it has probably been one of the least controversial. Nevertheless, these developments, paralleled by attempts at faculty upgrading through foreign training, were bound to spur important changes in the characteristics and performance of many members of the academic profession in Latin America.

## RECRUITMENT PATTERNS

One way of analyzing the recruitment patterns of contemporary members of the academic profession in Latin America is by comparing them with the alleged characteristics of the traditional role types—the full-time professional/part-time teacher—described earlier. According to this traditional view of the Latin American professor, recruits to the position were believed to be elderly established professionals of upper-class backgrounds who held professional degrees from local universities. The studies of professors in Argentina and Colombia, however, revealed that one of the most striking characteristics of contemporary academics is their relative youth. In Argentina, for example,

39 percent of the professors studied were under the age of 40 and only 28 percent were over 50. The Colombian professors were even younger, with 43 percent under 29 years of age and more than 75 percent under 40 (see Table 7.2). In both countries young and relatively recent recruits to the academic profession comprise the largest single group among both part- and full-time faculty.

Turning to the social origins of the professoriate, it was only natural to expect that individuals who occupied professorial positions would have upper-class origins since access to Latin American universities has traditionally been very limited, favoring the sons and daughters of the aristocracy and dominant classes. It was found, however, that contemporary professors in Argentina and Colombia were not uniformly the offspring of the established elite. Of the Argentine professors studied, only 30 percent came from what were classified as high social origins, with 42 percent coming from middle and 28 percent from low socio-economic backgrounds.* Among the Colombian respondents, if the professors whose fathers were owners of large farms and medium-sized businesses were added to those whose fathers were professionals or executives, then almost half would have origins that could be considered upper-and upper-middle-class (see Table 7.2). This should not obscure the fact, however, that the other half of the professors studied came from middle-class or lower origins. We are left then with a portrait of a university professoriate that on one hand is composed of more sons from the professional and upper class than from a highly underrepresented peasantry and working class, and on the other hand is dominated by the offspring of businessmen, prosperous farmers, and white-collar workers—the bourgeoisie—that make up Latin America's emerging middle class.

Confirming the traditional image of the Latin American university professor, the studies showed that men with professional degrees were the main source of recruits to the academic role in Argentina and Colombia (see Table 7.2). Many contemporary professors, however, had received advanced training either in their own or other countries. In Argentina, for example, 29 percent of the professors surveyed had some form of advanced training: 5 percent had earned Ph.D.'s, 11 percent had master's degrees, 13 percent had experienced one or two years of foreign advanced training but had not obtained an advanced degree; and a substantial number had received advanced training and degrees in their own country. In Colombia, by contrast, 10 percent of the professors studied had obtained foreign Ph.D. or master's degrees

---

*The classification used was based on an adaptation of a seven-point scale used by Gino Germani for an unpublished study of stratification and social mobility in Buenos Aires.

## TABLE 7.2

### Social and Educational Backgrounds of a Sample of Colombian Academic Staff (percent)

| Social and Educational Backgrounds | Total (N=190) | Part-Time Staff (N=106) | Full-Time Staff (N=84) |
|---|---|---|---|
| **Age** | | | |
| 29 or less | 43 | 41 | 46 |
| 30 to 39 | 35 | 39 | 30 |
| 40 or more | 22 | 21 | 24 |
| **Father's occupation** | | | |
| Professional | 14 | 22 | 4 |
| Executive | 9 | 8 | 11 |
| Owner of medium-sized business or large farm | 25 | 24 | 26 |
| White collar worker | 22 | 20 | 24 |
| Owner of a small business or farm | 26 | 24 | 29 |
| Worker (skilled or unskilled) | 4 | 3 | 7 |
| **Maximum education level attained** | | | |
| University degree unfinished | 11 | 17 | 4 |
| Licentiate | 16 | 12 | 20 |
| Professional degree | 47 | 50 | 44 |
| One or two years of graduate study | 13 | 9 | 17 |
| Master's degree or Ph.D. | 13 | 11 | 16 |
| **Foreign training** | | | |
| None | 77 | 84 | 69 |
| Six months or more | 13 | 10 | 17 |
| Master's degree or more | 10 | 6 | 14 |

*Source:* Pelczar 1973.

and 13 percent had experienced six months or more of foreign graduate study.*

While it is evident that a growing proportion of Latin American professors are receiving advanced training, it is important to point out that about an equal share in Colombia and many other Latin American countries have not even finished their first university degree. Although the quality of the professoriate may have diminished somewhat in those countries that have experienced the most rapid expansion in enrollments and faculty ranks, this may to a certain degree be balanced by the growing proportion of faculty who have received advanced training, mainly at foreign universities.

For a long time university professors in Latin America were recruited almost exclusively from among the most prominent and experienced professionals of the community. Expansion and the attempts to reform the professorial system, however, have led to the increased differentiation of the employment status of professors. Part-time positions, naturally, still exist and in some universities continue to predominate, but half-time, full-time and exclusive dedication positions have also emerged.† In many instances, in Colombia at least, the supply of leading professionals of the community who are willing and able to fill these positions has proved inadequate. This group continues to be well represented, but it is not unusual for unemployed, underemployed, and part-time professionals to also be called upon for university service. Moreover, as was already pointed out, advanced students with little or no professional experience are likewise increasingly being recruited as faculty members.

In summary, the Argentine and Colombian studies indicate that rapid growth in student enrollments created a demand for instructors that could only be met by the recruitment of younger and, in some cases, less qualified and experienced persons, from diverse social backgrounds. Although the qual-

---

*The educational backgrounds of the sample professors were not much different from those of their colleagues in Medellín's universities or from other professors in Colombia. The maximum educational levels attained by the 1760 professors teaching in Medellín's universities in 1968 were: degree unfinished, 15 percent; licentiate, 12 percent; professional degree, 66 percent; master's degree, 16 percent; and Ph.D. degree, 1 percent. The educational attainments of 7,165 professors teaching in Colombia's universities in 1968 were: degree unfinished 9 percent; licentiate, 14 percent; professional degree, 68 percent; master's degree, 8 percent; and Ph.D. degree, 1 percent (Associación Colombiana Universitaria 1968).

†Half-time professors usually teach from eight to ten hours per week, but do not have permanent appointments and do not receive other benefits. Full-time professors are allowed up to six hours per week of extra-university remunerated activities beyond the forty they are required to devote to university affairs. Exclusive dedication professors, on the other hand, enjoy a special status which entitles them to an extra monthly salary increment, the purpose of which is to make outside work unnecessary and thus ensure total commitment to academic pursuits.

ity of the professoriate may have suffered somewhat because of rapid expansion, more academics had received foreign training or had taken advanced degrees than might have been expected. Holders of professional degrees without specific training for teaching or research, however, remained the major source of recruits to the professoriate.

Thus, the recent changes in Latin American higher education do seem to have initiated a transformation of the academic profession. These changes have not only altered the structure of the academic role, they have also influenced the characteristics of its contemporary incumbents and the nature of the career contingencies that guided them to university positions.

## FACULTY MORALE

An important element in the study of any occupation is the satisfaction of the individuals who occupy it. In the two countries under consideration, one of the major, if not the most important, sources of dissatisfaction among members of the academic profession is inadequate salaries. In Argentina, 65 percent of the part-time and 40 percent of the full-time professors studied felt that their remuneration was unsatisfactory. In Colombia, 60 percent of the full-time and 50 percent of the part-time respondents were dissatisfied with their salaries. Colombian professors, especially those with full-time employment status, were also discontented with faculty fringe benefits, promotion systems, and library facilities, but they seemed quite satisfied with the capacity of their colleagues, the progress of their careers, and the preparation of students (see Table 7.3). Their Argentine colleagues, in turn, were very preoccupied with job security and external political pressures.

It is not difficult to find reasons for these sources of faculty dissatisfaction. Most professors are unhappy with their salaries because full-time academics generally earn less than other professionals with equivalent training and experience, while part-time professors are generally paid nominal hourly wages that often scarcely cover their travel expenses to the university. Faculty fringe benefits, where provided, offer limited and often inadequate services to the professors and rarely include members of their families. Facilities in the faculty and the central libraries that exist are often insufficient in terms of the number and quality of books and periodicals available and also in terms of organization and efficiency. Formal promotion systems are usually very rudimentary affairs based on level of training and seniority and little else. Many professors, notably part-time men, work under verbal or personal agreements and are often unaware that formal promotion systems exist or do not have access to them (see Table 7.3). Likewise, the shortcomings of informal promotion mechanisms riddled by nepotism, politics, and *amigismo* are readily apparent and add to professorial disaffection. Finally, there is a long history of government inter-

## TABLE 7.3

### Satisfaction with the Conditions of Work: Differences Between Colombian Part-Time and Full-Time Professors (percent)

| Conditions of Work | Very Satisfied or Satisfied | | Little Satisfied or Unsatisfied | | Did Not Exist or Unknown to Them | |
|---|---|---|---|---|---|---|
| | Full-Time Professors | Part-Time Professors | Full-Time Professors | Part-Time Professors | Full-Time Professors | Part-Time Professors |
| Capacity of colleagues (h=188) | 82 | 83 | 16 | 12 | 2 | 5 |
| Schedule (190) | 82 | 83 | 17 | 15 | 1 | 2 |
| Career progress (189) | 70 | 83 | 30 | 17 | 2 | -- |
| Preparation of students (190) | 51 | 64 | 46 | 36 | 2 | -- |
| Library facilities (190) | 40 | 55 | 58 | 41 | 1 | 5 |
| Present salary (190) | 39 | 39 | 60 | 50 | 1 | 11* |
| Fringe Benefits (190) | 20 | 35 | 62 | 34 | 18 | 31 |
| System of promotions(189) | 22 | 26 | 60 | 34 | 18 | 40 |

*Professors at the Autonomous University who worked voluntarily and thus collected no salaries.
*Source:* Pelczar 1973.

vention in university affairs throughout the region. Traditions of university autonomy and academic freedom have been repeatedly violated by hostile political regimes. The resultant fear and job insecurity created by these actions have naturally had a deleterious effect on faculty morale.

Additional clues to the sentiments of the professors are provided by their opinions concerning the existence of an academic community. Fifty-two percent of the Colombian respondents and 91 percent of the Argentine professors studied felt that an academic community characterized by professional interaction, communication, dialogue, and so on did *not* exist. As reasons for this, most cited problems that stemmed from the lack of communication. They mentioned, for example, the absence of permanent contact through professional meetings or associations, the lack of mechanisms for the diffusion of research findings, the deficiency of interinstitutional cooperation, and the imposing size of their universities. A large group indicated that things like personal ambitions, *egoismo,* and envy were also inhibiting the formation of a genuine academic community. Others blamed the university authorities for not being active enough and for not permitting professors sufficient time to devote to such pursuits. Among the Argentine professors, especially, there was a feeling that frequent political crises and government interventions had inhibited the emergence of an academic community because they created instability, distrust, and fear among the professors.

In most cases, as demonstrated above, full-time professors tended to be much more dissatisfied with their conditions of work and professional environments. These results suggest that there has been a considerable lag between hiring more full-time professors and creating the necessary institutional conditions to make university teaching a viable and satisfying career alternative. Consequently, full-time faculty members—especially those with advanced foreign training, who are expected to be better teachers, to spend more time with students, to do research, and to view university teaching as a career—have found their salaries insufficient and fringe benefits, promotion systems, library facilities, job security, and collegial interaction less than adequate. In general, therefore, the failure of Latin American universities to provide the necessary conditions and perquisites to complement the high expectations that society has for members of the academic profession has produced substantial numbers of professors who are professionally frustrated in their institutional settings.

## SCHOLARLY PRODUCTIVITY

Traditionally, the major social function of the Latin American university has been the training of professionals and future leadership elites. Increasingly, however, national governments and reform-minded university executives have come to realize that the demands of modernizing societies cannot be fulfilled by traditional academic structures whose major function is the transmission of knowledge. Over the years, the idea that the universities must also be involved in the creation of new knowledge and the adaptation of existing knowledge and technology to local development needs has gradually gained acceptance. Thus, one of the major concerns behind the movement towards a full-time professoriate and the attempt at faculty upgrading through advanced foreign training has been the desire to increase the scholarly productivity of the professors. The task has not been easy.

For a long time the professoriate has been dominated by the part-time teacher/full-time professional or the "taxi-professor" who was professionally trained and oriented and had little time for or interest in research. Because expectations concerning scholarly productivity have not been part of the expectations shaping the professorial role, the effort to institutionalize the research function in the Latin American university has had to start almost from scratch.

Thus, it was somewhat surprising to find that over half (55 percent) of the Colombian professors studied expressed a great interest in doing research. Another 34 percent expressed moderate interest in this activity and only 11 percent had little or no interest in it. Likewise, in Argentina one of the principal motives cited by the professors for entering university teaching was the desire to carry out research. This feeling was especially strong among full-time and foreign-trained academics.

Although there seems to be a growing recognition of the importance of research among university executives and professors, serious efforts to institutionalize it as a valued academic function have appeared only recently. It is, therefore, not unusual that a great discrepancy exists between expressed interest and actual research productivity. For example, despite the favorable orientations of the Colombian professors towards research only 43 percent felt their knowledge of research methods was good or very good. The remainder felt that their knowledge was average (52 percent) or minimal (7 percent). Furthermore, more than half the professors studied had not even completed one research project within the previous five years. Still, two-thirds of the full-time and a third of the part-time professors had done research during that time. Full-time professors were also twice as likely (16 percent versus 8 percent) as part-time professors to have completed between four to eight research projects. Research productivity was not measured in the Argentine study; instead, publishing activity was treated as an indirect indicator of research performance.

In addition to employment status, amount of foreign training was also associated with differences in research productivity. The great majority (89 percent) of the Colombian professors possessing a foreign master's degree or Ph.D. had completed one or more research projects within the previous five years. In contrast, 60 percent of those with no foreign training had not done any research at all during that time. Professors with six months or more of advanced foreign preparation who had not attained a degree fell in between, as 52 percent could claim completion of one or more research projects.

Moving on to publishing activity, we again encounter a disparity between preference and performance, but this time the gap between the two is not as great. The overwhelming majority (89 percent) of the Colombian professors thought that publishing books, articles, and essays was very important; however, 49 percent had not published enough (about two or three articles in national or international journals) to score more than low on the publications index devised for the study.* Again full-time professors outperformed their part-time counterparts as 61 percent scored medium or high on the publications index, compared to only 43 percent of the part-time professors who

---

*The publications index was based upon the following point system: low = 0-5 points, medium = 6-15 points, high = 16 or more points. Works published in the previous five years were scored according to this system: 1 point for each article in a faculty or university journal, press article, or translation; 2 points for each article in a Colombian (nationwide) scientific or professional journal; 3 points for each article in an international scientific or professional journal; 4 points for each book.

achieved such scores. Even greater distinctions occurred between professors with different amounts of foreign training. Here, 94 percent of those with foreign master's degrees or above and 72 percent of the men with six months or more of foreign preparation scored medium or high on the publications index, compared to 42 percent of the professors with no training abroad. In Argentina, by contrast, 82 percent of all the professors had published something within the previous five years, and there, too, full-time and foreign-trained professors outperformed their part-time and locally-trained colleagues.

From the foregoing discussion, it can be concluded that employment status and amount of foreign training are definitely important factors explaining differences in scholarly productivity. Yet, since neither study included information about the performance of the respondents before they experienced training abroad, there is some question as to whether achievement on the various measures of productivity is a result of foreign study or whether those who performed well were selected for advanced training abroad because they were already productive. Nevertheless, an analysis of the Colombian data, which took into account age, length of university service, etc. revealed that in the majority of cases advanced study abroad preceded major contributions to scholarly activity. Moreover, many professors even indicated that their foreign academic experience had been the key factor influencing their professional behavior.

The interaction among these variables is often complex. It was found in Colombia, for example, that employment status and amount of foreign training operate to affect research productivity independently of each other, with the possession of a foreign master's degree or above having a greater *relative* effect than having full-time status (see Table 7.4). In addition, these two variables have a greater combined effect than either of them has alone. Thus, part-time professors with no foreign training were by far the least productive of all the respondents, as 71 percent had done no research. Contrariwise, *all* of the full-time professors with a foreign master's degree or above had done some research and 42 percent had completed four to eight research projects.

With regard to the productivity of publications, it was found that in Colombia the positive relationship between the possession of full-time status and publication output essentially disappeared when amount of foreign training was held constant. The percentage of Colombian professors scoring medium or high on the publications index, with foreign training held constant, falls thus (Pelczar 1973): Equal proportions (72 percent) of both part- and full-time professors with some foreign training scored medium or high on the publications index. Similarly, almost all of the academics possessing a foreign master's degree or above scored medium or high *irrespective* of whether they had part- or full-time status, indicating that the relationship between full-time status and publication was largely spurious. Thus, full-time professors appeared to be more productive because a larger proportion of them had experi-

## TABLE 7.4

Research Projects Completed, by Employment Status,
Holding Amount of Foreign Training Constant, Colombia

| | Number of Research Projects Completed Within the Last Five Years | | |
|---|---|---|---|
| | None | 1 to 3 | 4 to 8 |
| No Foreign Training | | | |
| Part-Time Professors | | | |
| (N=89) | 71 | 23 | 6 |
| Full-Time Professors | | | |
| (N=58) | 38 | 50 | 12 |
| Six Months or More | | | |
| Part-Time Professors | | | |
| (N=11) | 55 | 27 | 18 |
| Full-Time Professors | | | |
| (N=14) | 43 | 50 | 7 |
| Foreign Master's or Above | | | |
| Part-Time Professors | | | |
| (N=6) | 33 | 50 | 17 |
| Full-Time Professors | | | |
| (N=12) | -- | 58 | 42 |

*Source:* Pelczar 1973.

enced foreign training than part-time professors, and in the study foreign-trained professors tended to produce more publications. These factors tend to interact similarly among Argentine professors.

Although there seemed to be general agreement among the professors about the importance of research and publication, the results indicate that there are still great discrepancies between desired behavior and actual outcomes. The scholarly work that has been produced has come disproportionately from the growing nucleus of full-time and foreign-trained professors. Emphasis on the recognition of research competence seems to be gaining in

| Amount of Foreign Training | Part-Time Professors | Full-Time Professors |
|---|---|---|
| None | 36 (89) | 52 (58) |
| Six months or more | 72 (11) | 72 (14) |
| Masters degree or above | 100  (6) | 91 (12) |

importance and incentives for contribution to knowledge are beginning to be created, but there has been little institutionalization of sanctions. Put another way, it will be some time before norms of "publish or perish" cause Latin American professors much anxiety or result in a flood of investigative and publishing activity.

## POLICY IMPLICATIONS AND PROSPECTS: THE NEED FOR AN ENABLING STRUCTURE

The foregoing analysis indicates that, on balance, the movement towards a full-time professoriate and attempts at faculty upgrading through advanced foreign training have had some positive consequences. It also reveals, however, that many professors are dissatisfied with their work conditions. It appears that faculty upgrading and the transition from a part-time to a full-time professoriate have not been accompanied by what might be called an adequate enabling structure. The problem of faculty morale looms as the major unanticipated result of attempts to reform the professorial system. Moreover, the evidence seems to indicate that an academic community in the scholarly sense hardly exists in Latin America. The kind of colleagueship, scholarly commitment, and supportive infrastructure needed to sustain such a community is only beginning to emerge. Yet, if having contented professors who feel they are members of a genuine academic community is viewed as a desirable end, then an effort must be made to create the enabling structure mentioned above.

The preceding discussion of some aspects of the development of the academic profession has signalled several policy issues that must be acted upon if such an enabling structure is to be created. What follows is a brief discussion of those issues and their implications for policy.

### Institutional Benefits

Full-time professors are dissatisfied with their salaries because they are among the most poorly paid professionals in Latin America. Generally, their salaries are not competitive with those of professionals having equivalent training and experience who work in the private and public sectors. This has been a contributing factor in the problem of rapid turnover in faculty ranks. Some of the most qualified professors have been forced to leave academic life because they could not refuse the attractive salaries that were offered elsewhere.

Clearly, unless salaries are raised it will be increasingly difficult to recruit and retain competent and committed staff. Failure to improve the attractiveness and holding power of the academic profession could increase necessity of hiring advanced students and other individuals who are not highly qualified.

Similar inadequacies exist concerning promotion systems and faculty fringe benefits. Formal systems of promotion do not even exist in some universities and if they do they are usually based on seniority and level of training. Placement and promotions are more often based on circumstantial needs and "cronyism" than they are on competence and achievement. Fringe benefits suffer much the same fate: if they exist at all they are woefully inadequate. It appears that the reason for these inadequacies stems from the fact that more thought has been given to structural reforms and administrative reorganization than to human organization. The need for formal promotion systems that incorporate merit criteria in addition to seniority is evident. The need to provide fringe benefits that are at least competitive with those offered by the private sector is similarly obvious. Unless a concerted effort is made to ameliorate these institutional sources of professorial frustration, faculty turnover will continue to rise and teacher militancy will increase.

## Full-Time Versus Part-Time Professors

The above analysis has shown that full-time professors clearly outperform their part-time colleagues when it comes to scholarly productivity. Although a similar distinction tends to exist on other measures of performance not discussed here, differences between the two groups for several role components —teaching methods, professional participation, community service, and so on —were not as great as anticipated. Full-time professors often carry heavy loads and have no more opportunity for such things as class preparation, student counselling, and research than part-time professors. Because of low salaries, many are forced to moonlight or take on part-time teaching positions in secondary schools or other universities. Complaints about this are common and reflect the fact that in some cases the change in the role structure represented by the movement towards a full-time professoriate has not resulted in a change in function.

In the light of these results, and given the necessity for the efficient allocation of scarce human and financial resources, it can be asked whether an unqualified policy of augmenting the number of full-time professors should be continued. Having one full-time professor teach ten hours a week or 40 hours a month may cost a university four times the amount needed to hire four part-time teachers to do the same job. In other words, the policymakers must ask whether or not the extra cost associated with having full-time professors is returning enough benefits to justify expansion of their numbers.

In spite of efforts to increase full-time staff, all indicators suggest that, in the short term, part-time teachers will continue to make up a large proportion of teaching staffs, especially in private universities. Instead of lamenting this fact, perhaps a strategy of upgrading and stimulating the part-time professors may be in order. If part-time teachers are to be kept at all, it should probably be in the applied or professional areas like law, engineering, business, and medicine, where the benefits of a part-time teacher's professional experience may be an asset in teaching.

If resources continue to be limited, policymakers may be better advised to set as a target a certain proportion or critical mass of full-time staff beyond which they will not expand. Resources that might have been invested in continued quantitative growth of full-time staff could then be utilized for the kind of qualitative academic improvements discussed in this chapter. What is being suggested is that there may be an upper limit beyond which the continued expansion in the number of full-time professors may become counterproductive either in terms of the cost involved or in terms of the qualifications and performance of individuals recruited to the professorial role.

## Faculty Upgrading and Scholarly Productivity

The attempt to upgrade university faculty by means of advanced foreign training does seem to have improved the academic performance and productivity of the Latin American professors who experienced it. Although the results of this effort have been generally beneficial, policies concerning foreign study need to be reformulated and its potential dysfunctional outcomes must be taken into account. First, there is the much publicized problem of non-return, the brain drain, that must be dealt with. Adequate safeguards must be built into training programs and grants for study abroad so as to minimize the dangers of nonreturn. There is also the question of the nature and adequacy of the training professors receive abroad. Complaints are often heard, for example, about the relevance of such training to local problems and needs and about the problem of overspecialization.

The third difficulty that can arise is indirectly related to the first two, and concerns what the faculty members does upon his return from study abroad. Often his previous position may be occupied by someone else, but another possibility is that he will find himself doing something he was not trained to do. It is not uncommon for professors who have studied abroad to quickly move into administrative positions for which they have had little preparation. Although the foreign-trained professor may end up doing what he was not trained to do, his occupation of an administrative position may enable him to fulfill a valuable leadership role in the transformation of academic life at his university. He may, for example, be more disposed to provide support for the next level of professors who need advanced training. There is also the danger, however, that the university may lose a good scholar and gain a bad administrator. More serious is the case of the academic with advanced training who returns to find inadequate research facilities and a generally unsupportive institutional environment preventing the accomplishment of the kind of scholarly work he has been trained to do. If conditions are too unsupportive he may flee the university for more favorable surroundings in business, industry, or in other countries.

Thus far, most of the unintended consequences of foreign training discussed here pertain more or less to individual faculty members, but they may also have direct and indirect institutional implications. If the professors of a faculty are constantly leaving for or returning from studies abroad problems of program continuity may arise. This suggests that faculty management must be given greater importance than it has received in the Latin American university. It also means that the planning of faculty development programs must become an integral part of larger, more comprehensive plans and programs for academic development.

In a similar vein, if too many professors who are products of foreign training move into key executive positions within a university they may form cliques or view themselves as a special elite group. The danger of this is that they may become a target for the resentment of the vast majority of professors who have not experienced foreign training as such training becomes the criterion for advancement or mobility of any kind in the academic system. Moreover, activist students who are sensitive to issues of cultural imperialism may not relish the thought of a foreign-trained elite running their universities.

One of the most important policy decisions that must be made is how long should organized programs of advanced study abroad continue. In other words, what proportion of the professors need to obtain advanced foreign degrees before viable graduate programs can be locally institutionalized. This is a key issue because the development of science, technology, and research may not be a realistic goal if a policy of advanced foreign training is pursued without at some point promoting the emergence of indigenous graduate programs. The objection that graduate programs are too expensive for developing nations is often heard, but this position must be examined in the light of ever increasing costs of advanced training abroad and its often dysfunctional consequences at home. It is doubtful that scholarly productivity can become a norm and an institutionalized part of the social system of science and academia in Latin America if graduate schools—the research training grounds of future investigators and scholars—do not flourish and provide the intellectual reinforcement and facilities necessary to stimulate contributions to knowledge and innovations in technology.

## CONCLUSION

The movement towards a full-time professoriate, in combination with a broader effort at university reform, does seem to have initiated a transformation of the academic profession in Latin America. Contemporary academics often exhibit characteristics and behavior quite different from those described by the traditional image of the Latin American professor. The impact of the changes may not have been as broad or deep as hoped and the effects may be uneven, but the trends are encouraging. Still, much remains to be done.

Unless measures similar to those described above are taken, professorial frustrations will continue to build and the discrepancies between professed aims and actual practices will continue. In other words, the adjustments alluded to earlier must be made if the structural reforms represented by the creation of full-time professorial positions are to result in significant functional changes in academic performance. Furthermore, unless a concerted effort is made to maintain and protect the advances that have been achieved, past gains in the development of the academic profession may prove illusory.

## REFERENCES

Arnove, R. 1967. "A Survey of the Literature and Research on Latin American Universities." *Latin American Research Review* 1.

Associación Colombiana Universitaria, Fondo Universitario Nacional. 1969. *Estadisticas de la Educación Superior en Colombia, 1968.* Bogota: ACU-FUN.

Atcon, R. 1965. *The Latin American University.* Bogota: Editorial ABC.

Bakke, E. W. 1964. "Students on the March: The Cases of Mexico and Colombia." *Sociology of Education* 3.

Benjamin, H. 1965. *Higher Education in the American Republics.* New York: McGraw-Hill.

Economic Commission for Latin America 1968. *Education, Human Resources and Development in Latin America.* New York: United Nations.

Harrell, W. A. 1973. "Changing a Professorial System: the Brazilian Case." *Focus on International Affairs.* (University of Houston) September.

ICFES. 1971. *Bases para la Reforma de la Educación Superior.* Bogota: Instituto Colombiano para el Fomento de la Educación Superior.

Inter-American Development Bank. 1967. *Socio-Economic Progress in Latin America.* Seventh Annual Report, Social Progress Trust Fund. Washington, D.C.: IDB.

_____. 1969. *Socio-Economic Progress in Latin America.* Ninth Annual Report, Social Progress Trust Fund. Washington, D.C.: IDB.

King, R. G.; Rangel, A. G.; Kline, D.; and McGinn, N. F. 1971. *The Provincial Universities of Mexico: An Analysis of Growth and Development.* New York: Praeger.

Lipset, S. M. 1970. *Revolution and Counter-Revolution.* Garden City, N.Y.: Doubleday.

Litten, L. 1973. "Foreign Education and the Scientific Communication Patterns of Academic Scientists in Developing Nations: A Study in Four Peruvian Universities." Ph.D. dissertation, University of Chicago.

McGinn, N. F.; Davis, R. G.; and King, R. G. 1968. *The Technology of Instruction in Mexican Universities.* New York: Education and World Affairs.

Pelczar, R. 1972. "University Reform in Latin America: The Case of Colombia." *Comparative Education Review* 2.

––––––. 1973. "The University Professor in Colombia: A Role Analysis." Ph.D. dissertation, University of Chicago.

Socolow, D. 1972. "The Full-Time Professorate in Argentina." Ph.D. dissertation, University of Chicago.

Waggoner, G. 1966. "Problems in the Professionalization of the University Teaching Career in Latin America." *Journal of Inter-American Studies,* April.

# 8

# In Search of Saraswati:
# The Ambivalence of the Indian Academic
## Philip G. Altbach

In the land of the guru, the profession which has taken over its obligations
is held in low esteem both by those who practice it and by others (Shils 1969,
p. 345).

The theme of this article is ambivalence, and its topic is the Indian
academic profession. This is a large topic, since there are 156,562 teachers in
the university system, with all but 26,569 of them in the undergraduate colleges affiliated to the universities. India's higher education system is the third
largest in the world, after the U.S. and the Soviet systems, and enrolls more
than 3 million students. The teaching community is, thus, a large and important element of India's society. Further, it has a long tradition. Universities
date from the mid-nineteenth century, and some colleges are even older. For
a general discussion of the Indian post-secondary education system, see P. G.
Altbach (1971). For general studies of Indian academics, see Shils (1969),
Chitnis (1969), Singh (1972), and Sinha (1969).

This discussion concerns, for the most part, college teachers, who constitute the majority of the teaching community, and not university staff, who are
better paid and have significantly better working conditions and a higher
professional status. We are concerned, specifically, with teachers in the arts
and sciences colleges, the large majority of the total. Conditions and orientations of staff in professional colleges such as law, engineering, and to some

This chapter is based on a paper given at the 30th International Congress of Human Sciences
in Asia and North Africa in Mexico City, August 3–8, 1976. I am indebted to Dr. Suma Chitnis,
Dr. Sheila McVey, and A. B. Shah for their comments on an earlier draft. Saraswati is the Hindu
goddess of knowledge.

extent commerce often differ. These latter institutions generally operate at a somewhat higher level than the arts and sciences colleges. This chapter is based on a case study of arts and sciences colleges affiliated with the University of Bombay, but it has relevance for the rest of India, since conditions do not differ markedly throughout the country.*

The postsecondary teaching community is an important yet often subtle social force in many Third World countries. In nations such as India, with a large educational system, it is numerically strong and diffuse geographically. In all Third World nations it is responsible for training the politically and economically articulate segments of the population, and thus even when the teaching community itself is not directly involved in political or social affairs it has an indirect role. While university teachers are expected to do research and publish, and many of them are in the top ranks of the nation's scientific and literary intellectuals, college teachers seldom contribute to cultural and political affairs through publication. It has not been uncommon, in India and in other Third World countries, for teachers to run for public office, to serve as government advisors or even as ministers (in 1977, at least three members of Mrs. Gandhi's cabinet were former academics). Until the 1976 emergency that effectively put an end to political opposition, a number of prominent and articulate political activists were from the academic community.

In India the political traditions of academics differ considerably from region to region. In Maharashtra, the state of which Bombay is the capital, the teaching community has not traditionally been involved in politics and was not especially active even during the struggle for independence. In Bengal and in Uttar Pradesh, however, teacher militancy has a long tradition and academics have been involved both in national and regional politics and in internal university politics, sometimes causing institutional disruption. One of India's best known universities, the Banaras Hindu University, was disrupted periodically for years in part because of academic politics. There are considerable differences between levels in the academic system and among the different parts of the country in terms of the political and intellectual participation of the academic community.

The academic community also plays a key intellectual role in Third World nations (Shils 1972). Colleges and universities provide a livelihood for many intellectuals in situations where free-lance writing and other intellectually based occupations are few. Many key journals and other means of expression are based in the academic community. In societies where the

---

*This study is based on pilot interviews conducted in Bombay in December 1975 and on available secondary materials. Chitnis (1969) provided additional information. For comparisons with Bihar, see Sinha (1969), and with Rajasthan, see Singh (1972).

"infrastructures" of intellectual life—the mass media, publishing firms, scholarly and other journals—are not well established, the academic community provides a home for a significant portion of creative intellectual work. This is true even in industrialized nations, but seems to be even more crucial in the Third World.

Undergraduate or college teachers have a somewhat ambivalent position in many countries, and India is one of these. They are, for the large majority of students, the embodiment of higher education. In a sense, they set the tone for postsecondary education. But they are not in the forefront of intellectual life. College teachers are seldom "creative individuals" and they seldom produce research or creative writing. They are, however, very much part of the intellectual system in that they transmit knowledge and culture to large numbers of students. College teachers are often not fully professional in that they do not have real autonomy over their working conditions and often do not control key elements of their teaching situations. In most university systems, the main burden of research and scholarship is carried by professors in university settings that offer a full range of graduate studies. These institutions have adequate research facilities and libraries and faculty members are expected, in many countries, to actively participate in the research enterprise. College teachers stand somewhere in the middle: they are part of the postsecondary educational system and have many of the expectations of their colleagues in universities in terms of social prestige, roles, and income, yet they do not often perform the "prestigeful" functions of research and graduate teaching that are the hallmarks of the university teacher.

It is my argument that the college teaching community finds itself in a particularly difficult situation and that, as a result of many factors, it has not developed fully into a profession and has not contributed substantially to the broader intellectual life of the nation. Perhaps more seriously, the standards of teaching are low and the teaching staff seemingly have neither the power nor the will to make the kinds of changes needed to improve standards. College teachers feel that they are not adequately paid, that they have little control over their conditions of work, that independent scholarly endeavor is not rewarded, and that standards of education are inadequate. While many teachers work to the best of their abilities and some colleges manage to engender a sense of commitment, in general the teaching community has little feeling of autonomy. College teaching, for most teachers, is not a calling but, rather, a job, and a poorly paid job at that.

The college has an important but somewhat subservient place in the Indian higher education system. Colleges are responsible for undergraduate education of virtually all Indian students, and handle approximately 90 percent of postsecondary education in India. In that sense, they are the key element of the system. However, most colleges are affiliated with a parent university. This means that the university, which is usually physically separate from the college and has relatively little intellectual contact with it, has minimal standards for the affiliation of new colleges in terms of collegiate facilities. The university sets all examinations and gives degrees—the colleges have no power to grant degrees. The university approves the syllabus, which is designed to dovetail with the examinations, and the colleges have little control over curriculum except through participation in university committees. Finally, the university sets salaries for college teachers and often legislates the means of hiring—and firing—teachers. The university administration has some participation in virtually every element of collegiate life, despite the fact that it has little role in the day to day operation of the colleges. The colleges, however, have participation, and sometimes a majority, on many of the committees that directly affect curriculum and other matters. For example, the majority of members on the boards of studies in the various disciplines are from the colleges. The overall situation, however, contributes to a situation of limited power, both by the teachers in the undergraduate colleges and by the colleges themselves.

College teachers, in India and the Third World especially, are in a particularly ambivalent situation. Academic traditions are largely Western in origin and orientation, and indigenous roots are sometimes weak. As a result, roles are often not well established. The postsecondary teaching profession has expectations based on Western models, and sometimes on a past in which the educational system was small and aimed at an elite. Postindependence reality has generally seen rapid expansion of the educational system and sometimes a declining standard of education. The teaching profession has been caught in this rapidly changing situation. Their own expectations relate to Western ideals of professionalism and autonomy, but reality dictates a different function for college teachers—a function more related to secondary education than to the university. The purpose of this paper is to describe the reality of the Indian college teacher and to place this reality in the broader educational and social environment of Indian society.

## THE INDIAN CONTEXT

The Indian academic profession emerged from a tradition of subservience and remains subordinate to the present time. Colleges and universities were patterned after British institutions, and the British colonial authorities were more interested in creating a reliable and obedient class of middle-level bureaucrats than in creating a high quality educational system. Even the prestigious Indian Educational Service, which constituted the pinnacle of the teaching profession until its dissolution, was very much under the thumb of the British authorities. Bureaucratic rules predominated, and academic freedom was restricted in many areas (Gilbert 1972).

The indigenous Indian intellectual and academic tradition also has an element of style that has inhibited the emergence of a strongly innovative intellectual life. The modern university system, established by the British for their own purposes, did not foster intellectual initiative and slavishly followed British models, both in terms of organization and style. The Hindu intellectual tradition also fitted well into this new organizational pattern. Reliance on commentary on established texts and on narrow scholarship was well established in traditional Indian scholarship, and coexisted neatly with the new university system. This dual subservience has inhibited Indian scholarship and has given some of Indian academic life a style that has limited creativity.

Like the Hindu family, the academic system is hierarchical, and this hierarchy provides relatively little mobility. Once placed in the academic caste system, it is very difficult to move. The *sudra* college teacher (*sudras* are the lowest caste in the Hindu caste system), particularly in a rural college, seldom has the opportunity to reach the *nirvanna* of the Brahmin university professor. The life style, remuneration, and ethos of the lower levels of the academic system differ from those at the top.

The curious bifurcation of higher education into undergraduate and postgraduate spheres contributes to the low status of college teachers, as does the system of affiliated colleges.* While some work at the master's level does go on in some of the better colleges, and an occasional college teacher who obtains the doctorate is able to more to a university department, the gulf between the university departments—and hence research work, upper level teaching, and prestige—and the colleges remains very wide. University teachers have a moderate teaching load (between four and nine classroom hours a week plus supervision of research), a higher salary scale, office facilities, some secretarial assistance in most cases, and often housing or other fringe benefits. Most university teachers hold the doctorate and many have been trained abroad. The standard degree for college teachers is the master's, and often a second-class master's at that. (The Indian academic system, like the British, awards degrees with differing ranks, first, second, or third, according to performance on final examinations.)

Even among the colleges in a large university like the University of Bombay there is a considerable hierarchy. While salary scales are legislated by the university and teaching responsibilities do not differ markedly from college

---

*In the British system, "postgraduate" translated into "graduate" work in the American context. "Affiliated" colleges are independent institutions affiliated with a university that examines students, sets the syllabus, legislates certain regulations, and in general maintains a minimum of standards for the colleges which are affiliated with it. The affiliating system is the standard form of undergraduate education in India, although there have been recent moves to provide the best colleges a degree of independence, freeing them from the lockstep of the present system.

to college, there is a clear hierarchy. The prestigious colleges tend to be located in the central part of the city, to be older, and to attract students from upper-middle-class or upper-class backgrounds with experience in English-language secondary schools. Facilities tend to be better, libraries larger, and amenities for teachers more adequate. The teaching staff from the prestigious colleges tend to have better qualifications and often to be graduates of those colleges. There is more sense of community among the teachers at the prestigious "downtown" colleges than in the rest of the academic community in Bombay. Of the 43 arts, science, and commerce colleges located in Bombay, perhaps five could be considered as having a separate identity and a degree of prestige.

Most studies of the teaching profession indicate that, at least in recent years, college teaching is not a particularly attractive occupation. Observers have pointed out that the academic qualifications of college teachers have declined as very able individuals tend to take jobs in the private sector or in government, where remuneration is better, prestige higher, and working conditions more favorable. Many teachers freely admit that the academic profession was not their first choice. Within academe, the sciences tend to have greater attraction than arts subjects, with students with high examination scores going into science more often than into arts. As a result, it is probable that better qualified teachers are in the scientific subjects.

The arts subjects, such as sociology, English, and foreign languages, have become increasingly female in recent years, as the prestige hierarchy of subjects has moved to science and commerce fields. It has been estimated that in many Bombay colleges up to 90 percent of the students in some arts fields are women, many of whom will not be seeking remunerative employment after graduation but who are in college to improve their marriage prospects. This situation provides dramatic evidence that women are increasingly well represented in the educational system (of the 141,714 students enrolled in the University of Bombay and its affiliated colleges, 93,126 are men and 48,588 women), although women seem to be concentrated in less prestigious and less remunerative fields. The teaching staff in these fields is gradually becoming predominantly female; this may have long-term implications for these fields and for the role of women in college teaching in India. It might be noted that college teaching has traditionally been a field that has attracted women, provided scope for advancement, and in which women have played an active role.

The teaching profession is less attractive mainly for economic reasons. As early as 1954, more than half of the teachers at the University of Bombay interviewed in a study of the conditions of faculty members complained about the inadequacy of their income (University of Bombay 1954). Given inflation and the fact that academic salaries have not kept up with the cost of living, many college teachers find it difficult to live adequately on an academic income. It is commonly felt that remuneration is better in other fields and thus the teaching profession cannot attract the most qualified applicants. Many teachers report that they do not advise their best students to enter academic life. Clearly, the economic burden weighs heavily on the teaching profession and is a crucial factor in its decline as a viable professional field.

## THE SITUATION IN BOMBAY

The University of Bombay is one of India's oldest institutions (founded in 1857) and remains among the more prestigious universities in the country. It is typical of the organizational structure of most Indian universities and is among the larger institutions in the country, with 141,000 students enrolled in its departments and affiliated colleges and with a total of 4,768 faculty members, the vast majority of whom are in the colleges. The university has a full range of postgraduate departments, some of which, such as economics and chemistry, have a national reputation. This analysis is largely concerned with the affiliated colleges, of which there are a total of 73 in Bombay, including medical and engineering institutions. The university's affiliated colleges are located throughout the metropolitan area of some 7,000,000 people and most are situated a considerable distance from the main university centers. Most college teachers seldom go to the university campus or the library and their professional lives are very much centered at their colleges. While the University of Bombay has a considerable influence over their academic situation, they feel that the university is quite distant geographically as well as intellectually, from them. Their hopes—and frustrations—are focused on the colleges. The university has responsibility for setting the syllabus, devising and administering examinations, awarding degrees, deciding conditions of work for teachers in the colleges, and devising salary scales. As such, it has direct relevance to the lives of college teachers; however, most feel that the levers of university power are far from their control. Indeed, many college teachers express considerable frustration at being unable to influence the policies of the university. Some feel themselves hamstrung by a curriculum that is rigid and difficult to change, but most seem to accept the university and its pervasive regulations and try to function effectively within these parameters.

### The College Environment

The college determines the working situation of the teacher and, as such, has the primary impact on professional life. While all colleges must function under the umbrella of university regulations, there are considerable differences among them, and some colleges have managed to create distinctive environments. A key element in the collegiate equation is the nature of the management, the group of individuals who are responsible in the corporate sense for the college and who make basic decisions concerning the internal management of the institution, including such matters as hiring and firing of staff and administrators and the nature of facilities. These questions are decided within the context of university regulations, but the managements of the colleges are left with considerable power.

For the most part, managing committees are self-perpetuating bodies of laymen reflecting the interests of the founders of the college. Members often come from business backgrounds and seldom have any expertise concerning education or management. The management is able, if it wishes, to create an atmosphere, an ethos, in its college that can have a profound effect, negative or positive, on the staff (Altbach 1972). Most colleges are managed by private groups, usually reflecting caste, regional, religious, or linguistic interests that seek to serve their communities by providing collegiate education. Colleges have also been founded by political interests or occasionally by profit-making groups. Most of Bombay's colleges are run by private groups. Some of the city's best colleges are administered by Christian missionary societies, both Roman Catholic and Protestant. While missionary colleges remain among the most prestigious in India, they have declined as a proportion of the total. A few, such as St. Xavier's in Bombay, exercise a national influence in terms of maintaining high standards and instituting innovative programs. A few colleges are managed directly by the state government, and these also have a distinctive flavor.

The managing committees of the individual colleges regulate various aspects of the lives of the teachers, such as setting maximum teaching loads (within university guidelines), and making various policies concerning other aspects of college life. One Bombay college, which adheres to an orthodox version of Hinduism, forbids its teachers to smoke on campus and legislates the attire of staff and students. The management also hires staff members— and can fire them. Much of the staff gossip concerns the policies of the management. The chief administrative officer of the college is the principal, who has substantial control over the college in its day-to-day operations. The principal is the direct instrument of the management, and is hired by the management and can be fired by them at any time. Most principals are very cognizant of their responsibility to management, and must carefully balance the interests of management with the sometimes divergent pressures from university policy, staff wishes, and student demands.

The basic structure of the college is autocratic. There is little pretense of collegial decision making or of participation by teachers (not to mention students) in policy making in many colleges. Indeed, the university structure allows for more participation from the teaching community through its boards of studies, senate and syndicate, all of which have at least some teacher representation. A few colleges have instituted means of allowing staff members a role in decision making, but this is not the norm. In general, policy within colleges is made by the management, usually in consultation with the principal. The exceptions to this autocratic norm are noteworthy because these colleges generally have a higher morale and a greater sense of professionalism. Several of the Christian-managed colleges, such as St. Xavier's and Wilson, have teacher representatives on college governing bodies. The most democratic institutions are Ruia, Podar, and Kirti colleges, which are managed by Maharashtrian groups and in which the faculty has virtually total control over the internal arrangements of the institution.

Job security is a key issue for Indian college teachers, particularly in a situation of considerable unemployment of skilled individuals. The formal legal safeguards for job security are minimal in Bombay, although university or college authorities must engage in a lengthy series of procedural steps to fire a "confirmed" teacher. Confirmation, which is akin to permanent tenure, generally is granted after two years of service in a college upon the decision of the management. These university rules have provided considerable job security for college teachers: very few have actually been fired in Bombay. Unconfirmed teachers can be fired without cause, and many colleges have increasingly resorted to temporary appointments in order to provide more flexibility—on occasion, government or university authorities have supported a policy of not confirming teachers. The Bombay University Teachers Union has supported stronger legal guarantees of both academic freedom and job security, although some thoughtful academics have argued that such laws would strengthen the hand of government in educational affairs, and that reliance on internal university regulations would be better in the long run. Despite the fact that very few teachers have been dismissed from their jobs in Bombay, there is a general feeling that neither job security nor academic freedom is very well protected.

The college management and its administrative embodiment, the principal, have considerable impact on the college teacher. Day-to-day working conditions are determined to a significant extent by the atmosphere created by the management, as are physical facilities and amenities. Teachers generally have no role in policy making and only a limited voice in determining their own teaching schedules. In some colleges department heads consult with the principal on most key matters relating to the academic affairs of the institution. Nonetheless, there is basically no involvement of the rank and file of the teaching community in any of the key decisions affecting their working conditions or environment in the majority of colleges.

The college environment helps to determine the nature of teaching and to some extent the orientations and attitudes of faculty members. In general, the colleges in Bombay do not provide the kind of physical environment that encourages professional development or quality academic work. It should be noted that Bombay colleges are, in general, better endowed physically than similar institutions in most other parts of India: the many newer colleges founded in smaller towns are particularly deficient in terms of physical facilities. In Bombay, few college teachers have their own offices or even their own desks. In many colleges, department heads cannot claim a work space of their own. Typically, the teacher has only a seat in the staff common room where it is possible to relax, discuss matters with colleagues, or engage in academic work such as preparation for class or grading of papers. Common rooms are often fairly noisy, poorly lit, and in general not conducive to serious work. Teachers seldom have a place where they can meet informally with students, and it is rare that a faculty member will be found in the student canteen socializing with students. Students are not allowed in the staff common rooms.

The general facilities of most Bombay colleges provide undergraduate students with minimum standards of quality. College libraries, with a few exceptions, are small, fairly poorly maintained, and inadequate for faculty research. Classrooms are antiquated and the opportunities for teacher-student interaction are quite limited. Laboratory facilities, again with some exceptions, are only minimally acceptable for undergraduate science teaching. Most of Bombay's colleges are housed in old buildings in need of renovation. Some of the newer colleges, often located in the suburbs, boast new buildings but these facilities were constructed with limited funds and meet only the minimum standards set by university authorities for affiliation.

Working conditions in the colleges also directly affect the morale, orientation, and professional standards of the teaching community. The University of Bombay has legislated a maximum of nineteen 45-minute lectures a week for any teacher. Most teachers work at or near this maximum and thus have very heavy teaching schedules. In some subjects tutorials are part of the teaching responsibility, although in many cases tutorials are more like classes, since they involve up to 15 students at a session. Similarly, some science teachers include laboratory sessions as part of their teaching responsibilities. College teachers who are professionally ambitious will often attempt to teach postgraduate classes in their subject. While there is a modest financial remuneration attached to such teaching, the main motivation is to qualify for a higher salary scale as a result of competence in postgraduate teaching. Thus, there is considerable competition for opportunities to teach these classes despite the additional work that is involved. There is generally a small reduction in the number of undergraduate lectures given if postgraduate courses are offered.

Teaching schedules are often not very well coordinated, as many staff members teach in the "morning colleges" (classes beginning as early as 6:40 A.M. and aimed at students who also hold full-time jobs) as well as in the regular college program. Many teachers complain that they have little time for preparation of new lectures because of a heavy teaching load. Classes in most subjects tend to be large—often more than 150 students in a single lecture, and this inhibits much direct interaction between teachers and students. There are few innovations made in teaching methods. This is due in part to the lockstep curriculum dictated by the university-sanctioned syllabus and reinforced by the pervasive centralized examination system. The individual instructor does not have the opportunity to examine students, and assessment is provided through university-administered tests.

It is clear that there is little professional autonomy in the teaching community. Class schedules are heavy and leave little opportunity for research or reflection even if there were stimuli for this element of academic life. Schedules are not usually under the control of the individual staff member, and the teacher does not have control over the curriculum or over the assessment of students. There is no assessment of teaching quality in most colleges, and teachers have little incentive to spend much time improving their teaching. The dominant method of teaching is lecturing and there is neither incentive nor much opportunity to vary this method. Indeed, many teachers dictate notes directly to their students. This is done in part because it requires little imaginative effort by the teachers, and in part because many undergraduate students, particularly in the newer colleges that attract students with limited academic ability and backgrounds, demand that the teacher provide information that will be clearly understood and useful in the examinations.

## Salaries and Alternate Sources of Income

Academic salaries do not permit a professionally rewarding life, even by the standards of the Indian urban middle class. Exact salary scales are now in flux in many parts of India, and it is likely that there will be some improvement, particularly for those at the upper reaches of the system in the universities. However, the income of the college teacher will improve only marginally in most cases and the basic situation will not change much. In Bombay, the basic college lecturer's salary ranges between about Rs 400 and about Rs 1,000.* Additional compensation equivalent to $60-200 is provided because of Bombay's high cost of living (exact correlation is difficult because of cost of living differences). This salary structure is now in the process of upward revision to meet the increased cost of living. It is considered possible for a college teacher with some other source of income—often a working spouse— to barely make ends meet and to survive in Bombay's middle class, but few amenities are possible and a medical bill, family crisis, or other economic disruption can cause havoc.

_____

*In 1977, eight rupees was equivalent to U.S. $1.00.

Few college teachers can afford to live lavishly. Most seem to be able to participate in an urban-middle-class life-style, but only with considerable struggle. Most teachers must commute considerable distances to their jobs, often under uncomfortable conditions. It is not unusual for a teacher to spend more than one hour each way in commuting since academic salaries do not often permit living in the expensive neighborhoods close to many colleges. Few teachers can afford to purchase books and few use the major libraries available in Bombay. Thus, it would seem that college teachers read relatively little, although interviews indicate that they participate in various kinds of cultural activities, such as films and drama.

In addition to fairly low salaries, college teachers have virtually no fringe benefits, thus contributing to their economic insecurity. There is no medical insurance available from the university, and only a fairly insignificant provident fund to which teachers may contribute as a kind of retirement insurance. It is, moreover, not uncommon for salaries to be paid late. As a result of these elements, it is clear that the economic status of the academic profession leaves much to be desired, and certainly contributes to insecurity, fear, and low morale and job commitment.

The majority of teachers in Bombay do seem to have some alternative source of income. Some come from wealthy families and have income from family sources. Many teachers have working spouses, and rely on these earnings. Quite a few teachers are forced to take outside jobs of various kinds. Some of these are related in some way to academe, but others are not. Most teachers grade university examinations, and thereby earn a modest additional income. Some teachers do "tuitions," or tutor students privately for a fee. Both of these sources of income are officially sanctioned by university rules. Some faculty members participate in "coaching classes" or private-enterprise tutorial schools which flourish by providing students with cram sessions aimed at passing university examinations. Such activity is against university regulations. Faculty members also author guides that are widely used by students as quick reference sources for examinations. While both the writing—and the use—of such reference books is not considered academically respectable, this can be a source of considerable income to authors. A few college teachers write textbooks in their fields. Since publishers will favor authors who can hope to get their books adopted as part of the university syllabus, it helps to be a member of the Board of Studies or somehow able to exercise influence. The author of a popular textbook can earn considerably more than his college salary in royalties. In addition to these activities related to academic life, some teachers hold jobs which are entirely unrelated: they may work in family businesses, provide consultation to business firms, or have other sources of income. While exact figures on the proportion of teachers who must earn income in addition to their academic salaries are unavailable, it is likely that, in Bombay at least, a large number have a second job or some alternative sources of funds.

There is relatively little mobility in the Indian academic profession, and this is also the case in Bombay. It is uncommon for a teacher to move voluntarily from college to college, although there is a good deal of circulation at the junior ranks when a teacher fails to achieve confirmation and tries to find a position at another college. This situation makes the average teacher more dependent on the particular college in which he is employed than would be the case in a more mobile academic system. Individual teachers must, therefore, be especially careful not to alienate powerful elements in their colleges so as to maintain their positions.

## The Sociology of Indian College Teachers

The background, orientation, and training of the college teacher helps to determine his professional role. College teaching is clearly an occupation that has lost a good deal of its social prestige and economic rewards in the postindependence period. As higher education expanded, salaries remained steady and the elite role of teaching declined. Relatively few teachers interviewed in several studies indicate that they chose college teaching as their first occupational choice (Sinha, 1969; Chitnis, 1969). It also seems that the social class origins of the teaching community have declined in recent years as well, although in Bombay some individuals from wealthy families enter college teaching more as an avocation than as a profession. Y. Singh (1972, p. 231) points out that, at least at the University of Jaipur in Rajasthan, most teachers come from upper-caste, urban, and professional backgrounds.

An increasingly large number of teachers, especially at the newer and less prestigious colleges, come from families that have not traditionally been educated, and for whom a college teaching career is a matter of importance and signals considerable upward social movement. This segment of the teaching community sees itself as highly successful and is generally content with current salary levels. These individuals are not often research-oriented and are tied to their colleges.

It has been mentioned that the proportion of women in the teaching community has risen, particularly in arts subjects. Many of the women entering teaching are married and have family responsibilities: they are unable to take on a full professional role due to lack of time. Many of these women are also from fairly affluent backgrounds and see college teaching as a supplement to family income rather than as a career.

The educational qualifications of many college teachers are not outstanding, and have probably declined somewhat in recent years. Many college teachers hold second-class master's degrees, largely from the University of Bombay. Some teachers hold a doctorate or are working on a research degree, particularly at the older downtown colleges. At present, there is little or no incentive to complete the advanced degree, as added qualifications result in no higher salary or other benefits. There is now some discussion of requiring college teachers to pursue an advanced research degree. It is often the case that an individual, especially in the sciences, who does well on the university examination will be able to obtain a remunerative job in government or industry, and thus the academic profession is left with those individuals who could not qualify for these better positions. The public image, as well as the internal perception, of the expertise of the academic profession has clearly declined in recent years.

All of these elements mitigate against an orientation towards research and scholarly work. The educational background, reward structures, internal socialization process, time and schedule constraints, and other factors all work against the college teacher having any concern with making scholarly contributions. Most teachers seem to try to do their best within the constraints of the situation and their own abilities, but this does not generally include participation in any broad intellectual community or scholarly enterprise.

## BOMBAY'S RECENT CRISIS

The final section of this paper deals with the contemporary situation of the teaching community in Bombay. This situation embodies many of the key elements of controversy concerning higher education and the teaching profession. The impact of the state of emergency on the political activities of teachers, efforts to improve working conditions for teachers, and issues of unionization of academics are all intertwined in Bombay's crisis. While the situation is at present tranquil, due in large part to the restrictions of the emergency, the potential for considerable unrest exists. There is no question but that the teaching community is in turmoil, and that many frustrations and contradictions lie under the surface.

The University of Bombay, traditionally one of India's most orderly universities, has in the past year been involved in a struggle concerning staff-related issues. The basic issue has concerned the implementation by the university of higher salary scales mandated by the University Grants Commission (UGC). The new scales would have modestly raised the bottom of the salary scale by about Rs100 a month and would have substantially raised the top of the scale so that college lecturers would have the potential of earning up to Rs1,100 a month (about $130). In fact, due to technical elements such as adjustments in salaries for "Dearness Allowance" (additional income to offset Bombay's high living costs) and other matters, the new scales would not have meant dramatic increases for most college teachers—they were more impressive for postgraduate university staff. Because of a complicated financial and political situation that would have required the Maharashtra government to provide a part of the salary increases, and because of the fact that the dominant element in the ruling party consists of rural areas uninterested in the financial well-being of urban academics, the implementation of the new salary scales was delayed. This delay, after initial promises from the government, combined with other grievances to agitate the academic community.

Issues such as uncertainty about the possibility of large scale retrench-ments of staff under a reform plan proposed by the Maharashtra government, the firings of several teachers in local colleges, and other matters stimulated the growth of the Bombay University Teachers Union (BUTU), which was founded in 1967 but achieved real strength only in 1972.* The BUTU leader-ship, consisting of a small number of college teachers, most of whom had some background in political affairs, was able to mobilize considerable support around the salary scale issue. Other issues, such as fears of college teachers that what little job security they had would be damaged by broad-scale retrench-ments, a proposed revision of the Bombay University Act, and several moves by local colleges to lay off individual teachers, contributed to BUTU's appeal. It is significant that the BUTU mobilized around trade union issues and attempted to use trade union tactics to achieve its goal.

The BUTU has worked to obtain legal safeguards for job security and more clearly defined and improved working conditions for teachers. After considerable pressure, the BUTU convinced the university that the require-ment that college staff be confirmed after a maximum of two years probation or dismissed be implemented—it had been widely ignored and many teachers remained on probation for long periods. The result of this initiative was that a large number of probationary teachers were fired. This was very much contrary to the result that the BUTU had desired. Similarly, the dispute concerning the implementation of the UGC salary scales resulted in a solution that is probably not in the best interests of the teachers, although this and several related matters are under litigation in the courts.

In order to force a recalcitrant Maharashtra government to implement the new and improved salary scales, the BUTU organized a teacher boycott of grading the university's final examinations, thus bringing the operation of the university to a halt and creating massive pressure on university authorities from parents and others demanding examination results. This pressure was successful in forcing the government to agree to the implementation of the UGC scales. However, shortly after this agitation, Prime Minister Indira Gandhi declared the emergency, effectively stopping all political activity and outlawing strikes and other forms of agitation. The government of Maharash-

---

*Information concerning the BUTU comes from interviews with members and from a pub-lished paper by a BUTU activist. See also "Code of Conduct for Teachers" (1975) and "The Sen Committee and After" (1975).

tra, taking advantage of this situation, attached to the new salaries a series of additional conditions that were unacceptable to the BUTU and to most teachers ("Code of Conduct for Teacher's" 1975).

These conditions are significant because they indicate some of the issues that are of concern to the government with regard to the teaching profession: this matter indicates the degree to which the university is dominated by government authorities, in terms of major policy decisions. Perhaps most important in the financial sense, the new salary scales were tied to an elimination of additional payments to teachers for grading examinations. Teachers would be expected to grade examinations without remuneration and as a part of their normal academic duties. In addition, in order for teachers to be permanently given the new scales, they would be required to obtain an additional research degree beyond the master's—either the Ph.D. or the newly established, research-oriented master of philosophy (M. Phil.) degree. Teachers not completing this degree within a specified period of time would revert to the old salary scales. A series of very specific rules of conduct were promulgated, effectively removing many elements of the limited academic freedom available to the teaching community and making it easier for administrators to discipline or dismiss teachers for infractions of these rules. The Maharashtra authorities, with the approval of the University of Bombay administration, chose to implement all of the recommendations of the UGC for upgrading and systematizing the teaching profession, without regard to local conditions (Report of the Committee University Grants Commission 1973). The new conditions and scales would result in considerably less autonomy for the teaching community; would increase qualifications for teachers, which would be difficult to implement and would place a tremendous burden on the university departments that would have to greatly increase the number of postgraduate degrees conferred; would place teachers under increased administrative rules and constraints; would further limit the possibility of political involvement; and would only marginally increase the salaries of most teachers.

The response of the teaching community and the BUTU was wholly negative. But it was impossible for the teachers to mobilize against the new rules, since under the emergency political and trade union activity was strictly controlled. Police officials would not permit a public meeting to discuss the matter, and two of the BUTU leaders were imprisoned without charges under the emergency regulations. The BUTU did institute a legal action against the university in order to stop the new rules, but without much success. The situation has left the teaching community demoralized and essentially powerless. The outcome cannot be a positive one for the growth of professionalism and commitment in the academic community in Bombay.

This recent crisis points out several significant factors concerning the teaching community. The Bombay University Teachers' Union has been able to mobilize support only for issues that are related to economic benefits or job security. This has seemingly fitted into the trade union approach of the BUTU leadership. The teaching community has not been very interested in having the BUTU concern itself with educational issues, even though many teachers agree that the educational system is in need of considerable reform. Despite the BUTU's impressive victory in forcing the government to implement the UGC scales, the organization does not have very solid support from the teaching community. Indeed, many teachers support it on specific issues, such as salary scales, but do not trust its leadership.

The outcome of this crisis is as yet unclear. Given the present situation, it is unlikely that the matter will be settled to the satisfaction of the teaching community.* Teacher morale has been damaged and it is likely that the small degree of self-esteem and autonomy that the teaching community has had will be further eroded. Teachers will have less academic freedom, and less control over their working situations. The perquisites of administrators will be increased, and while salaries for many teachers will increase to some degree, the added income of grading examinations will be lost and the final result is not likely to be a significant increase. In addition, about 500 teachers were fired as the result of a government-imposed reorganization of the educational system in Maharashtra. Most of those fired were from the ranks of unconfirmed staff, and efforts are being made to find other positions for them.

Bombay's crisis highlights a number of elements of the situation of the teaching community. In Bombay, as in most parts of India, there is no strong trade union movement among college teachers, although it is possible to organize the teaching community around specific issues, usually relating to their own working conditions or salaries. Despite a common perception that teaching conditions are in need of improvement and that, in fact, the entire educational system requires basic reforms, there is no consensus concerning these reforms and very little militancy concerning direct improvement of conditions. The leadership of the BUTU has been somewhat ideological, in the sense that some key figures have been involved in political activism, but the BUTU itself has kept away from political questions and ideological matters. The teaching community is pragmatic, not notably radical in its orientation, and not basically committed to either social or educational change.

Although it is possible that the BUTU gained quiet support as a result of the emergency, the organization remains controversial. Many teachers oppose its political stance on some issues. Some feel that one result of BUTU agitation has been to bring governmental authorities more directly into the educational equation, and that this in the long run will further weaken concep-

---

*This chapter was written before the end of the emergency. The academic situation is now in flux, but the balance of power has shifted in the direction of the teachers.

tions of academic autonomy. BUTU officials have tended to seek government intervention when they could not obtain their aims within the academic system, and have not hesitated to use confrontation tactics when this seemed useful. Given the generally poor conditions of the teaching community, however, any group that claimed to champion the demands of teachers could count on considerable support, especially when it proved effective on several occasions.

The role of government in education, particularly at the state level, is crucial (for a discussion of the relationship between politics and higher education in India, see Rudolph 1972). The informal role of government officials in university decisions has grown in recent years, not only because state authorities have ultimate control over expenditures for education and have attempted increasingly to make sure that their policies have been implemented at all levels of the educational system, but also because university authorities and others within the academic system have turned to government for assistance on matters that traditionally would have been settled within the university. While in the constitutional sense, universities are governed by acts passed by the state legislatures, and direct governmental interference in the affairs of institutions is thereby precluded, informal involvement has increased. The university budget, for example, is provided in a block grant from the state government, and can be spent by the institution without direct interference. But when the government asked that universities and colleges not fill staff vacancies, the institutions complied without regard to their staffing needs. This increased government involvement—and Maharashtra has been relatively free of direct meddling in academic affairs—colors the entire academic environment.

## CONCLUSION

The Indian academic community, and especially that large segment teaching in undergraduate colleges, finds itself in an ambivalent and in general an unenviable position. A number of reasons for this ambivalence have been suggested by the foregoing analysis. This conclusion will summarize some of the structural and other factors that contribute to the present state of affairs in most of Indian academic life.

The historical tradition of subservience, strong within Hindu intellectual life and nurtured by the history of British colonial higher education in India, has been an inhibiting factor of major proportions. Hindu intellectualism has stressed a derivative scholarship based on established texts. British colonial policy built academic institutions that were not supposed to develop an active and independent intellectual life; rather, they were aimed at training bureaucrats and professionals, not scholars and thinkers. Colleges and universities had little autonomy, and academics who strayed too far from established policy found it difficult to function. While some academics were involved in the independence movement, it is perhaps not surprising that the majority of college and university teachers were inactive throughout the dramatic events leading to independence in 1947. Students were active and militant, but not teachers.

Indian higher education has, from the beginning, been politicized. Universities and colleges were founded with certain policy orientations in mind, and were kept under close governmental scrutiny during the British period. After independence, considerable academic freedom was available to the academic community, but the direction of higher education was very much a matter of public policy. Higher education expanded very rapidly in the post-Independence period, resulting in overcrowding, deteriorating conditions, and an increasing rate of unemployment of graduates. While academics have spoken out against these declines and against overly rapid growth, their voices have not been effective. The universities themselves have been unable to shape the direction of higher education in India. Major direction has come from political leaders responding to public pressure. It is not surprising that under these conditions an autonomous and self-conscious academic community did not emerge.

Colleges and universities have been dominated by petty internal politics as well. Impelled in part by the severe competition for remunerative jobs in India, and by the need to retain a position once it is obtained, academics have engaged in factional politics within their educational institutions. While Bombay has been relatively free of disruption based on academic politics, it is not unknown in India for colleges and universities to be severely hampered in their operation by factional politics. In many instances, productive scholarship and teaching are limited by nonacademic considerations that are part of the institutional environment. In a society of scarcity and in an institutional framework that does not have clear norms of behavior it is not surprising that internal politics play an important yet disruptive role.

The emergence of professional norms depends on appropriate institutional and societal conditions. These conditions do not, for the most part, exist in India. Institutional autonomy is very limited and the teachers, especially in the colleges, have little control over their own work conditions, teaching, schedules, or other elements of everyday academic life. The fact that the academic profession has not, in many cases, been able to recruit the most qualified individuals has resulted in a teaching body that is sometimes not especially well trained. A key element is the lack of autonomy at any level of the college structure. Teachers naturally do not regard themselves as independent intellectuals with self-imposed responsibilities for teaching and academic life, but rather as employees of large bureaucratic structures that they often fear. It is not surprising that professionalism has failed to emerge in such an environment.

The economic status of both the colleges and the teachers contributes to the present situation. Colleges receive only limited assistance from university or governmental bodies, and are dependent for their survival on student fees. The more newly established colleges have inadequate facilities and are unable to find funds to create a more adequate teaching and learning environment. The teaching staff has traditionally been underpaid and inflation has further eroded income levels. In the cities it is virtually impossible for college teachers to live in a middle-class style, although teachers fare better in less urban settings, where the cost of living is lower. Low salaries have forced teachers to take other jobs, reducing their commitment to their college responsibilities and dividing their loyalties.

College teachers are not creative intellectuals in most societies. They are, rather "consuming intellectuals," transmitters of knowledge from those who do write and who participate in creative work to students. Thus, it would be unfair to expect Indian college teachers to publish very much, and indeed their job responsibilities do not, for the most part, include publication. Yet, it is increasingly rare for college teachers even to keep up with the latest developments in their academic fields and in the broader world of intellectual life. Without this current awareness, it is difficult to impart to students the latest and most exciting knowledge. The picture is, of course, mixed, with many teachers taking their roles seriously and participating in intellectual life; however, it would seem that these individuals constitute only a minority in the teaching profession.

The role of the college in the Indian social structure dictates to a considerable degree the status and role of the teacher. Colleges have become mass institutions, providing access to education to the urban middle- and lower-middle-classes and, increasingly, to the rural bourgeoisie as well. With a few exceptions, they no longer train an elite for positions of power and prestige in the society. Given this societal position, it is not surprising that the colleges themselves and their teachers do not have a prominent position in society. In this sense, the college teacher occupies a place that, in fact, fits logically with the function of the college in the Indian social structure. To expect dramatic change in the light of this situation, given India's "society of scarcity," is probably unrealistic.

## REFERENCES

Altbach, Philip R. 1971. "Higher Education in India." In B. Burn, P. Altbach, C. Kerr, and J. Perkins, *Higher Education in Nine Countries,* pp. 317–44. New York:McGraw-Hill.

————. 1972. *The University in Transition: An Indian Case Study.* Cambridge, Mass.: Schenkman.

————, Chitnis, S. And Kulkarni, J. 1977. *The Academic Profession in Maharashtra.* In preparation.

Chitnis, S. 1969. *The Teacher Role in the College System.* Ph.D. dissertation, Tata Institute of Social Sciences, Bombay.

_____. 1974. "Teachers in Higher Education." In A. Singh and Philip G. Altbach, eds., *The Higher Learning in India,* pp. 237–50. Delhi: Vikas.

"Code of Conduct for Teachers." 1975. *Economic and Political Weekly* (November 15), pp. 1754–55.

Gilbert, I. 1972. "The Indian Academic Profession: The Origins of A Tradition of Subordination." *Minerva* 10 (July), pp. 384–411.

University Grants Commission. *Report of the Committee on the Governance of Universities and Colleges,* Part II *Teachers.* 1973. New Delhi: University Grants Commission.

University of Bombay. *Report of the Inquiry on the Problems of Teachers in the University of Bombay.* 1954. Bombay: University of Bombay.

Rudolph, L. and S., eds. 1972. *Education and Politics in India.* Cambridge, Mass.: Harvard University Press.

"The Sen Committee and After." 1975. *Economic and Political Weekly* (November 22), pp. 1790–91.

Shils, E. 1969. "The Academic Profession in India." *Minerva* 7 (Spring), pp. 345–72.

_____. 1972. "Toward a Modern Intellectual Community in the New States." In E. Shils, ed., *The Intellectuals and the Powers and Other Essays,* pp. 335–71. Chicago: University of Chicago Press.

Singh, A. and Altbach, P., eds. 1974. *The Higher Learning in India.* Delhi: Vikas.

Singh, Y. 1972. "Academic Role Structure and Modernization: A Study of University Teachers." In S. Saberwal, ed., *Beyond the Village: Sociological Explorations,* pp. 195–244. Simla: Indian Institute of Advanced Study.

Sinha, B. N. 1969. *The Problems and Attitudes of University Teachers in Bihar.* Ph.D. dissertation, Ranchi University.

# 9

# Faculty Women in the American University: Up the Down Staircase
## Bonnie Cook Freeman

Academic women for the most part have been invisible until very recently. The ivory tower was assumed to be a legitimate male preserve. Those few scholars who even mentioned the subject agreed that female faculty were on the fringes of the academic mainstream. For example, Caplow and McGee in their classic work, *The Academic Marketplace* (1958), noted that women scholars could not look forward to normal professional careers. As most early descriptions of university life were profiles of the average professor ("the academic man"), the costs to women making it in a man's world were not enumerated. With the advent of the women's movement in the last decade, academic women have become a more popular research area and, consequently, our understanding of the female professoriate was significantly increased by a series of works beginning with Jessie Bernard's *Academic Women* (1964). This essay will contribute to this relatively recent genre of academic investigation.

The argument will be divided into three parts. First, I intend to document the degree of inequality that exists between academic men and women (particularly at Quality I institutions of higher education*) and to show it is the product of discrimination. Second, this material will serve as the context

---

I would like to acknowledge Gary Freeman and Jan Ford for comments on an earlier draft of this paper.

*Quality I institution refers to a classification of institutions of higher education assigned by the 1969 National Survey of Higher Education sponsored by the Carnegie Commission. Institutions of higher education participating in the survey were ranked according to their quality in three broad groupings: universities, colleges, and junior colleges. Within the first two categories, three quality classes (I, II, III) were created, of which I was most highly rated. At Quality I institutions, there were 12,094 faculty men and 1,559 faculty women (13,653 total)—the respondents to whom

within which an overview of the political movement of academic women in the past eight or ten years is set. I will argue that inequality and discrimination are the basis for the discontent and anger manifested by academic women in the late sixties and early seventies in the United States. Finally, I include a brief assessment of the impact of women's political activities on university campuses. I will devote special attention to the progress of affirmative action programs and try to determine how current economic and political trends will affect the future status of academic women.

## THE STATUS OF ACADEMIC WOMEN IN THE UNITED STATES

After World War II the United States experienced an unprecedented expansion in the demand for higher education, in the provision of educational facilities, and in the financial commitment of the federal and state governments to higher education. Between 1956 and 1966, total expenditures of institutions of higher education increased from $4.1 billion to $15 billion, an increase of 258 percent (Harris 1972, p. 819). During the same decade new colleges opened at the rate of one a week and student numbers expanded from 3 to 7 million (Lowi 1970, p. 238). From 1949–50 to 1967–68, the percentage of faculty involved in residential instruction increased by approximately 150 percent (Harris 1972, p. 483). In 1957–58, the number of faculty was 260,486: in 1967–68 it was 481,000, an increase of 85 percent (Harris 1972, p. 483). In 1974–75, the total was 654,000, an increase of 68 percent (U.S. 1976, Table 97, p. 95).

Although women shared in the educational growth of the last three decades in absolute terms, they lost ground relative to their male counterparts. Contrary to popular belief about the rising status of women, this downward trend has continued to be the dominant pattern from 1970 through 1976. In 1920 women constituted 26 percent of all faculty and in both 1930 and 1940 they constituted 27 percent (U.S. 1973, Table 100). But by 1960 the overall proportion of women faculty in colleges and universities had fallen to 19–20 percent, where it remained until 1971 (Kilson 1976, p. 937).

---

I refer in this essay. For a more detailed exposition of these data, see the author (1975) and Martin Trow (1975). Other sources drawn on are the 1969–70 survey data of all institutions, from the Carnegie Study, reported by Alan Bayer (1970); the 1972–73 information collected by the American Council on Education and reported by Bayer (1973); the 1976–77 data from the National Center for Educational Statistics reported in the *Chronicle of Higher Education;* a 1972–73 survey conducted by the author among University of Wisconsin faculty women and men, reported in Freeman (1975); and the study of women doctorates conducted by Helen Astin (1969).

While several scholars have emphasized that the proportion of women faculty has risen slightly at four-year institutions during the past decade (Carnegie Commission 1973, p. 111), they have not pointed out that the gains were in the lower, off-tenure track positions. In fact, there has been a decrease in the proportion of tenured women faculty, from 17 percent in 1971–72 to 13 percent in 1974–75. During the same period the proportion of tenured male faculty only declined from 59 percent to 57 percent (Kilson 1976, p. 937). At the more prestigious and influential institutions of higher education, female faculty are even more underrepresented (they constitute 11 percent of the faculty) and are more intensively concentrated in the lower professional ranks (Bonnie C. Freeman 1975, Chap. 3).

Figures on the total number of women faculty in institutions of higher education tend to conceal very remarkable differences between male and female faculty on a number of dimensions. Before looking specifically at the question of inequalities in status, rewards, and work environment, it may be useful to explore the social backgrounds and adult family lives of male and female faculty. Academic women are in many ways survivors, exhibiting the talents and qualities that are required to make it in a men's world. They also bear the scars of their struggle. The ways in which the lives of academic men and women differ are an indication of the requirements and costs of academic careers for each of the two sexes.

## Social Backgrounds of Male and Female Faculty

Social origins exert considerable influence on the individual's chances of occupational and educational success. The major factor determining a person's opportunities for upward mobility is usually the socioeconomic level at which that person begins—academics are no exception to this social norm.

Both male and female professors are drawn disproportionately from the higher status elements of the society. This is clearly evident with respect to the occupational and educational characteristics of their parents. At Quality I institutions, 17 percent of both men and women had fathers who had either a graduate or professional degree. Women were slightly more likely than men to have well-educated fathers—54 percent of women faculty had fathers with at least some college, compared to 48 percent of the men. Furthermore, there were only minor differences between male and female faculty with respect to the educational attainments of their mothers—12 percent of the females had mothers with at least some graduate training, while 8 percent of the men were in this category.

The same general pattern is found when one examines the occupational backgrounds of the parents of faculty. At Quality I institutions, only 17 percent of the men and 16 percent of the women reported that their fathers had held manual positions. No data on the occupations of mothers were collected in the Carnegie surveys. In a 1972–73 study of University of Wisconsin female faculty, it was discovered that only one-fourth of the women had mothers with any occupation, and only 16 percent of those were classified as professional or semiprofessional (Bonnie C. Freeman 1975, p. 34).

In summary, both parents of male and female faculty tend to be educated more than the general population and to hold higher-prestige jobs. It seems safe to conclude that the socioeconomic milieu from which these men and women were drawn constitutes a supportive and facilitative influence on their careers. For our purposes, the most interesting conclusion is that these differences between male and female faculty are not important and in fact are much smaller than those which separate faculty of both sexes at elite schools from those at less prestigious schools (Ladd and Lipset 1975, p. 174).

These basic similarities are not duplicated when one is looking at two other socioeconomic variables—race and religious affiliation. Representing over half of the population of the country, women hold almost 20 percent of all professorships while blacks, who make up 11–12 percent of the population, hold only 2.2–3.0 percent of all professorships (U.S. 1973, pp. 90, 94). For Quality I schools the story is told in Table 9.1. It is clear that while women and blacks (as well as Chicanos and Native Americans) make up a smaller

TABLE 9.1

Racial Composition of the Professoriate at
Quality I Schools, by Sex

| Race | Percent | Number |
|------|---------|--------|
| White | | |
| Male | 86.28 | 11,657 |
| Female | 10.93 | 1,502 |
| | | |
| Black | | |
| Male | 0.49 | 70 |
| Female | 0.15 | 21 |
| | | |
| Oriental | | |
| Male | 1.97 | 281 |
| Female | 0.19 | 27 |
| | | |
| Total | 100.00 | 13,558 |

proportion of the professoriate than they do of the population as a whole, Orientals are slightly overrepresented among faculty. While they represent approximately 1 percent of the population, they comprise over 2 percent of the professoriate at Quality I institutions. Blacks, on the other hand, hold only 0.64 percent of the professorships at Quality I institutions.

Within each ethnic group, women are less numerous than men. That means that, while the most fortunate group in terms of acquiring professional status is white males, followed by Oriental males, the least fortunate group is black women closely followed by Oriental and white women. Both being female and being colored are stigmata limiting the individual's opportunities for success: when they occur in conjunction the effect is cumulative. It is difficult to ascertain whether femaleness or blackness is the more serious handicap for an aspiring professor. It is true, as I have pointed out, that blacks are more underrepresented on faculties than are women. But that is misleading without further explication. Blacks tend to be clustered in the lower socioeconomic strata of our society. Since college professors are not normally recruited from those strata, a large part of the explanation for underrepresentation of blacks is to be found in class-related factors. That blacks come from low-income backgrounds and experience poorer educational preparation because of racism is, of course, true: that is another question in itself. Women, on the other hand, are spread evenly across class lines. Strictly class-related factors cannot explain their underrepresentation on faculties and we are forced to resort to sex-linked explanations. The most striking evidence of the importance of sex is simply that, within each racial group, women are the least well represented in faculties.*

Men and women at Quality I schools come from slightly different religious backgrounds. Of the men, 60 percent—and 65 percent of the women—reported that they were brought up as Protestants. More women (16 percent) than men (12 percent) had been reared as Catholics and more men (18 percent) than women (10 percent) had been brought up in the Jewish religion. On the whole there has been a significant decline in the percentage of both men and

---

*As there were so few black and Oriental women at Quality I schools, separate analyses of sexual differences within racial groups were not possible. This is quite unfortunate, as there is some suggestion of patterns of distinctive behavior among Oriental women and black women. A study of these groups, using samples of all institutions to increase the $N$, should be quite rewarding. However, analysis on sexual, racial, and ethnic characteristics for either degree recipients or faculty members in general has been difficult due to the inadequacy of data collection by federal agencies, research foundations, and institutions of higher education. Major research foundations, such as the American Council on Education and the Carnegie Commission, have used a catch-all "other" category that included Native Americans, Mexican Americans, Puerto Ricans, and other unspecified groups. Also, most data on minorities, such as that collected by the National Research Council, has not included breakdowns by sex.

women claiming any religion: 36 percent of the men and 31 percent of the women say they now have no formal ties to any religious group. The religious stability of academics is somewhat surprising in that professors are thought of as being committed to both the "institutionalization of the spirit of doubt and skepticism" and the intellectual's duty to "re-examine critically any proposition about the observable elements of the world in which we live" (Lenski 1961, pp. 253–55), either of which would seem to be in contradiction to steadfast religious belief or orthodoxy.

Of course, mere membership in a church or a synagogue says little about the depth of the sentiment involved. The respondents were asked, therefore, if they were very or moderately religious, indifferent, or basically opposed. In every instance, except for the Jews, female respondents expressed more religious intensity than did men. The most intensely religious of the women were Catholics, of whom 95 percent reported they were moderately or very religious compared to 88 percent of the men (again, the most religious of any group of men). Jews were the least intense for either sex (J. Freeman 1975, p. 46).

## Adult Family Life of Faculty Women

The route to professional certification in any field, for men or women, exacts certain costs—prolonged study, financial sacrifices, foregone alternatives, uncertain outcomes. Perhaps the most demanding professions are those religious orders where the initiate takes vows of poverty and chastity and gives up, as it were, the rest of the world. Of all the aspects of an individual's life —social origins, attitudes, professional activities—none more sharply distinguishes the female professor from her male colleague than family relationships. In choosing to marry or not, in selecting a spouse, and in deciding whether to have children, females face a much different set of options and costs than do males. Thus, in the process of becoming a professor, the terms of bargaining and exchange for women are quite distinctive from those for men. The area of life most affected is the most personal, marriage and family.

In the following, it is not my intention to demonstrate that the exchanges demanded of the female and not of the male are fully articulated or even conscious. But I will show that there is remarkable evidence that different exchanges are in fact made; and I will. argue from this that the woman is coerced subtly or directly into paying a higher price than that demanded of her male counterpart in order to be accepted into the academic world.

### Marriage

Possibly the single factor that most clearly distinguishes male and female faculty is marital status. Almost all male faculty marry at some point in their lives. From one-third to over one-half of female faculty never marry. The rate of marriage for women with doctorates is very low when compared with either men or women in general or with male academics and women in comparable professions.

Of the women at Quality I institutions, 40 percent were single. At a highly prestigious institution like the University of Wisconsin, the figure rises to 55.6 percent. In the general population only 3 percent of the adult women are single and 4 percent of the men. On the other hand, of the male faculty at Quality I schools, only 8 percent have never married (Bernard 1973, p. 187).

Traditionally, learning and domesticity have been considered incompatible. If a woman married, her colleagues assumed she would retire from the academic scene. That these social expectations still persist can be illustrated in the differences between the marriage rates of male and female professors (on their face quite dramatic). To anyone acquainted with academic mores and socialization, the wide gap is in fact not surprising. "Everyone knows" that the expectations for women and men are different, and it is not necessary for them to be formally spelled out. To be taken "seriously" an academic woman knows that it is best not to marry; however, remaining single does not guarantee serious treatment. For men, on the other hand, marriage is usually understood to be an asset and is often taken to be an indicator of stability and maturity.

The most persuasive evidence that marriage does have deleterious effects on the careers of women and beneficial effects on those of men is produced when one inquires into the academic rank held by men and women with different marital statuses. The results show rather conclusively that single women hold higher positions than married women and that married men hold higher positions than single men.

Of the men in the Carnegie Quality I sample who reported that they were currently married to their first wife, 38 percent were professors, 22 percent were associate professors, and 28 percent were assistant professors. Of those who were currently married to their second, or later, wife, 52 percent were professors, 22 percent were associate professors, and 17 percent were assistant professors. For those never married, 16 percent were professors, 18 percent were associate professors, and 41 percent were assistant professors. Rank, therefore, is strongly related to the marital status of these men and being married is a great advantage.

For the women in the elite group the story is much different. Of those who were currently married to their first husband, 6 percent were professors, 12 percent were associate professors, and 36 percent were assistant professors. Of the women currently married for the second time, or more, 6 percent were professors, 23 percent were associate professors, and 36 percent were assistant professors. But of the women who had never married, 17 percent were professors, 23 percent were associate professors, and 30 percent were assistant professors. The percentage of the women who hold positions below the rank of assistant professor (that is, instructor or lecturer) declined markedly for the single women. Forty-six percent of the once-married, 36 percent of the remarried, but only 30 percent of those never married were in these lowly positions. Rank is consequently related to marital status for women and being single is a relative advantage.

One may ask, of course, if this relationship is not spurious to some degree and if it is not the result of the intervention of some third factor. In an attempt to discover if this were the case, I examined the relationship between sex, marital status, and rank, controlling, for the highest degree of accuracy, the individuals held, their age, the number of years they had been teaching, and the year they had received their degree. In no case was the original relationship between marital status and rank attenuated for either sex.

In summary, married women are not as likely to be promoted as single women who never married and married men are more likely to be promoted than single men who never married. The exact reasons why this is so seem quite complex. One immediate possibility is that married women, because they must normally take on the primary responsibility for managing a household and rearing children (not to mention actual time lost on the job during pregnancy and childbirth) are simply unable to produce professionally at the rate of their single female colleagues. Furthermore, following this logic, one might surmise that the married man, benefiting from the assistance and support of a wife, is free to produce more scholarly research and publications. The data do not support the hypothesis as it relates to women, but do with respect to men.

Married men publish both articles and books at a higher rate than single men; however, there is no difference between the publication rates for married and single women. Of the once-married women, 6 percent have 3–4 books, 3 percent have 5 or more. Of the remarried, 5 percent have 3–4 books, 4 percent have 5 or more. Of the never-married women, 5 percent have 3–4 books, 4 percent have 5 or more. There is no difference, then, in the publication rates of married and single women; but, as I have shown, there are differences in rank between the two sets of women. My hypothesis that marriage is a facilitative factor for the scholarly labors of man is consistent with the data, although my suggestion that marriage is a disadvantage for a woman in terms of scholarly output is not upheld. Married women publish as much as unmarried women, regardless of their family burdens. However, in terms of professional advancement, marriage proves to be a severe handicap.

While marriage creates obstacles for academic women, remaining single does not necessarily secure professional success and personal happiness. First, single women constitute a clearly defined minority group of social deviance, and conceptions about single women are contradictory and paradoxical. What's more, single women are considered fair game for exploitation. Defined as the weaker sex, women exchange the independence for the appearance of protection and economic support from the men they marry. It is ironic that the single woman, who is at times considered a pathetic spinster, may also be thought of as threatening to the male. For, lurking in the background is the subtle suggestion that she may have rejected the passive role that society had set for her, and thus the protection of the male of her choice. Therefore, the single woman is sometimes perceived as "asking for it." She is open to sexual advances, economic exploitation, and social harassment and intimidation. Although the single woman fares better in the academic marketplace, she pays another and perhaps equally high price for remaining alone.

## The Educational Attainments of the Spouse

People tend to marry persons with similar educational backgrounds and intellectual interests. Women usually do not marry men whose educational attainment is lower than their own, but men do often marry women of similar or lower educational attainment. Thus, it comes as no surprise that, of the married women in the Carnegie sample, most report that their husbands have professional or graduate degrees. Of the married women at Quality I schools, 81 percent had husbands with professional or doctoral degrees.

When these figures are compared with those for male faculty at Quality I schools, the results are striking. Only 45 percent of the males who were married had wives with professional or doctoral degrees. In other words, women were almost twice as likely as men to choose persons with advanced educations as spouses. This finding fits the cultural norm of the marriage gradient—women marry men brighter than themselves, or at least as well educated and men marry women who are slightly less well educated or similarly educated. This norm may also account *partially* for the large number of faculty women who have remained single. There is no one for the women at the top to look up to: there are no men superior to them.

## Children

If the careers of academic women are somewhat impeded by marriage, motherhood is an even greater drawback. Even with affirmative action supporting maternity leaves and university day-care centers, many universities have prejudicial policies regarding maternity and day care. Some institutions provide for no leave for maternity and assume women in such circumstances will quit. Others provide leave but no pay. Few universities have part-time, on-track positions, which would be particularly helpful for men and women dedicated to professional *and* family life. Even fewer universities have adequate day-care centers. Most universities seem to be run on the premise that if women "get pregnant" it is their problem.

For academic women, children may or may not be desired; yet there is no way they do not present a time-consuming responsibility. Indirect, but suggestive, evidence on this point is provided by the Carnegie data on Quality I faculties. Married women faculty have significantly fewer children than married male faculty. Of those men who were married only once, 20 percent had no children and 33 percent had three or more. Once-married women, in contrast, were much more likely to have no children (46 percent) or to have fewer children (only 15 percent reported three or more). As with marriage itself, I have no way of knowing if women who prefer to remain childless are self-selected into university careers, but it seems safe to conclude that the rigors and demands of such careers have an independent effect on the child-bearing propensities of faculty women.

### Summary

This section has shown that male and female academics are quite similar in most of their social background attributes. Except for those matters dealing with marriage and the family, these men and women share similar social origins and experiences. As we shall see in the following section, however, they diverge radically in their professional success.

## The Professional Lives of Faculty Women at Quality I Institutions

In comparing backgrounds and present positions of men and women faculty at Quality I schools, we are dealing with individuals who have made it to the top of their profession. This is not primarily an essay on inequalities between male and female professors in general. We have ignored those who are trapped at the bottom or have fallen by the wayside. Data here indicate the professional situation of the most successful women. As a consequence, this section understates the real inequalities between male and female professors.

The path to a doctorate is always a long and difficult one, with many obstacles along the way. It is a very common practice for a particular faculty member to act as a sponsor for individual graduate students. In performing this role, the major advisor guides and directs the student's general education, the preparation of his or her thesis, and, very importantly, helps him or her secure the first job.

The career plans of graduate women have been found to be affected more significantly by the quality of their relationship with their major professors than are those of graduate men. The data on faculty women at Quality I institutions support the conclusion that as graduate students they encounter greater difficulty acquiring a sympathetic *patron* than do their male peers.

Of these individuals now at Quality I institutions, 52 percent said that they had enjoyed the services of a sponsor and 48 percent said that they had not. When one looks at the answers by sex, one sees that men are quite a bit more likely than women to have answered "yes": 54 percent of the men had such assistance, compared to only 38 percent of the women.

The evidence on sponsorship suggests some very interesting differences in the processes of occupational mobility that men and women academics experience. It appears that many women move up the ladder even without the encouragement and assistance that one receives from an established sponsor. They seem to exhibit an ability to stick it out, even if doing so means that they must overcome the resistance of either their professors, whose lukewarm endorsement they ignore, or of their peers, with whom they must compete for status and recognition. Most men report that their own professional lives were facilitated by an older professor who paved the way for them by giving them encouragement and assistance. They are then spared the necessity of promoting their own careers directly or challenging the academic judgment of their graduate departments.

## Financial Assistance

When one examines the elite sample for differential financial rewards by sex, one finds that men teaching at Quality I institutions are more likely than women to have received all three of the basic forms of financial aid as graduate students. Sixty-three percent of the men and only 54 percent of the women reported ever having received teaching assistantships or graduate assistantships as graduate students. The greatest disparity between men and women is with regard to the awarding of research assistantships: while 51 percent of the men had received such an award during their graduate years, only 33 percent of the women had.

## Distribution of Women Among Academic Disciplines

Women are not found in equal proportions in all academic fields. The Carnegie survey data for all colleges and universities (including Quality I institutions), show that there is a tendency for faculty women to cluster in a few fields stereotypically thought of as feminine, such as nursing, home economics, library science, and foreign languages (Feldman 1974, p. 43). The percentage of women in all disciplines tends to decrease as one moves from the undergraduate to the faculty level, and from less to more prestigious universities. Furthermore, the tendency for women to cluster in "feminine" fields is more marked the higher up the educational hierarchy one goes, and the fields women vacate enjoy better academic reputations within the university than the departments to which they move. Surprisingly, however, in no single field do women constitute a greater proportion of faculty than they do as undergraduate majors. Even in "feminine" fields where women constitute a majority, there is a tendency for the proportion of female faculty to be smaller than that of undergraduate majors or graduate students (Bonnie C. Freeman 1975, p. 81).

## Professional Status and Activities

Women tend to populate the lower professional ranks and nontenure track positions. The more prestigious and influential the institution, the greater is the inequality in status between men and women (see Table 9.2). One study that matched women and men statistically on a number of variables ostensibly related to academic reward found that women were still likely to be below men in both rank and salary (Astin and Bayer 1973, p. 355).

### TABLE 9.2

Academic Rank of Men and Women,
Quality I Institutions (percent)

| Rank | Men (base N=11,549; total N=12,094) | Women (base N=1,356; total N=1,559) |
|------|------|------|
| Professor | 38 | 12 |
| Associate Professor | 22 | 18 |
| Assistant Professor | 28 | 34 |
| Instructor | 7 | 22 |
| Lecturer | 5 | 14 |

Promotion in academia, of course, depends on a number of criteria—
degrees earned, years of employment, teaching, and research. As I will show,
women are not as likely to hold the Ph.D. as are men. On first sight this might
seem to account for the disparity in academic rank one finds between the sexes,
as shown in Table 9.2. But this is not the case, as Table 9.3 clearly demon-
strates. Regardless of what type of degree the female holds, she is much more
likely than her male counterpart to be in one of the lower classifications. *In
fact, a greater percentage of males with bachelor's degrees are full professors
than are women with Ph.D.'s:* 23 percent of the men with only a B.A. are full
professors, while only 15 percent of the women with Ph.D.'s hold that rank.

The differences in the distribution of academic rank between the sexes are,
therefore, striking. Even more dramatic, however, is the disproportionate
concentration of males in the higher ranks because of their greater numbers.
Men hold 96.5 percent of all full professorships at Quality I institutions. In
addition, they account for 91 percent of all associate professorships, 88 percent
of all assistant professorships, 73 percent of all instructorships, and 76 percent
of all lectureships. In other words, as one ascends the academic ladder of
success the proportion of each rank held by women, never large, declines so
swiftly it almost disappears altogether.

Academic rank is not simply a matter of status, prestige, and income. In
most cases, ranks below that of associate professor are not accompanied by

## TABLE 9.3

### The Academic Rank of Male and Female Faculty, by Highest Degree Earned, Quality I Institutions

| Degree | Professor | Associate Professor | Assistant Professor | Instructor | Lecturer | Base N | Total N |
|---|---|---|---|---|---|---|---|
| **Ph.D.** | | | | | | | |
| Males | 42 | 24 | 29 | 2 | 3 | 7070 | 7154 |
| Females | 15 | 22 | 46 | 4 | 13 | 493 | 511 |
| **Other Doctorate** | | | | | | | |
| Males | 39 | 22 | 26 | 6 | 7 | 588 | 602 |
| Females | 29 | 30 | 20 | 5 | 16 | 103 | 108 |
| **Medicine/Law** | | | | | | | |
| Males | 31 | 22 | 30 | 14 | 3 | 1892 | 1950 |
| Females | 11 | 16 | 36 | 33 | 4 | 108 | 113 |
| **M.A.** | | | | | | | |
| Males | 23 | 14 | 19 | 27 | 17 | 866 | 1081 |
| Females | 4 | 15 | 22 | 41 | 18 | 381 | 455 |
| **First Professional Degree** | | | | | | | |
| Males | 30 | 17 | 20 | 13 | 20 | 353 | 380 |
| Females | 10 | 14 | 35 | 24 | 17 | 150 | 167 |
| **B.A.** | | | | | | | |
| Males | 23 | 9 | 26 | 27 | 15 | 304 | 420 |
| Females | 6 | 2 | 23 | 58 | 11 | 53 | 118 |

tenure. Since most women are clustered in these strata, they are likely to experience a sense of job insecurity much more sharply than males.

While the failure of academic women to achieve advanced ranks at Quality I institutions cannot be attributed to the types of degree they hold, it is nevertheless true that women are much less likely than men to hold the Ph.D. Of the men, 62 percent have earned a doctorate, while only 35 percent of the women have done so. The best explanation for this lies in the fact that many women faculty teach in fields that either developed doctoral programs rather late or do not normally require the doctorate for faculty status. To some extent, however, the disparity between men and women in degrees earned must reflect simply the greater difficulty a woman faces in obtaining a degree. For all the reasons already suggested in this chapter, it is easier for men to acquire doctorates.

In recent years the situation of women with respect to academic rank has actually worsened. In 1975–76 women made up 24 percent of faculty teaching at all institutions of higher education (a rise of one percentage point since 1972–73). However, they held a smaller share of full professorships (9.8 percent) than they did one year before (10.1 percent). At universities the figure is only 6 percent. The proportion of women at the assistant-professor level rose slightly from 24 percent in 1972–73 to 29 percent in 1975–76, and the proportion of women in nontenure track positions jumped from 24 percent in 1972–73 to 35 percent in 1975–76. Therefore, while the proportion of women at the bottom of the educational heap is increasing, the proportion of women at the top is shrinking slightly.

## Teaching Responsibilities

Faculty women at Quality I schools (and in general) bear a disproportionate share of undergraduate instruction and have less contact with graduate students. At Quality I institutions, there is a tendency for women to teach more classroom hours than men. However, the gap is even larger when one looks at the entire Carnegie survey. Fully 30 percent of all women professors questioned by Carnegie were teaching 13 or more hours, while only 21 percent of the men were (see Table 9.4). Furthermore, men were more likely to have graduate teaching assistants assigned to them (Bonnie C. Freeman 1975, p. 98).

The evidence in this section suggests that women at Quality I institutions are in many cases little more than faculty teaching assistants. They tend to do the hard, boring work of handling large introductory courses, while their better-paid, higher-ranked male colleagues teach the more exciting and professionally rewarding, upper-level undergraduate and graduate courses.

## TABLE 9.4

### Classroom Hours of Male and Female Faculty, Quality I Institutions and All Institutions (percent)

| Class Hours Per Week | All Institutions | | Q I Institutions | |
|---|---|---|---|---|
| | Men (N not given) | Women (N not given) | Men (base N=11,976; total N=12,094) | Women (base N=1,517; total N=1,559) |
| 0 | 7.9 | 7.6 | 11 | 12 |
| 1-4 | 16.2 | 11.9 | 32 | 28 |
| 5-8 | 26.8 | 17.7 | 38 | 31 |
| 9-12 | 28.3 | 32.8 | 12 | 15 |
| 13+ | 20.7 | 29.9 | 7 | 14 |

*Source:* Bayer 1970, p. 14.

### Research and Publications

More and more, publications are used as a measure of scholarly abilities and as a basis for promotion and financial reward in the academic world. As publications are more observable and quantifiable than success as a teacher, their number has become the primary criterion of job performance. Evidence, such as that in Table 9.5 comparing men and women faculty, shows that women publish less than men; however, much of the difference can be shown to result from disciplinary variations in expectations and encouragement in regard to research and publication.

Women are more likely than men to be in departments that do not provide strong normative incentives to publish, either because they are practitioner-oriented (for example, nursing, home economics, social work) or because academic achievement is supposed to be demonstrated in artistic accomplishments (for example, the fine arts) rather than in written research. However, this clearly cannot be the whole story, because, although men in these fields also exhibit a tendency to publish less than men in other fields, they still publish at higher rates than women. And women in heavily research-oriented fields do not publish as much as men, although the differences are not as great as for the sample as a whole.

Other factors that may keep women from publishing are male domination of the publishing industry, the "stag effect" in academic life that excludes women from participation in important aspects of intellectual life, and discrimination in the allocation of research funds. While all these considerations, taken together, explain most of the gap between male and female publishing rates, there also is some suggestive evidence that women value the teaching,

## TABLE 9.5

### Articles and Books Published by Male and Female Faculty, Quality I Institutions (percent)

|  | Men (base N=11,790; Total N=12,094) | Women (base N=1,493; Total N=1,559) |
|---|---|---|
| **Books** | | |
| 0 | 51 | 68 |
| 1-2 | 29 | 22 |
| 3-4 | 11 | 6 |
| 5+ | 9 | 4 |
|  | Men (base N=11,818; Total N=12,094) | Women (base N=1,498; Total N=1,559) |
| **Articles** | | |
| 0 | 15 | 38 |
| 1-4 | 24 | 33 |
| 5-10 | 16 | 12 |
| 11-20 | 15 | 9 |
| 20+ | 30 | 8 |
| TOTAL | 100 | 100 |

student-related aspects of their jobs more than men, and it is reasonable to assume that at least some women *choose* not to publish.

## Salary

Probably the most telling evidence as to how an individual is evaluated in a Western capitalist society is the salary accorded that individual. In 1975–76, the average salary for a faculty male was \$17,312, while for a faculty woman the figure was $14,242. If one looks only at public universities the figures were $18,638 and $14,458, respectively. When rank and type of institution are held constant, these differences persist—male full professors received $24,093, women only $21,497. In the academic year 1975–76, faculty members received the largest pay increases in seven years, but male gains (6.3 percent) outstripped those of women (5.8 percent) (*Chronicle of Higher Education,* February 9, 1976).

## Summary

I have shown thus far that, in the graduate careers of male and female faculty, the very best women receive less encouragement, material and emotional, and encounter more serious obstacles than do their male colleagues. Also, the proportion of women in all disciplines declines steadily from the undergraduate to the faculty level.

In their professional careers women are second-class members of the academic community, especially at elite institutions. My examination indicates that women sacrifice more in personal terms than men do to become professors, work harder (in terms of their teaching, at any rate), and receive far fewer pay-offs and rewards for their efforts.

While inequality piled upon inequality does not directly measure discrimination, it does suggest a systematic pattern of discrimination. In the late 1960s and early 1970s, American academic women became aware of their increasingly inferior status and the nature of sex discrimination. Academic women began to organize to express collectively their sense of exploitation and misuse. The new awareness involved a redefinition of events. Rather than considering themselves personal failures, women began to analyze their experience with discrimination within a political framework. It is to this issue I now turn.

# THE POLITICAL ORGANIZATION OF ACADEMIC WOMEN

## The Women's Movement on Campus

The academic women's movement is a part and a consequence of a more comprehensive women's movement and of changes in the size and structure of American higher education in the 1960s. It is difficult to pinpoint exactly when the movement emerged on campus. Some of the founders of the National Organization for Women (NOW) were academic women who carried the broad issues of equal employment and equal educational opportunity back to their campuses after their first national conference in 1966. Around the same time, women on campus had been reading Simone de Beauvoir's *The Second Sex* (1952) and Betty Friedan's *The Feminine Mystique* (1963).

Some of the women involved in the New Left had begun to argue that the inferior status of women, not class, was the fundamental inequality. Thus the campus reflected the women's movement in microcosm, with separate groups developing out of the various strata of women in the university community. A variety of groups, responding to different stimuli, began to address the problem of the inferior status of academic women. What brought them together was a common recognition of the need to deal with the issue of sex discrimination in the political arena. They were redefining their smaller allocation of the economic and academic pie as discrimination instead of just desserts for inferior capability.

At most universities the number of women faculty has been relatively small and it has been difficult to develop strong organizations. Yet, by 1969, political organizations of academic women were emerging around the country. Their form and strength depended on the prevailing political conditions on individual campuses but, generally speaking, they were more common in the Northeast, Midwest, and West than in the South and Southwest. The major purpose of most faculty women's organizations was to improve the professional status of women in academia, but investigations of that status eventually spilled over into broader questions about their very existence as women on campus. This was reflected in new concern over maternity leave, day care, and nepotism rules. In some instances, organizations whose functions had been primarily social were transformed into political bodies expressing the concerns of female professors. In other places, faculty women created new organizations (both on-campus and state-wide). Some of these groups focused primarily on protecting and advancing the professional status of their members. Others took a much broader perspective and became immersed in the general problems of women in the society.

On the national level, numbers were not so constraining. Within most academic disciplines there are sufficient women to allow caucuses to be formed within the professional associations. In addition, faculty women have renewed and developed other organizations. In the American Association of University Professors (AAUP), the Committee W (the Committee of the Status of Women within the AAUP) was reactivated. Through these organizations academic women began to gather and exchange information about sex discrepancies (for example, as regards salary). Their findings indicated a greater gap by sex than anticipated and outraged faculty women to the extent that they were willing to break from the informal, unwritten norms that members do not seek outside assistance (interpreted as interference) but abide by the "rational" decisions of "reasonable" colleagues in judging merit and rewarding that merit in salary, promotions, and retention *à la* tenure. Faculty women initiated appeals for assistance from federal agencies created by the executive to deal with discrimination and lobbied for new legislation where statutes were nonexistent or inadequate.

## The Attack on the Sexist Tower

As academic women moved to file charges of discrimination against institutions of higher education, they were surprised to discover that sex discrimination was not clearly illegal and that, as a result, legal remedies were not assured by existing U.S. federal statutes. Title VI of the Civil Rights Act of 1964 prevented discrimination against beneficiaries of federally assisted programs on the basis of race, color, or national origin; it did not do so with respect to sex. Furthermore, although Title VII of the same act forbade sex discrimination in employment, until it was amended in 1972 it specifically exempted college faculties from coverage. However, under Executive Order 12375, issued by President Johnson as a part of the guidelines for implementing the 1964 Civil Rights Act, contractors with the federal government (including universities and colleges that receive funds from federal contracts) were ordered to practice "non-discrimination" and to take "affirmative action" to remedy the effects of past discrimination with regard to race, sex, and other categories (Sandler 1973). One newly formed women's organization, the Women's Equity Action League (WEAL) filed charges in 1970 against American institutions of higher education for not abiding by the guidelines of this executive order. Because of these initial charges of sex discrimination by WEAL, the federal Department of Health, Education, and Welfare (HEW) was brought into the conflict by initiating investigations of universities suspected of violating federal contract agreements.

The university response to attacks by WEAL and other women's groups, and to investigations by HEW, has been varied, but in general one may conclude that university administrators have tried to stall inquiries and deny criticisms. They have seemed genuinely wounded that anyone would question the integrity or motives of the "gentlemen" who run the academic community and that complaints came from members inside higher education circles. After recovering from their initial shock, university administrators sought to evade the pointed requests of HEW and women's groups for information about hiring and personnel decisions on the grounds that such demands threatened to violate the university's autonomy and academic freedom, and endangered the very existence of the meritocracy in higher education. There has, of course, been some compliance and cooperation with HEW officials, but it has been slow and begrudged and has come only after repeated requests, demands, and threats from federal agencies of enforcement.

Since 1970, university officials have learned the tactics of delay and impression management and, for their part, HEW officials have been slow to respond to complaints, focusing (when they have responded) on the form of compliance (the letter of the law) rather than on the substance of compliance requirements (the spirit of the law). There are many problems with the ways in which the agencies of enforcement were set up, in addition to problems in determining compliance with any of the legal directives. Until recently there were no legal guidelines from which staff could determine sex discrimination. Within the agency, those who were responsible for higher education were underfunded, understaffed, and uninformed about academic norms of promotion and salary. Furthermore, the administrative process and administrative codes are unwieldy, confusing, and unenforceable. Although funds from federal contracts are supposed to be withdrawn by HEW enforcement agencies if an institution of higher education has no affirmative action plan, in actuality, with a few minor exceptions,* there has been only rhetoric and posturing in the form of brief delays and weakly announced threats to cut off funding. No university has actually suffered financially because of permanent or long-term suspension of funds.

Because a climate exists (even within enforcement agencies) in which many believe that the penalties for discrimination are disproportionate to the crime, the officials in the federal agencies hesitate to use available sanctions; when they have tried, they have been thwarted by other federal agencies or the university has moved reluctantly and only symbolically towards satisfying HEW requirements. University officials, initially frightened by the possibility of government intervention, have noted the internal fighting and sensed the inability of HEW to act. Such officials have developed a repertoire of tactics (such as stalling and lobbying internally within HEW) to pressure enforcement agencies into backing down. While there seem to be individuals within the Office of Civil Rights dedicated to their task and sensitive to the problems of discrimination, the inadequate level of funding, personnel, and training, and the absence of understanding on the part of many HEW officials themselves have raised serious questions in the minds of the affected university personnel concerning the intent or capability of HEW to enforce the statutes. Complaints filed with HEW are backlogged up to as much as five years, with 1,800 complaints awaiting action (*Chronicle of Higher Education,* May 10, 1976,

---

*HEW cut off federal funds at the University of Maryland, only to have a federal judge restore them through an injunction. There were also temporary contract suspensions at Rutgers University and Columbia University. The University of Texas was informed that it was ineligible for new contracts until it resolved a pending complaint and submitted an acceptable affirmative action plan. In June 1976, the University of Texas was informed that it had filled these criteria and was again eligible for new contracts.

p. 1).* Because the evidence indicates that HEW is failing to live up to its delegated responsibilities under federal law, organizations representing academic women and other professional women's organizations—WEAL, NOW, Association of Women in Science, Federation of Organizations for Professional Women, and so on—have filed numerous lawsuits against HEW on the grounds that they are not enforcing the executive order, reviewing contractor records, conducting precontract award reviews or continuing compliance reviews, demanding affirmative action plans where absent, reviewing and evaluating the ones sent, and initiating sanctions when necessary. At this writing, these lawsuits have not been resolved.

While the events here described are interrelated and ongoing, in this final section I will assess the headway academic women have made thus far in righting the balance against sex discrimination.

## EVALUATING THE SUCCESS OF THE WOMEN'S MOVEMENT ON CAMPUS: A TIME TO TRY MEN'S SOULS?

It is clear that the events that occurred in the late 1960s and early 1970s on the nation's campuses were intimately linked to the women's movement as a whole. Institutions of higher learning were one of the primary objects of the feminist critique of society. Certainly, the 1970 WEAL class action complaint against universities as federal contractors served as a catalyst for academic women to join both general and specific professional women's organizations committed to achieving equity for women. Being highly educated, academic women were able to gather data on their oppression and develop arguments necessary to make their case. For these reasons, one could expect that the women's movement would experience more success on campus than in almost any other arena. And this is all the more so since universities, as the seat of liberal and humane values, would *prima facie* seem more likely to be open to the just aspirations of women than, for example, corporations. But when one turns from these rather ethereal and innocent expectations to the frank reality of modern universities, the picture is anything but clear. What has been the impact of efforts to eliminate sex discrimination in higher education?

Perhaps some of the most tangible outcomes, partially a result of the civil rights movement in the early 1960s and partially the result of women's efforts, have been the passage of the legislation relevant to women and education, the

---

*In the spring of 1976, HEW took the unprecedented step of requesting assistance in *The Federal Register,* seeking recommendations for different guidelines in the handling of discrimination complaints filed with them.

creation of new administrative areas—for example, the Equal Employment Opportunity Commission (EEOC) and the Office of Civil Rights (OCR)—and several executive orders that provide guidelines for federal administrators to determine sex discrimination. Recently passed legislation dealing with academic women includes: Women's Educational Equity Act of 1973; Title VII of the Civil Rights Act of 1964; Title IX of the Educational Amendments of 1972; Title VII of the Public Health Service Act; Equal Employment Opportunity Act of 1972, which expanded the jurisdiction of EEOC to cover public and private institutions of higher education; Comprehensive Health Manpower Training Act of 1971; and Equal Pay Act of 1963, as amended by the Education Amendments of 1972, which expanded EPA coverage to all professional employees in higher education.

In addition to legislation, there has been a willingness on the part of some congressional representatives to hold public hearings on sex discrimination in higher education. Such hearings gave academic women a public platform from which to state their case and to widen the audience familiar with sex discrimination in academia. And there have been other notable advances. For some women who "made it" in academia but have not been rewarded as well as their male peers, there have been promotions and equity increases in salaries to make up for past years of discrimination. And the general climate of expectations has not left other women untouched. The greater visibility of professional women and the efforts of the Women's Liberation Movement to widen women's roles in society have also raised the aspirations of young women now entering college and served as support for older women who are returning to complete degrees. One recent study found that an unprecedented number of freshman women are moving from the stereotypical career choices of education and nursing to majors in business and economics, engineering, pre-med and pre-law—in essence, younger women are preparing now for line, rather than staff, positions (*Chronicle of Higher Education,* January 12, 1976).

Yet the overall record of women in wringing concessions from the universities in which they work has been quite mixed. Academic communities have shown a surprising ability to resist compliance with the law, and only where tightly organized groups of women or intrepid individuals have stood firm has any significant change taken place. It is obvious that something more than the pressure of isolated groups or individuals is needed if major advances for women on campus are to occur. Because of the decreasing number of academic positions, the weak enforcement powers of agencies responsible for investigations, and university resistance affirmative action has not produced significantly greater hiring, retention, and promotion of women or members of minority groups than existed before such policies were announced.

For the most part, academic positions still go unpublicized and the "old boy" network continues to operate—even for the filling of affirmative action officer positions. Universities know that all they have to do is look good on paper and even that is necessary only after an HEW preliminary review and a call for an affirmative action plan. And (wittingly or unwittingly) HEW has failed to demand vigorous implementation and to establish a reputation for enforcing sanctions.

One of the most heatedly argued questions about affirmative action concerns the goals that such a policy should pursue. Some opponents of affirmative action have argued that women are so underrepresented at present that to achieve parity with the percentage of Ph.D.s earned by women in a field (a minimum goal of affirmative action) would require the virtual end of the hiring of white males for the next decade or more. This, they conclude, is patently unfair to men (Lester 1974).

As the reaction has organized against the women's movement, the debate over affirmative action has ironically transferred the label of victim from women (and minorities) and placed it on white men.* This represents a strategy of divisiveness under the guise of concern for equality and fairness to all. White males are told that they cannot be hired because of the pressure to hire women and members of racial minorities. Furthermore, women and members of racial minorities perceive themselves as pitted against each other for the small number of positions made available to them. In a declining academic market, women or minorities serve as readily available scapegoats to explain the inability of white males to find jobs. An absurdly false impression is generated that women and minorities are taking all the available positions and that affirmative action is pressuring university administrators to hire unqualified persons in positions which are beyond their abilities (Lester 1974).

With a declining birthrate, a sluggish economy, and diminishing financial support for education, the prospect for affirmative action against sex discrimination is not positive. Current status differentials between men and women faculty will have serious consequences in the future. The increase of women in the professions has nearly all been at the assistant and instructor levels. As faculty cutbacks are based on seniority, those hired last are most likely to be fired first. And, given the conservative political and budgetary climate of the 1970s in universities throughout the United States, it seems reasonable to predict continued losses in the areas of minority and female recruitment and hiring.

At present, unemployment for women is six times as great as it is for men in the professions (*Chronicle of Higher Education,* December 22, 1975). For

---

*The reactions of academic men to the issue of sex discrimination have ranged from cool indifference to overt hostility. In a recent study, M. Elizabeth Tidball reported that many male professors are not very concerned about discrimination against women in higher education and that some others have indicated opposition to participation of women in academia and the changing role of women (*Chronicle of Higher Education,* April 5, 1976, p. 8).

women with doctorates, the unemployment rate is more than four times as high as that of their male counterparts (Sandler 1975, p. 403). Throughout the country, the overall picture for women employed in teaching positions in higher education has not changed significantly—gains at the instructor level have been lost at the rank of full professor. During this same period of time, the percentage of total recipients of doctoral degrees earned by women has been increasing (Gittell 1975, p. 42). If the organizations representing women and minorities cannot even maintain the status quo, the traditional sexist practices that initially created inequalities between male and female faculty could regain possession of the field. Jo Freeman notes that in the field of women's rights those groups that are in violation of the law, not their victims, are most likely to be effectively organized to protect their interests (Jo Freeman 1975, p. 81). The outcome of this pattern of organization is legislation or executive action that performs primarily symbolic or rhetorical functions rather than providing real protection for the less well organized. That the meager advances won by academic women have been bought at a high price in time, energy, and emotion suggests the difficulties inherent in significant reform of the sexist nature of American higher education, as well as the problems in maintaining recent redistributive policies in the United States in relatively hard economic times.

## REFERENCES

Astin, Helen. 1969. *The Woman Doctorate in America.* New York: Russell Sage Foundation.

_____.. and Bayer, A. E. 1973. "Sex Discrimination in Academe." In Rossi, A. and Calderwood, A., eds., *Academic Women on the Move.* New York: Russell Sage Foundation.

Bayer, Alan E. 1970. *College and University Faculty: A Statistical Description.* Washington, D.C.: American Council on Education.

_____. 1973. *Teaching Faculty in Academe: 1972-73.* Washington, D.C.: American Council on Education.

Beauvoir, S. de. 1952. *The Second Sex.* New York: Alfred A. Knopf.

Bernard, Jessie. 1964. *Academic Women.* University Park: Pennsylvania State University Press.

_____. 1973. *The Future of Marriage.* New York: Bantam.

Caplow, T. and McGee, R. J. 1958. *The Academic Marketplace.* New York: Basic Books.

Carnegie Commission on Higher Education. 1973. *Opportunities for Women in Higher Education.* New York: McGraw-Hill.

Carnegie Council on Policy Studies in Higher Education. 1976. *Making Affirmative Action Work.* San Francisco: Jossey-Bass.

Feldman, S. D. 1974. *Escape from the Doll's House: Women in Graduate and Professional School Education.* New York: McGraw-Hill.

Freeman, Bonnie C. 1975. *A New Political Woman: The Politicization of Faculty Women.* Ph.D. dissertation, Madison: University of Wisconsin.

Freeman, Jo. 1975. *The Politics of Women's Liberation.* New York: McKay.

Friedan, Betty. 1963. *The Feminine Mystique.* New York: Norton.

Gittell, M. 1975. "The Illusion of Affirmative Action." *Change* 7:39.

Harris, S. 1972. *A Statistical Portrait of Higher Education.* New York: McGraw-Hill.

Kilson, M. 1976. "The Status of Women in Higher Education." *Signs* 1:935–42.

Ladd, E. C. Jr., and Lipset, S. M. 1975. *The Divided Academy.* New York: McGraw-Hill.

Lenski, G. 1961. *The Religious Factor.* Garden City, N.Y.: Doubleday.

Lester, R. A. 1974. *Antibias Regulation of Universities.* New York: McGraw-Hill.

Lowi, T. 1970. "Higher Education: A Political Analysis." *Liberal Education* 56:238–57.

Sandler, B. 1973. "A Little Help from Our Government: WEAL and Contract Compliance." In Rossi, A. and Calderwood, A., eds., *Academic Women on the Move.* New York: Russell Sage Foundation.

⸻. 1975. "Backlash in Academe: A Critique of the Lester Report." *Teachers College Record* 76:401–19.

Tobias, S. 1974. "Action and Reaction." *Change* 6:56–57.

Trow, Martin, et al. 1975. "Appendix A: A Technical Report on the 1969 Carnegie Commission Survey of Faculty and Student Opinion." In *Teachers and Students.* New York: McGraw-Hill.

U.S. Department of Health, Education, and Welfare. 1973, 1976. *Digest of Educational Statistics.* Washington, D.C.: U.S. Government Printing Office.

# 10

# The American Professoriate
# and the Movement Toward Unionization
## Lionel S. Lewis & Michael N. Ryan

In his stinging and still mostly unrefuted observations on American academic life, Thorstein Veblen, after pointing out that many academic incomes "compare . . . with the lower grades of clerks and salesmen" remarks that "there is no trades-union among university teachers, and no collective bargaining. There appears to be a feeling prevalent among them that their salaries are not of the nature of wages, and that there would be a species of moral obliquity implied in overtly so dealing with the matter" (1957, p. 118). More recently, Ladd and Lipset, in estimating that the faculties at 294 colleges and universities now have bargaining agents to represent their interests, concluded that "unionization is the wave of academe's future" (1976, p. 11). This is consistent with the extensive study of faculty unionization published in 1975 by Kemerer and Baldridge, which also noted the dramatic progress of the union movement. According to Kemerer and Baldridge, by the mid-1970s, almost "one-eighth of the 3038 colleges and universities in the country [had] bargaining agents" (1975, p. 1). They too predicted that "faculty collective bargaining will almost certainly be a major force in the governance of higher education" (1975, p. 3). Likewise, Joseph W. Garbarino feels that while "it will be many years before a majority of colleges and universities are organized . . . academic unionism is well established, and, unless something unforeseen happens, it will continue to expand" (1973, p. 18). A survey published as late as the spring of 1976, by presenting figures for unionized faculties significantly greater than those of Ladd and Lipset, lends support to the forecasts that it will still be some years before the growth in academic unionization reaches a plateau (Semas 1976, p. 5). While estimates of the number of unionized faculty vary, there is little doubt that collective bargaining has become a major influence in academic governance, on the structure of academic authority, and on the nature of academic work. Ladd and Lipset argue that "if student activism and reactions to efforts to politicize academe explicitly proved to be the major developments affecting American campuses in the latter half of the 1960s, faculty trade union organization and formal collective bargaining are likely to constitute the most important new intramural issues in the 1970s" (1973, p. 1).

| Institutions | Number Unionized |
|---|---|
| Four-year public | 128 |
| Four-year private | 60 |
| Two-year public | 266 |
| Two-year private | 7 |
| Total | 461 |

Institutions of higher learning in the United States vary considerably in terms of educational orientation and status. Among academics, the junior, or community, colleges have the lowest status and their faculties are said to be lacking the professionalism that presumably characterizes those at four-year institutions. It has generally been assumed that inroads made by the union movement have been, and would continue to be, largely confined to the two-year college. However, Terrence N. Tice, and others, now argue on the basis of recent trends that "the conjecture that faculty bargaining would be largely a junior college phenomenon is not holding up" (1973, p. 181). As Duryea and Fisk note, "unionism is strongest in the public two-year colleges, but is moving decisively into four-year colleges and some major universities. Similarly collective bargaining in higher education has centered in the northeast . . . and in the northern Middle West . . ., but the evidence confirms that it is spreading to other regions" (1975, p. 7). Current developments have, then, at least cast a shadow of doubt over Veblen's contention.

There have been numerous attempts to explain the change in faculty attitudes towards unionization. Carol H. Shulman believes that the movement is the result of the following: a depressed academic job market during the 1970s; the financial problems currently plaguing many institutions; the centralization of decision making that accompanied the growth of large state-wide systems of public colleges and universities; increasing intrusions by elected officials into institutional affairs with a concomitant loss of local autonomy; a lack of faculty involvement in the governance of the newer state liberal arts colleges; the passage of legislation giving faculty the right to bargain collectively (1972, p. 1).

Ladd and Lipset also refer to a buyers' market and the decline of collegiality with increased bureaucratization. Nonetheless, they, along with Garbarino, place more emphasis than Shulman on changes in the law that have allowed public employees to organize and negotiate. To them, such "permissive legislation is the key explanation for the burst of academic unionism in the late 1960's and early 1970's" (1973, p. 4). The same authors believe that unionization "became a *conservative* force vis-a-vis student power" (1973, p. 4) that was primarily aimed at the erosion of faculty prerogatives. While Kemerer and Baldridge are in general agreement with Shulman's assessment, they add declining student enrollments and the rising expectations of faculty to the list. On the latter point they argue that "whether those who-join unions are really deprived or not is immaterial. It is enough that they perceive themselves to be" (1975, p. 43).

Taking a slightly different tack in explaining the dramatic growth of academic unions in the past decade, Duryea and Fisk emphasize changes in values. They contend that "by the early 1960s, the trend to shared authority among faculty members and administrators seemed inevitable" (1973, p. 197). However, "by 1970 tens of thousands of professionals in an expanding number of institutions had accepted bargaining agents. . . . In effect, these individuals turned away from a primary dependence on shared authority to a more pragmatic reliance upon the power of organization outside the disciplinary and professional societies" (1973, p. 198).

Garbarino, while citing many of the causative factors mentioned above, focuses some attention on the built-in limitations of traditional faculty senates as a potent faculty voice in institutional affairs. He argues that "as the area of shared goals has narrowed and as economic issues have become more important, faculties are more interested in organizations that can effectively represent their interests as an occupational group" (1971, p. 7). Typically, senates have been most influential in more general academic matters.

While all of these explanations of the increase in collective bargaining make sense on one level, they seem to be more symptomatic than causative. For example, academics in the United States have experienced depressed job markets many times over the years, and higher education has regularly been confronted by a shortage of funds. Yet, the union movement did not take hold until very recently. While it is true that the increase in size and complexity of colleges and universities has resulted in a more centralized decision-making process, administrators and trustees are probably less autocratic today than in previous decades when Veblen's captains of erudition insolently dominated academic government. Legislation enabling faculty to bargain collectively could be seen as little more than a reaction to social forces already in existence. It is highly unusual for American politicians to lead or initiate change. There is considerable evidence to suggest that elected bodies generally follow, react, legitimize, or formalize changes that have previously occurred.

The assumption that the union movement is a defensive reaction to "student power" is also highly suspect. In another paper, we argue that students have never been central in the academic decision-making process, in spite of all the publicity that accompanied the campus disruptions of the late 1960s and early 1970s (Lewis and Ryan 1971, p. 249). The rising expectations of faculty may account for some restiveness but feeling deprived does not explain why the union rather than the professional association has been increasingly thought to be the most effective vehicle for the expression of dissatisfaction.

It may be that Duryea and Fisk's observations about a change in faculty attitudes is significant; yet, the impetus behind this shift needs to be identified. Lastly, faculty senates have always labored under the burden of numerous limitations. Garbarino's recognition of these shortcomings still does not explain the choice of the union over the professional association.

## PROFESSIONALIZATION OR UNIONIZATION: ANOTHER HYPOTHESIS

We believe that the contemporary union movement is better explained as a manifestation of growing awareness, among more and more academics, of the failure of the professional association, in this case the American Association of University Professors (AAUP), to see the relationship between power and occupational autonomy. The focus of this study is, then, on the question of why increasing numbers of academics are turning to the union, rather than the professional association, to effectively represent their interests. Our analysis seeks to identify and explain the genesis of the movement away from the AAUP which, like all professional associations, has traditionally attempted to serve as a vehicle for the expression of "consciousness-of-kind" (Greenwood 1957, p. 51) among the occupation's members. It is our contention that, while all the factors mentioned above have contributed to the union movement, the limitations of the professional association are most central, even critical, to an understanding of this phenomenon.

The professional model of the academic occupation, as exemplified by the ideological orientation of the AAUP, presupposes considerable autonomy. However, two important points need to be mentioned: first, academics are not independent professionals. They are salaried employees who must practice their occupation in complex bureaucratic organizations; second, there is an inherent conflict between this professional model and bureaucratic principles. The AAUP has failed to comprehend that those who work in a bureaucratized institution cannot control all aspects of their occupational activities and, therefore, lack the autonomy necessary for the fulfillment of such a professional expectation. In their attempt to further occupational ends, proponents of this professional association have adopted an accommodating posture vis-a-vis the bureaucratic system, and this position does not address the structural roots of the tension between the two systems. Consequently, the union movement can be seen as another phase in the professoriate's struggle to achieve the autonomy associated with the occupational role of the independent professional.

## ACADEMICS AS PROFESSIONALS IN BUREAUCRACIES

In their work, American academics are involved in two different social systems. As scholars and teachers, they are part of a professional system concerned with self-determination. At the same time, they routinely carry out their research and pedagogical functions in bureaucratic structures. Logan Wilson was not the first to recognize that "unlike many other professional intellectual workers, the professor is always an employee and has to conform to basic administrative controls common to all organized undertakings" (1942, pp. 120–21). Control over employees is a central feature of the bureaucratic system. Since the objectives of these two systems are fundamentally incompatible, there is an inherent and persistent tension created as each system—the professional and the bureaucratic—seeks ascendancy in the academic world. This is because, as Kornhauser's research revealed, *"professionalism has as its primary function the protection of standards for creative activities; organization has as its primary function the efficient coordination of diverse activities. . . .* For the combining of professionalism with bureaucracy entails certain contradictory principles" (1962, pp. 195–96).

The bureaucratic system is characterized by a centralized authority that coordinates activities with formal rules and a hierarchical chain of command. Power is delegated to positions within the hierarchy in proportion to their proximity to the top. Since the professoriate is placed in the authority hierarchy in institutions of higher learning not at the top but somewhere below the controlling apparatus, it has less power than administrators and trustees who occupy such positions. It is this situation that has created special problems in the professoriate's attempt to attain the autonomy necessary for full professional status. This is to be expected, for, as W. Richard Scott has observed,

> when professionals are employed by organizations, there is a fundamental change in their situation. They must sacrifice some of their autonomy and conform to certain organizational rules for a simple reason: they do not possess all the basic skills for doing the work but are part of a larger and more complex system in which they perform only some of the required activities. Their activities must be regulated to fit in with the over-all organizational purpose as well as coordinated with the activities of others (1966, p. 270).

Since administrators are responsible for the functioning of the entire organization, the power relation between them and the faculty is, and must be, tipped in favor of the bureaucratic system. Although it is true that "confronted by other organized groups protecting their own special interests . . . the rank and file of academic men are highly dependent on the discretion of superiors"

(Wilson 1942, p. 121), it would be overstating the case to suggest that academics are supine in the face of administrative sovereignty. It is essentially correct to argue thus:

> That he has been an employee for centuries has not left the professor without important freedom. Control over the terms and conditions of work is certainly weakened by being an employee rather than an entrepreneur in a favorable marketplace. Nonetheless, control over the *content* of work is not necessarily so weakened (Freidson 1973, p. 36).

## THE AAUP

American academics have aspired to autonomy and other benefits of professional status since they ceased viewing themselves as schoolmasters sometime near the end of the nineteenth century. Laurence R. Veysey points out that their aspirations were given additional momentum in the first 15 years of the twentieth century when, in growing numbers, professors made "the claim for exemption from interference on the ground that they were "professional experts". . . . The plea for a "professional" definition of academic goals . . . culminated in the establishment of the American Association of University Professors in 1915" (1965, pp. 355–56), between the time Veblen completed his manuscript *The Higher Learning in America* and its publication in 1918. The founding of the AAUP represented the first attempt to unite the professoriate on a national scale and lead it to professional status.

The AAUP has been central in the efforts to promote the ends of the professoriate; until recently it has been the only national organization speaking on behalf of the occupation as a whole. Like other professional associations, it made decided efforts to persuade the public that the greater the rewards, status, and power of its members, the better society would be served. As Vollmer and Mills point out, such "occupational associations are essential to the process of professionalization" (1966, p. 153). "The American Association of University Professors has other purposes than increasing the bargaining power of members, but this [the protection and advancement of in-group status] is its most important objective" (Wilson 1942, p. 119).

Since its founding, the AAUP has given its attention to a wide variety of professional issues, and initially 16 committees were established to monitor and keep abreast of matters bearing on the academic profession. in 1965, its fiftieth year as a professional organization, it completed an extensive self-survey of its activities, a report of what its officials perceived as its role "as the spokesman for those engaged in teaching and research" (AAUP 1965, p. 101). In the words of the report, the "principles for which the Association stands

[are] . . . academic freedom and tenure, academic responsibility, participation of the faculty in institutional governance, the academic freedom of students, appropriate compensation schedules" and so on (p. 117). About one-third of the lengthy analysis focused on activities surrounding the first, second, third, and fifth concerns, in addition to those pertaining to accreditation and the relationship of the profession to federal and state governments.

> The substantive functions of the Association . . . from the viewpoint of the Washington Office . . . [are] (1) the setting of standards for the profession, (2) efforts to secure acceptance of these standards and improve the profession generally through information, education, and persuasion, and (3) the protection of members of the profession in individual cases" (AAUP 1965, p. 140).

## THE PRESIDENTIAL ADDRESSES

In order to identify the parameters of the professoriate's claim for autonomy and the characteristics of the posture adopted by the AAUP, a content analysis of each of the biennial convention addresses of AAUP presidents was completed. These addresses, usually delivered near the end of the incumbent's term, are not taken to be literal representations of the state of all or most academics at any particular point in time. They are considered as artifacts that might reveal recurring themes or patterns, or trends from which inferences might be drawn.

The speeches of 32 AAUP presidents were analyzed. These addresses cover the years from the organization's founding in 1915 through to 1974. Table 10.1 shows the presidents whose speeches are contained within this study and the years of their tenure in office. Relevant statements were identified and coded according to their subject matter. Once the content of each speech was placed in the appropriate category, themes, patterns, or trends were identified, and then grouped, labeled, and counted within each category. The count summarized the number of speeches in which reference to a specific phenomenon appeared and the total number of times the topic was addressed in all of the speeches.

While codification and tabulation are customarily associated with exacting empiricism, it is important that the figures generated by the content analysis not be reified. Coding the content of speeches requires the use of judgment. There were parts of these presidential addresses that could not be neatly fitted into a coding system. In addition, some of the broader issues that were raised were placed into more than one category since a number of topics were discussed within a paragraph or series of sentences. In sum, there is no attempt to convey scientism that is not justified by the nature of the data.

## TABLE 10.1

### Presidential Addresses

| Tenure | President | Year of Publica- tion | AAUP Bulletin Volume | Pages |
|--------|-----------|------|------|-------|
| 1915-16 | John Dewey | 1915 | 1 | 9-13 |
| 1916-17 | John H. Wigmore | 1916 | 2 (No.1) | 8-10 |
| | | | 2 (No.5) | |
| 1917-18 | Frank Thilly | 1917 | 3 | 11-24 |
| 1918-19 | J. M. Coulter | 1918 | 4 (No.7) | 11-12 |
| | | | 4 (No.1) | 3 |
| 1919-20 | Arthur O. Lovejoy | 1919 | 5 | 10-40 |
| 1920-21 | Edward Capps* | | | |
| 1921-22 | Edwin R. A. Seligman | 1922 | 8 | 6-26 |
| 1922-24 | Joseph Villiers Denney | 1924 | 10 | 18-28 |
| 1924-26 | A. O. Leuschner | 1926 | 12 | 90-99 |
| 1926-28 | W. T. Semple | 1928 | 14 | 162-166 |
| 1928-30 | Henry Crew | 1928 | 14 | 167-168 |
| | | 1930 | 16 | 103-111 |
| 1930-32 | W. B. Munro | 1932 | 18 | 6-17 |
| 1932-34 | Walter Wheeler Cook | 1934 | 20 | 84-96 |
| 1934-36 | S. A. Mitchell | 1936 | 22 | 93-97 |
| 1936-38 | A. J. Carlson | 1938 | 24 | 9-18 |
| 1938-40 | Mark H. Ingraham | 1940 | 26 | 13-34 |
| 1940-42 | Frederick S. Deibler | 1942 | 28 | 32-45 |
| 1942-44 | William T. Laprade | 1944 | 30 | 176-195 |
| 1944-46 | Quincy Wright | 1947 | 33 | 43-54 |
| 1946-48 | Edward C. Kirkland | 1948 | 34 | 15-26 |
| 1948-50 | Ralph H. Lutz | 1950 | 36 | 18-32 |
| 1950-52 | Richard H. Shryock | 1952 | 38 | 32-70 |
| 1952-54 | Fred B. Millett | 1954 | 40 | 47-60 |
| 1954-56 | William E. Britton | 1956 | 42 | 256-267 |
| 1956-58 | Helen C. White | 1958 | 44 | 392-400 |
| 1958-60 | Bentley Glass | 1960 | 46 | 149-155 |
| 1960-62 | Ralph F. Fuchs | 1962 | 48 | 104-109 |
| 1962-64 | Fritz Machlup | 1964 | 50 | 112-124 |
| 1964-66 | David Fellman | 1966 | 52 | 105-110 |
| 1966-68 | Clark Byse | 1968 | 54 | 143-148 |
| 1968-70 | Ralph S. Brown, Jr. | 1970 | 56 | 118-122 |
| 1970-72 | Sanford H. Kadish | 1972 | 58 | 120-125 |
| 1972-74 | Walter Adams | 1974 | 60 | 119-125 |

*Capps' death while in office necessitated the appointment of Vernon L. Kellogg as acting president, and he did not formally address association members at the annual meeting.

## Academics as Independent Professionals

There is little question that academics hold the professional ideal. The speeches reveal that physicians and lawyers, because they enjoy the kind of professional autonomy to which the professoriate aspires, serve as such models. But many are aware that the employee status of academics imposes formidable problems. As Richard H. Shryock (1952) notes: "All would probably agree . . . that the quasi-employee status of academic men . . . lowers their general prestige. In contrast, the professional independence of physicians and lawyers may contribute something to their social standing" (p. 54). Yet, this does not preclude Ralph F. Fuchs from arguing in 1962 that

> there is a need for a formulation that extends beyond the matter of participation in academic government, to the entire set of activities and responsibilities attaching to faculty members as such. As a basis for it we need to study . . . the tradition of individual professional responsibility which we share with such largely self-employed groups as the practitioners of medicine and law (p. 107).

Working in a bureaucratic setting requires some modification of this professional model. The answer apparently has been found in the relative independence of faculty in certain European universities, particularly in Germany and England. Physicians and lawyers set the standard against which the degree of autonomy can be measured while the conditions enjoyed by some European faculty represent an accommodation to the bureaucratic system. European faculties were on the mind of A. O. Leuschner in 1926: "Many presidents have been chosen from the ranks of professors. After all, the title of this officer . . . does not matter much, but it is of great importance that his functions should permit of faculty cooperation in university government in accordance with the successful traditions of the Old World" (p. 94). In 1938, A. J. Carlson still held that "those who are afraid of permitting or encouraging an increasing democracy in university organization and university life should take a look at some of the well-known universities in Europe" (p. 12). The evidence suggests the intention of establishing an academic guild.

The AAUP is seen as eventually playing a role comparable to that of the American Medical Association and the American Bar Association. This aspiration has been evident from the outset. Frank Thilly in 1917 restates a position outlined in the "Call for the Meeting for Organization of a National Association of University Professors," issued in 1914, by suggesting that a "society, comparable to the American Bar Association and the American Medical Association in kindred professions, could be of substantial service to the ends for which universities exist" (p. 11). In 1922, Edwin R. A. Seligman felt compelled to reiterate that "it has . . . been made abundantly clear that our

Association must be regarded not as a trade union, but rather as an association comparable to the American Bar Association, or the American Medical Association" (p. 6). Ten of the 32 speeches contain references to either doctors and lawyers, their professional organizations, or to European faculty. The issue is unflagging, being found in speeches given in 1917, 1918, 1922, 1926, 1930, 1938, 1952, 1962, 1966, and 1974, with a total of 21 such comments.

Although not an exclusive area of concern, establishing the autonomy of the occupation has been of primary interest. Twenty-one of the speeches, with 38 references in all, address this objective. The speeches rarely contain explicit demands for autonomy; however, it is often an implicit objective, as it was in the following statement, made in 1944, by William T. Laprade: "A university is a great and indispensable organ of the higher life of a civilized community, in the work of which the trustees have an essential and highly honorable place, but in which the faculties hold an independent place, with quite equal responsibilities" (p. 186). In 1946, Quincy Wright attempts to establish the parameters of this autonomy. He cites "freedom from censorship; freedom from the explicit directives of superior authority; freedom from pressure to produce practical results; periods of freedom from time schedules and the coercions of an operative institution" (p. 48).

## Means and Ends

Adopting means that are appropriate to both the mission of the organization and the milieu within which it operates is of critical importance: the degree to which ideals, or objectives, are achieved is dependent upon the tactics employed. The speeches indicate that the American professoriate has rested its hopes for success upon the efficacy of the following: reason, debate, publicity, and moral rectitude; cooperation with the representatives of the bureaucratic system; and involvement with administrators and trustees in institutional government. The table below shows the frequency with which each of these three tactics appears in the thirty-two presidential addresses.

John H. Wigmore (1916) was the first to identify the use of rational argumentation and publicity: "Immediate Utopia cannot be hoped for. We must patiently proceed to formulate our own views of the needs of our own time, and must then endeavor to impress these views on the community at large. Our function is to build up a sound public opinion" (p. 14). This can be done, W. T. Semple (1927) suggests, through "the recourse to reason and argumentation" (p. 163). And David Fellman, nearly 40 years later, in 1966, points out that "our principal weapon is moral influence; our principal method is to appeal to the opinions of the public. In the hard-core cases, where our efforts at mediation and conciliation have failed, we resort to our ultimate weapon, which is to pronounce public anathema in the name of the academic community (p. 106).

|  | Reason, Debate, Publicity, Moral Rectitude | Cooperation | Involvement in Government |
|---|---|---|---|
| Number of speeches in which topic appears at least once | 20 | 16 | 14 |
| Total references (all speeches) | 34 | 39 | 36 |

Just how overawing this "ultimate weapon" might be remains to be seen. Implicit here is the assumption that reasonable and honorable representatives of the two systems—the professional and the bureaucratic—can work out their differences. This process, if successful, is facilitated by the support of an interested and sympathetic general public.

The speeches also indicate that tension between the two systems can be reduced by fostering a spirit of cooperation. In 1922, Edwin R. A. Seligman optimistically reports that

> we may look forward in the not distant future either to a virtual inclusion of most of the administrative authorities in our membership or at least to a situation where we can count upon the sympathetic cooperation of those who at one time were active in our own management and deliberation. . . . Mutual understanding, good-will and whole-hearted cooperation will do more to bring us together and to solve our outstanding problems than dozens of independent reports and reams of separate discussions (p. 24).

A. O. Leuschner, speaking in 1926, states that

> this association has not set itself the goal of gaining absolute control of functions hitherto exercised in most institutions exclusively by trustees, presidents, and administrative officers. It is investigating and reporting on suitable methods of cooperation between recognized authorities and faculties which may raise institutions of higher education to the highest degree of efficiency (p. 91).

In passing, it is worth noting the use of the word "efficiency." It is possible that the choice of this word reflects a certain deference to the businesmen who since the Reconstruction Era have dominated academic boards of trustees.

The speeches give no indication that trustees and administrators share the association's cooperative spirit embodied in Henry Crew's (1928) effervescence: "This organization was conceived in a spirit of good sportsmanship. Cooperation is written large in the first article of our Constitution. The charter members . . . clearly recognized the need for more conference and less regimentation in university control" (p. 167). It seems reasonable to assume that this posture was intended to bridge the gap created by the power differential between the professional and bureaucratic systems. Apparently, there was the implication and hope, until 1952 when no further mention is made of what Frederick S. Deibler (1942) called "cooperative attitudes" (p. 39), that the bureaucratic system would voluntarily share some of its excess power with the professional system.

Becoming involved in institutional governance is the final tactic identified in the addresses, a tactic that reflects both the influence of European faculty and the problem of establishing occupational autonomy within a bureaucratic setting. An alternative to the creation of a separate power base is the sharing of the power concentrated in the bureaucratic system. This approach represents an attempt to maximize the autonomy of the occupation by integrating it into the institutional power structure. Presumably, the intention is to create an arrangement somewhat comparable to that which exists in hospitals where physicians sit on governing boards. Fourteen speeches refer to this strategy, and a total of 36 such references are made to it. Early on, Arthur O. Lovejoy (1920) argues "that the body of scholars composing the faculty of any university or college should, either directly or through its chosen representatives, have a definitely recognized and an important part in the shaping of all the policies of the institution, except with respect to technical financial questions" (p. 39).

Joseph Villiers Denney (1924) expands upon, and adds specificity to, this position:

> The mode of utilizing the wisdom of the Faculty in university control will vary in different institutions. Faculty membership in boards of trustees, instituted at Cornell University on recommendation of ex-President Schurman, has established one mode in practice. This mode may come to be adopted rather widely in time since in many institutions no change in charter or law would be needed to bring it about.... It would not be surprising if the Governor of a state in which regents are appointed, seeing the advantage of introducing into the Board a representative Faculty element ... should signalize his administration by calling upon the Faculty of his state university for nominations from their own members. His example would doubtless be followed (p. 23).

Denney's optimism is noteworthy. More faculty control, Ralph F. Fuchs (1962) argues, would mean fewer intramural problems: "Many of the strains in our institutions tend, I think, to diminish when faculty authority is clearly bestowed" (p. 107). It is curious that the mechanics involved in bringing about the hoped for reforms in governance are not mentioned; the assertion of their desirability appears to be assumed sufficient for the initiation of this kind of institutional realignment.

These three methods, either singly or in combination, are the means upon which the professoriate apparently rests its hopes for success. The issue, of course, is whether they are equal to the task. In other words, can academics win their autonomy by relying on this course of action? Given the inherent tension between the bureaucratic and the professional systems, with, as has already been suggested, the balance of power weighed in favor of the former, and given that autonomy and power are closely related, these tactics must be capable of altering structural characteristics. The professional system must be able to generate power sufficient to challenge the bureaucratic system, and this seems unlikely.

## Obstacles to Success

There are distinct themes, commonly found somewhere near the end of each speech, that suggest why the tactics employed by academics to achieve autonomy may not always be appropriate, and why the approach of the professional association has not been more successful. While the AAUP may claim credit for some progress, it has not been able to further the interests of its membership as well as have the American Medical Association or the American Bar Association. Nor has the American professoriate been elevated to the status enjoyed by many European academics. The content analysis reveals fundamental problems in the posture adopted by the AAUP. Two questionable assumptions are apparent: first, a tendency to emphasize the individual, or personality, characteristics of representatives of the bureaucratic system rather than focusing on the structure of, and distribution of power within that system. Second, the commitment to an accommodating role when reacting to an intrusion by outside forces into the affairs of the occupation. The table below shows the relative frequency of these obstacles to success. Almost two-thirds of the addresses make some reference to individual characteristics of administrators. Focusing on this point rather than on the structural characteristics of colleges and universities represents what appears to be a serious error, as the assumption that "better people" will improve the position of the professoriate probably accomplishes little more than to reinforce any existing state of affairs. Altering the relationship between the professional and bureaucratic systems would seem to require structural change.

| | Emphasis on Individual Characteristics | Commitment to Accommodating Role |
|---|---|---|
| Number of speeches in which topic appears at least once | 20 | 29 |
| Total references (all speeches) | 42 | 159 |

John H. Wigmore (1916) is the first to personalize: "In my own opinion, not so much depends upon the governmental structures as upon the spirit of the institution. . . . And this will ultimately go back to the personality at the head of all" (p. 18). A. J. Carlson (1938) expands on this theme as follows: "The better men and women in executive positions in the university . . . have usually had an uncommon amount of common sense, good leadership, and some sense of justice. . . . This seems to bring the problem down to men and women rather than to organizations and laws" (p. 12).

Frederick S. Deibler echoes these sentiments in 1942 when he observes that "the mechanism of government is of less importance than the spirit which operates the mechanism" (p. 38). Most recently, Walter Adams (1974) has observed that "what we need, alas, is not a PPBS [program-planning-budgeting-systems] deus ex machina, but a new brand of academic leadership—administrators capable of analytic thought and endowed with civilized values" (p. 124). There is little evidence to suggest that these spokesmen have seriously considered the distribution of power in the bureaucratic system. It seems clear that the balance of power between the two systems cannot be altered by focusing on personalities.

An even more prominent theme revolves around the reluctance of AAUP presidents to suggest anything resembling an assertive or activist position. The addresses repeatedly skirt around the question of power and give precious little indication of an offensive thrust to the professioriate's efforts to attain its autonomy. Rather, they reflect an accommodating and mostly passive posture, one that dictates a responsive or reactive stance. The ability of outside forces to keep the AAUP, and by inference the professoriate, on the defensive, coupled with its seeming distaste for the rough-and-tumble inherent in a more activist approach, may be seen as another shortcoming in the tactics employed. Yet, A. O. Leuschner (1926) assesses the situation somewhat differently:

> There has been much misunderstanding of the attitude of the Association. No educational association has the power or intent to impose its will on the educational public, not even on its own members. It stands in an advisory relation to all concerned. In general, principles adopted in the form of resolutions are intended as carefully considered recommendations (p. 91).

Of the 32 speeches analyzed, 29 contain comments that reflect this reluctance to adopt a more adversary role, and 159 different references to this are contained within these addresses, although how an organization is to proceed if its "recommendations" are ignored is not once made clear. Even without an explanation Henry Crew (1930) can exult thus: "If Herbert Spencer's definition of progress as an increasing adaptation to environment is correct, we may, I believe, modestly claim to have been progressive without being radical and conservative without being reactionary" (p. 105). There is, however, a serious question of whether adaptation is the road to autonomy.

There are, of course, creditable reasons why the professoriate should react rather than act. William T. Laprade (1944) explains that

> the necessity that scholars and teachers have the cooperation of executives and administrators and in some degree of the trustees of institutions in which they work if freedom and tenure are to be maintained should preserve the Association from the temptation to become a pressure group, primarily concerned with the personal interests of its members (p. 189).

However, there is some doubt that the occupation can achieve its objectives without becoming a pressure group; furthermore, it is unclear what the interests of the AAUP should be if not those of the members of the occupation. In 1972, Sanford H. Kadish again affirms the thesis that has become a paradox for the professoriate: academics must demonstrate that they are worthy of full professional status by always putting the interests of others before their own, even if this necessitates abandoning the means to that end.

> Since our classic claims to autonomy from the outside and to academic freedom have rested in large part on the concept of a university as a neutral and nonpartisan haven for intellectuality, such super-citizen activist roles for the university and the faculty reduce the authority of our claim. . . . [We] lose the only persuasive argument we have for our extraordinary claim to support without control: a haven for research and teaching is one thing; a special lobby is another (p. 123).

It is doubtful that a haven can be created without a somewhat more sophisticated approach to the problem of power than is reflected in these 32 presidential addresses.

Taken as a whole, these spokesmen always seem to be responding: to the attacks on academic freedom in the 1920s, to the consequences of the economic depression of the 1930s, to the censorship that accompanied both world wars, to the renewed attacks on freedom of speech during the McCarthy era, to the attacks by student activists in the 1960s and, finally, to the effects of the financial retrenchments of the 1970s. From all of this, it is apparent that the AAUP has not perceived the nature of the problems associated with the achievement of autonomy within a bureaucratic setting. In particular, it has not been sensitive to the dilemma posed by the differential distribution of power between the bureaucratic and professional systems. As a consequence, the professoriate is still denied what it believes to be the autonomy necessary for the achievement of its objectives. It also seems clear that the tactics adopted by the AAUP are not equal to the task. Put simply, there is a discontinuity between means and ends. It is not surprising that the failure to understand the nature of the problem has led to the selection of inappropriate tactics.

## STALEMATE AND ITS EFFECTS

If these addresses represent something more than random comments, and if the analysis to this point is correct, it could be expected that a pattern of consequences would emerge from what are here suggested as apparent shortcomings in the posture adopted by the AAUP. Such is the case, and the patterns that have been identified include the following.

1. The location of members of the occupation along the employee-professional continuum is problematic. While it is generally assumed that academics are, by and large, fully professional, there seems to be a need to defend repeatedly this contention.

2. Since the status of the professoriate is open to debate, it is similarly unclear whether the professional association or the trade union is the most appropriate organization to further its interests. Invariably the argument is made for the professional association, although there seems to have been a need to reaffirm continually this position against those critics, real or imagined, who would select the trade union.

3. There are also ambiguities relative to the internal structure of the AAUP. It has not been satisfactorily resolved whether professional interests are best served by a centralized type of organization with decision-making at the national level or through the encouragement of activities at the local, or chapter, level. This leaves a question of how power within this organization should be distributed. Clearly, this is not a problem shared by representatives of the bureaucratic system.

4. In spite of the best efforts of the AAUP, violations of academic freedom and tenure continue to occur. While most representatives of the bureaucratic system accept these principles in theory, the professional system has had mixed success in their enforcement—particularly when the issue is the reinstatement of an individual once the bureaucratic system has become committed to dismissal.

It is our contention that these four phenomena would be less prominent if the professoriate had more accurately perceived the nature of its situation or, better yet, predicament. The following table presents the results of the content analysis relative to these consequences.

Frank Thilly (1917), for one, has difficulty deciding whether faculty should be supervised employees or autonomous professionals.

A thoroughly conscientious man will carefully question himself whether he has really been conscientious enough in examining his judgments and whether he is justified in promulgating ideas which may be dangerous to the public welfare. While we cannot leave the decision of the correctness of his

| Topic | Number of Speeches in Which Topic Appears at Least Once | Total References (all speeches) |
|---|---|---|
| Ambiguity of status | 15 | 34 |
| Rejection of trade union model | 15 | 27 |
| Ambivalence regarding structure of organization | 18 | 49 |
| Continued violations of academic freedom/tenure | 20 | 54 |

> behavior ... entirely to his own individual conscience, we are surely not
> prepared to leave it to any group of persons who would deny him the right
> of a fair defense against specific charges (p. 20).

Note that the emphasis is on the "right of a fair defense," and not on the right
of the professional to reach his own conclusions. On the other hand, Frederick
S. Deibler (1942), after observing that faculty "have been forced more and
more into the status of employees" (p. 37), contends that

> an educational institution is in fact a great cooperative undertaking. To
> relegate the faculty to the status of employees is tantamount to dwarfing
> much of the driving force which contributes to the success of an institution.
> Within his own sphere of learning the faculty member is more like an
> entrepreneur than an employee (p. 38).

More recently, Sanford H. Kadish (1972), offers a variation on this theme:
"Their status as employees, as well as professionals, places them, like any
industrial or business employee, under the economic control of those who
employ him. . . . But professors are the essence of the university enterprise, as
well as its employees" (p. 122). As has been pointed out, since autonomy is
one of the crucial distinguishing features of the professional, it is difficult to
be autonomous and an employee at the same time. It is the incompatibility of
these two roles, of course, that creates a paradox for the professoriate.

Although there is some uncertainty as to where to locate the professoriate
on the professional-nonprofessional continuum, there is little question in the
minds of AAUP officials that the professional association rather than the labor
union can best serve its interests. Thus, the defense of the general ideology of
the professional association is continuing. Again, almost half of the speeches,
from the 1920s to the 1970s, contain references to this question. W. T. Semple
(1928) speaks in support of the professional association thus: "It was really odd
to perceive at times how quickly and how vigorously I have responded to the
suggestion . . . on the part indeed of some of our best friends among adminis-

trative officers that the American Association of University Professors is a "professors' union." Thus Semple defends his position: "there are degrees of difference as to the emphasis laid upon the moral and the spiritual aspects of . . . labor. As the labor rises in moral and spiritual value, so also does delicacy in the relationship between employer and employed increase" (p. 162).

It should be remarked that Semple, in contrast to many, seems to be assigning faculty to employee status. In 1940, Mark H. Ingraham argues:

> I still believe we should be guided by a philosophy of partnership, not a philosophy of control. A philosophy of control may lead to a violence of reaction that has come . . . to be expected of labor. Some already believe that the best type of organization to represent our profession is one modeled after and affiliated with those created in industry to wring the maximum from a system of management which at times seems to desire to yield a minimum. This I believe is a mistake and represents an unnecessarily defeatist attitude, but it is a belief to which the system of government of many institutions lends credence (p. 30).

Although the structure of many bureaucratic systems lends credence to the union model, Ingraham still continues to defend the professional association. David Fellman (1966) emphatically declares:

> Of course we defend the right of professors to join a trade union if they so desire, and we are strongly opposed to the imposition upon them of reprisals of any sort for so doing. Nevertheless, our Association is not a trade union, it is not part of the trade union movement, and it does not seek that identification with organized labor which trade union status would imply (p. 106).

Such a strong affirmation of the AAUP's posture is taken to be a response to mounting pressure from alternative kinds of organizations. Sanford H. Kadish (1972) again defends the professional association as follows:

> Take the economic strike . . . which some unions seeking professional representation urge as the standard policy to resolve bargaining impasses, after the industrial model. . . . [The] strike proceeds by deliberately harming the educational mission, although temporarily, in order to promote the personal employee interest, in contradiction to the service ideal of subordinating personal interest to the advancement of the purposes of the university (p. 122).

This statement provides an indication of how the association's assumptions may inhibit its chances for success. In order to move along the continuum towards professional status, members of the occupation must look after their own interests. Certainly it would be too much to expect the bureaucratic system to relinquish voluntarily its control over institutional affairs. Administrators are simply not likely to place the personal employee interest ahead of institutional needs. Needless to say, relying on an approach typically taken by the professional association to advance the ends of an occupation whose members are not even sure whether they qualify as full professionals is at best risky and at worst ineffective.

The addresses also reflect a lack of consensus over the internal organization of the AAUP. On the one hand, centralization would be required in order to exert a unifying force, to present a united front, and to challenge the power of the bureaucratic system. On the other hand, a partnership of equals, diffused power, and occupational diversity would require both 'local, and individual, independence. As the last table (p. 207) shows, the association has been unable to reconcile these competing claims. Joseph Villiers Denney (1924) attempts to limit the role of local chapters by suggesting that

> on local questions no chapter may assume support from the national association unless the latter has already adopted a principle that clearly governs in the specific case. It is, therefore, necessary and proper, when a chapter has reached a conclusion on a local question, that the subject should be introduced into the Faculty, not as the decision of the chapter, but as a motion by an individual member of the Faculty (p. 25).

It is not clear why such a low profile is being recommended. Conversely, Walter Wheeler Cook (1934) stresses the importance of the local chapter: "If the purposes of the Association are to be accomplished, it is clear that it can be done only with the aid of active local groups" (p. 93). At the same time, he adds that "obviously it would not be fair to the national association for the action of a single chapter to appear as the official action of the Association" (p. 95). It appears that local support is welcome as long as the national association is not drawn into a visible intramural controversy, an unlikely possibility. In 1940, Mark H. Ingraham sends an equally ambivalent message to the local units: "In trying to obtain the goal of enlarged faculty responsibility our chapters must be active, but also exhibit a form of self-restraint that will keep them from building loyalties that later . . . might hamper the usefulness of their members in the faculty. The chapter's purpose often should be to work itself out of a job" (p. 30). Thus, we are left with a division between the local chapters and the national organization, along with one between the various disciplines and the occupation as a whole, and, according to Bentley Glass (1958), between the "hard" and the "soft" sciences.

The problem of internal organization is a prominent and persistent theme throughout these addresses. Again, the failure of the AAUP to develop a structure capable of exerting the kind of force necessary to achieve its objectives is seen as a direct consequence of a lack of understanding about the nature of the organization of work within a bureaucratic setting, and the ultimate distribution of power.

Although the defense of academic freedom and tenure is seen as central to the successful performance of the work of the professoriate, the addresses reflect a keen awareness of, and concern over, their continual violation. The inability of the professional system to protect its members' fundamental rights can be viewed as yet another consequence of the posture of the organization. Unquestionably, substantial progress in the protection of faculty rights has been achieved since the turn of the century. Nevertheless, the bureaucratic system generally remains a catalyst relative to the application of the principles involved with academic freedom and tenure, while the professional system assumes a more dependent role, often reacting to the initiatives of administrators, trustees, and legislators. Once more, the association's stance is defensive and reflects the institutional roots of the power differential between the two systems.

The speeches reinforce the findings of the self-survey by indicating that, from the very beginning, the defense of faculty rights has consumed a large amount of time and energy (AAUP 1965, p. 141); 20 of the addresses contain 54 comments on this issue. In 1932, W. B. Munro points to one recurring pretext for violations of academic freedom and tenure:

> This warning needs more emphasis today that at any time heretofore because a few institutions have not scrupled to use the existing business depression as an excuse for releasing teachers of long and efficient service. Pleading shortage of funds they have grasped the opportunity to rid themselves of instructors whose only shortcoming has been an intellectual restlessness under administrative constraint (p. 14).

When Walter Adams (1974) makes somewhat the same point 40 years later, it is still, unfortunately, relevant.

> In the current atmosphere of retrenchment, it is perhaps not surprising that the ancient controversy over the institution of tenure has suddenly been revived. Citing financial stringency as their justification, some administrators have found it convenient to condemn tenure as a built-in and systematic commitment to increasing costs (p. 122).

It seems clear that the bureaucratic system remains on the offensive.

William T. Laprade (1944), reviewing the association's activities in defense of academic freedom and tenure, notes that "the volume of this activity shows no tendency to abate." In subsequent years, after the Cold War had become a well-rooted part of normalcy, there is the apprehension that the state of academic freedom, in turn, has become especially precarious. In 1950, Ralph H. Lutz worries: "In this present period of international tension particularly, there are controversies relating to the application of the principles of academic freedom and these principles, as heretofore interpreted, are being seriously challenged by some college and university administrators and governing boards and by some legislatures" (p. 26). The situation seems to have changed little by the time David Fellman comments in 1966 that "the steady flow of complaints from all over the country, to the Washington Office of the Association, from members of the teaching profession, testifies to the persistence of basic pressures in the American scene which compels us to continue to be preoccupied with the defense of academic freedom" (p. 108). It is these basic pressures that are at the heart of this study. The problem is that they have not been clearly identified, nor has an appropriate response been developed.

It seems reasonable to conclude that the professional system has yet to achieve the autonomy necessary to control the workplace fully. The bureaucratic system, in the end, retains the power to employ and dismiss faculty. For the academic profession, the ability to control entry into and exit from their occupation is limited, and when there is a clear conflict of interest between the professional and bureaucratic systems, the predominance of the latter apparently still emerges from the maze of faculty committees.

In passing, it should be mentioned that during the 1960s a few outspoken faculty did seek to challenge the ascendancy of administrators, trustees, and legislatures. Not surprisingly, there was a reaction from the bureaucratic system and some of these faculty were dismissed. In an earlier paper examining those published contested dismissals where the faculty member was represented by the AAUP, the authors concluded that

> There is little to suggest that administrators are going to be easily divested of their power. . . . There is some evidence to suggest that when there is a threat to their position, they will sacrifice academic freedom to retain their power. The information generated from these contested dismissals between 1963 and 1970 bears out this proposition. . . . In most cases, administrators still operate from the premise that institutional needs take precedence over individual needs (Lewis and Ryan 1971, p. 257).

Although these addresses provide some indication that the association sought to develop general principles of academic freedom and tenure based on precedent and commonly accepted norms, it has been inclined to focus its efforts primarily on the defense of individual faculty. The time and resources demanded by these individual cases have diverted attention from strengthening more universally applicable principles. This set of circumstances has also limited the professional system's ability to challenge the power of the bureaucratic system.

It is taken for granted that the most fundamental responsibility of academic administrators is to maintain the integrity of their institutions. This charge, usually originating from trustees and legislatures, can be met by insuring the continued functioning of the college or university. The operation of an institution is facilitated by the maintenance of the existing distribution of power. And because professional efforts are focused on the defense of individual faculty, the bureaucratic system is not impeded in meeting what is seen as its basic responsibility. While institutional integrity is maintained, individual cases may be debated endlessly. There is relatively little pressure under these conditions for the bureaucratic system to alter the way it has been performing its functions. To date, the AAUP has relied mostly on publicity and persuasion to elicit an administrative response. This tactic seems to have been a limited success. The analysis of the contested dismissals revealed that the reinstatement of a faculty member, even when a violation of academic freedom or tenure was probable, is rare (Lewis and Ryan 1971). If the position taken by the bureaucratic system has been formalized, the best the victimized individual can hope for is a "moral victory." For some, this might be little consolation.

It may be that the entire faculty would have to be mobilized in such a way that the bureaucratic system is unable to fulfill its most basic responsibility— keeping the institution running—unless individual faculty are allowed to meet their responsibilities unimpeded. If something as essential to professional work as academic freedom and tenure are violated, then collective faculty action could challenge the bureaucratic system in a manner that directly affects a critical aspect of its work. In this case, greater pressure would be brought to bear on the representatives of that system. One assumption here is that professional needs are as important as institutional needs. With this assumption, the power differential between the bureaucratic and professional systems would of necessity be reduced, and the defense of faculty rights concomitantly strengthened. There is no indication, however, from the material we have gathered, that this kind of collective approach on behalf of endangered faculty members is seen as a viable alternative.

## CONCLUSION

In the course followed to further its interests, the professoriate has relied more on the professional than the union model. Since academics are not independent practitioners, however, this approach—though the process has been followed true to form—has been less than totally successful. The high road, so to speak, taken by those who make the professional claim can only be taken if they have and are able to use concomitant power effectively to advance their ends. By definition, employees under the direction of others are not so armed. The AAUP seems to have ignored both this fact and the sociological commonplace that "*the distribution of rewards in a society is a function of the distribution of power, not of system needs*" (Lenski 1966, p. 63).

It may be that the collective approach nurtured by the union movement in higher education in the past decade will be more capable of confronting the power of the bureaucratic system than the cooperative, publicity-oriented strategy of the AAUP. Although the AAUP has been moving gradually into collective bargaining, it gives little evidence of relishing this trend. Once again, the organization's posture is defensive and reactive. This time, however, the initiative comes not from the bureaucratic system but from the union movement. The response of the AAUP seems to be more of an expedient in the face of a possible, or actual, loss of influence than a change in tactics resulting from a more accurate critique of the problem of power. As late as 1968, Bertram H. Davis, then general secretary, argued as follows:

> Even if power were the key to faculty success, one would have to take issue with those who insist that the faculty can achieve that power only by placing exclusive reliance on an external bargaining agent. The truth is that there are few, if any, reasonable goals that a faculty cannot accomplish for itself if its members are persistent and imaginative, and if it draws when necessary upon the experience of the professional association (1968, p. 320).

He goes on to suggest that if faculty resort to union tactics, "boards and administrators will look to the sources of their own power, and institutions may have lost the opportunity for that cooperative effort which is indispensable to their welfare" (1968 p. 320). Although Davis appears to have had second thoughts (1973, p. 146–49), there is a lingering suspicion that there still springs the hope, among the association's traditionalists, that if administrators, governing boards, and legislators were "better people" and a new period of expansion and prosperity were to return to higher education, unionization would retrogress. They might be correct, and, if so, the myths incorporated in the professional model could continue to comfort academics while the problem of power goes unresolved.

## REFERENCES

AAUP. "Report of the Self-Survey Committee of the AAUP." 1965. *AAUP Bulletin* 51:99–209.

Davis, B. H. 1968. "Unions and Higher Education: Another Look." *AAUP Bulletin* 54:317–320.

———. 1973. "Report of the general secretary." *AAUP Bulletin* 59:146–49.

Duryea, E. D., and Fisk, R. S. 1973. "Epilogue: Analysis and Perspective." In Duryea, E.D., and Fisk, R. S., eds., *Faculty Unions and Collective Bargaining,* pp. 197–216. San Francisco: Jossey-Bass.

———. 1975. *Collective Bargaining, the State University and the State Government in New York.* Buffalo: State University of New York at Buffalo.

Freidson, E. 1973. "Professions and the Occupational Principle." In Freidson, E., ed., *The Professions and Their Prospects,* pp. 19–38. Beverly Hills, Calif.: Sage.

Garbarino, J. W. 1971. "Precarious Professors: New Patterns of Representation." *Industrial Relations* 10:1–20.

———. 1973. "Emergence of Collective Bargaining." In Duryea, E. D., and Fisk, R. S., eds., *Faculty Unions and Collective Bargaining,* pp. 1–19. San Francisco: Jossey-Bass.

Greenwood, E. 1957. "Attributes of a profession." *Social Work* 2:45–55.

Kemerer, F. R., and Baldridge, J. V. 1975. *Unions on Campus.* San Francisco: Jossey-Bass.

Kornhauser, W. 1962. *Scientists in Industry.* Berkeley: University of California Press.

Ladd, E. C., Jr., and Lipset, S. M. 1973. *Professors, Unions, and American Higher Education.* Washington, D. C.: American Enterprise Institute for Public Policy Research.

———. 1976. "The Growth of Faculty Unions." *Chronicle of Higher Education* 9:11.

Lenski, G. 1966. *Power and Privilege.* New York: McGraw-Hill.

Lewis, Lionel S., and Ryan, Michael N. 1971. "In the Matter of University Governance During the 1960's." *Social Problems* 19:249–57.

Scott, W. Richard. 1966. "Professionals in Bureaucracies—Areas of Conflict." in Vollmer, H. M. and Mills, D. L., eds., *Professionalization,* pp. 265–75. Englewood Cliffs. N.J.: Prentice-Hall.

Semas, P. W. 1976. "Faculty Unions Add 60 Campuses in 1975–76 Academic Year." *Chronicle of Higher Education* 12 (May 31), p. 5.

Shulman, Carol H. 1972. *Collective Bargaining on Campus.* Washington, D.C.: American Association for Higher Education.

Tice, T. N. 1973. "The Situation in the States." In Tice, T. N., ed., *Faculty Bargaining in the Seventies,* pp. 177–238. Ann Arbor, Mich.: Institute of Continuing Legal Education.

Veblen, Thorstein. 1957. *The Higher Learning in America.* New York: Hill and Wang.

Veysey, Laurence R. 1965. *The Emergence of the American University.* Chicago: University of Chicago Press.

Vollmer, H. M. and Mills, D. L., eds. 1966. *Professionalization.* Englewood Cliffs, N.J.: Prentice-Hall.

Wilensky, H. L. 1964. "The Professionalization of Everyone?" *American Journal of Sociology* 70: 137–58.

Wilson, Logan. 1942. *The Academic Man.* New York: Oxford University Press.

# About the Editor and Contributors

PHILIP G. ALTBACH is professor of higher education and foundations of education at the State University of New York. He previously taught at the University of Wisconsin and Harvard and is North American editor of *Higher Education,* an international journal. He is the author of a number of books on higher education, including *Comparative Higher Education* (Washington, D.C.: American Association for Higher Education, 1973), *Student Politics in America* (New York: McGraw-Hill, 1974), *Publishing in India* (New York: Oxford University Press, 1975), and *The University in Transition: An Indian Case Study* (Bombay: Sindhu, 1970). He has also edited several volumes, and has contributed to such journals as the *Harvard Educational Review, Comparative Education Review,* and others.

IKUO AMANO is associate professor in the Faculty of Education, Nagoya University, Japan. He was recently a visiting fellow of the Program in Comparative and Historical Studies on Higher Education at Yale University. Professor Amano is the author of several articles on higher education in Japan.

WILLIAM K. CUMMINGS is assistant professor of sociology at the University of Chicago. He has taught at Tsuda College, Tokyo and has been a visiting fellow of the Research Institute for Higher Education, Hiroshima University, Japan. Dr. Cummings has written extensively on education in Japan in such journals as the *Journal of Asian Studies, Comparative Education Review, Japan Interpreter,* and others. His book on the academic profession in Japan was published in Japanese.

THOMAS EISEMON is assistant professor of social foundations in the Faculty of Education, McGill University, Montreal. He is author of *U.S. Educated Engineering Faculty in India* (1974). He has been on the staff of the UNESCO Institute for Education, Hamburg, and has contributed to such journals as *Interchange, Higher Education, Teachers College Record,* and others.

BONNIE COOK FREEMAN is assistant professor in the College of Education, University of Texas at Austin. At present, she is editing a volume on *Texas Women: Myths and Realities* (Austin: University of Texas Press, forthcoming). She has written on children's rights, women, and the politics of education. Her current research, supported by the Spencer Foundation, deals with the politics of textbook choice.

ALBERTO GIASANTI teaches sociology at the University of Messina, Italy. He is co-author of *Citta e conlitto sociale* (1972) and is co-editor of *Sociologia del diritto.*

GRANT HARMAN is on the staff of the Education Research Unit in the Research School of Social Sciences, Australian National University, where he specializes on higher education and the politics of education. He has compiled *The Politics of Education: A Bibliographical Guide,* co-edited *Readings in the Economics and Politics of Australian Education,* and co-edited *Australian Higher Education: Problems of a Developing System.* He was recently a visiting scholar at the University of California at Berkeley.

LIONEL S. LEWIS is professor of sociology and adjunct professor of higher education at the State University of New York at Buffalo. He is author of *Scaling the Ivory Tower: Permit and Its Limits in Academic Careers* (Baltimore: Johns Hopkins University Press, 1975), and co-editor of *Social Stratification* (New York: Macmillan, 1974). He has also contributed many articles to such professional journals as the *American Journal of Sociology, Social Problems,* and others.

GUIDO MARTINOTTI is professor and chairman, Faculty of Political Science, University of Turin, Italy. He is author of *Gli studenti universitari, profilo sociologico* (Padua: Marsilio, 1969), *Citta a analisi sociologica* (1971), and other publications.

RICHARD PELCZAR is on the staff of the Inter-American Development Bank in Santiago, Chile. He was previously assistant professor of comparative education at the University of Illinois. He has written on Latin American higher education, and has contributed to the *Comparative Education Review* and other journals.

JAKOV M. RABKIN is on the staff of the Institut d'histoire et de sociopolitique des sciences, University of Montreal. Educated at the Institute for the History of Science and Technology in Moscow, he has worked as science advisor at the National Council for Research and Development in Israel.

MICHAEL N. RYAN teaches sociology at Niagara County Community College, New York. He served as chairman of the Department of Sociology from 1974 to 1976. He has written for such journals as *Social Problems* and *Education and Urban Society.*

JANET SCARFE is a graduate student in higher education at the University of Toronto. She has previously studied at the Universities of Adelaide and Sydney in Australia.

EDWARD SHEFFIELD is professor emeritus of higher education at the University of Toronto. He has served as director of the Education Division, Statistics Canada, and has written extensively on higher education in Canada.

GARETH L. WILLIAMS is professor of educational planning and director of the Institute for Research and Development in Post-Compulsory Education at the University of Lancaster, England. He was formerly on the staff of the London School of Economics and has worked for the Organization for Economic Cooperation and Development. He is co-author of *The Academic Labour Market* (Amsterdam: Elsevier, 1974), *Patterns and Policies in Higher Education* (Harmondsworth, England: Penguin, 1969), and other publications. He is an editor of *Higher Education,* at international journal.